THE ARTIST'S TAX GUIDE

and

FINANCIAL PLANNER

CARLA MESSMAN

Lyons & Burford, Publishers

Printed in the United States of America

10 9 8 7 6 5 4 3 2 1

LIBRARY OF CONGRESS CATALOGING-IN-PUBLICATION DATA

Messman, Carla.
The artist's tax guide and financial planner / Carla Messman.
p.   cm.
Rev. ed. of: The artist's tax workbook for 1990. 1990.
Includes bibliographical references and index.
ISBN 1-55821-130-6
1. Artists—Taxation—Law and legislation—United States.   2. Self-
employed—Taxation—Law and legislation—United States.   3. Income
tax—Law and legislation—United States.   4. Artists—United States—
Finance, Personal.   5. Self-employed—United States—Finance,
Personal.   I. Messman, Carla. Artist's tax workbook for 1990.
II. Title.
KF6369.8.A7M47   1992
343.7305'26—dc20
[347.303526]   92-7631
CIP

Contents

Preface to the 1992 Edition   vii

PART I: The Artist as Business Owner

1   Bookkeeping   3
2   Receipts and Recordkeeping   8
3   Setting Up Your Books   12
4   Books as Business Tools   32
5   Reporting Requirements   48
6   Capitalization   61

PART II: Special Tax Topics

7   Depreciation   69
8   Using Your Personal Automobile for Business   86
9   Home Office   96
10   Travel   103

11 Business Structure   111
12 Employee or Independent Contractor?   121
13 Business or Hobby?   125
14 Sales and Use Tax   133
15 Inventories   142
16 Sale of Business Equipment   156
17 Pricing and Profits   173
18 Audits   181
19 Retirement Plans   190
20 Paying Your Taxes   207
21 "Qualified Performing Artist"   215

PART III: Appendices

Glossary of Terms   223
A Quick Guide to Income and Deductions   240
Index   265

Preface

This book first appeared in 1985 as *The 1984 Tax Workbook for Artists and Other Self-Employed Persons*. I wrote it after seeing a client use a 1980 edition of a colleague's tax book to gather the information for her 1983 tax returns. In the interim two major tax bills had been passed, leaving my client dazed and confused as she tried to reconcile 1983 tax form requirements with 1980 tax form instructions. I realized then that artists needed a comprehensive and comprehensible annual guide to income tax preparation.

From 1986 through 1988 the book appeared as *The Art of Filing, A Tax Workbook for Visual, Performing and Literary Artists and Other Self-Employed Professionals*. From 1989 to 1991 it was entitled simply *The Artist's Tax Workbook*.

For all those years the book combined nuts-and-bolts tax advice with financial and business information. But I found that many readers were using the book mainly as a reference, having their tax returns prepared by their accountants. Inevitable delays in the release of tax forms by the IRS made for a last-minute rush to have the book ready by tax time, leading to frustrations for everyone and often a book that was too late to help. And over the years, the financial and business part expanded to occupy a larger and larger share of the book. *The Artist's Tax Guide and Financial Planner* is the result of that evolution.

This book attempts to provide as close to a one-to-one consultation on financial and business issues as I can provide in writing. If you already have an accountant, this book provides an excellent base from which to work effectively on tax return preparation and business planning.

Use the *Artist's Tax Guide and Financial Planner* as a reference book. Keep it next to your dictionary and local arts community guide. As a specific tax or business situation becomes real to you, turn to this book for guidance on the options you have.

In writing the book and choosing what I hope are illustrative examples, I've tried to keep my sense of humor. I do so in the hope of making the task of sorting out pages and pages of information to get to the part that affects *you* less daunting.

I also hope using humor helps keep the business and tax aspects of what you do in perspective. I frequently tell clients there's no individual part of tax law that's not easily understood. The problem is the volume of information available, on the one hand, and the complexity of the individual problem, on the other. You have to be able to sort and pick out the information from the former that pertains to the specific, stripped down issues of the latter before you come up with a treatment that feels, looks, and is right. That's what I want this book to help you accomplish.

A well-done tax return is like a thousand-piece jigsaw puzzle of a wave: every piece fits together perfectly to create a realistic visual from apparent chaos and disorder. No piece was forced into place. There are no gaping holes. Solutions to problems appear simple, clear, and understandable, to you and to an auditor (if it comes to that). Well-done tax returns keep your conscience clear and keep you in the studio where you belong.

I'm eager to hear your comments and impressions of this book. As in the past, I also solicit your inquiries and will do my best to respond to written questions. Please direct comments, critiques, and other correspondence to the publisher, Lyons & Burford, 31 W. 21 Street, New York, New York 10010.

Carla Messman
St. Paul, Minnesota
November 1991

PART

I

> # THE ARTIST
> # AS BUSINESS
> # OWNER

▫ 1 ▫

Bookkeeping

Who Needs It?

A mental image of the myopic accountant, eyes shielded by a green visor from the harsh glare of an overhead lamp, struggling to make each column of numbers add up vertically and horizontally (and, you suspect, diagonally as well), may have kept you from keeping books on your business.

Alternate scenario: a teacher. Not the kind, role-model type who develops your hidden talents, but rather the rap-'em-on-the-knuckles, how-could-you-be-so-dumb type who knows there is only one correct answer—and you don't have it.

Either image is enough to sour you on bookkeeping, just when you need it most. The bad news is that you *should* be keeping books; the good news is that there are few right or wrong answers in bookkeeping. You may find it easier to set up books on your business than you've been led to believe.

To keep books on your business:

1. You need not balance your checking account every month. If

your financial affairs are in good order, by all means balance and continue to balance your checking account. Banks occasionally (but rarely) make errors. Balancing your checking account forces you to review checks written over a particular thirty-day period—a kind of "prudent consumer" audit. Furthermore, it alerts you to bank charges—no small matter these days. But *need* to balance your checkbook? No.

2. Your books do not need to balance, nor do they need to correspond to your checking-account balance. For one thing, your books may not contain some items that appear in your check register. Gasoline, for example, may be purchased by check, but the deduction for business use of your personal automobile is best handled by a year-end tally of receipts for actual expenses balanced against the standard mileage rate deduction. Don't put gas receipts into your books as if they were a real business expense. For another, you may have cash expenses your checks don't cover: copying, or a business lunch, or parking.

3. You don't need to keep books on a daily or even weekly basis. Keep them monthly, to cut down on the time you spend chained to your desk. Waiting until year's end to pull your records together is a formula for disaster: too many papers, too little time, too short a memory.

4. You don't need an elaborate system that tracks everything in your life. Start with the basics: Keeping track of how you earn the money that supports you. As an add-on, keep track of expenses you can deduct against that income so the government doesn't take more than it deserves.

What You do Need is Discipline

Make yourself sit down on the last day of the month (or the first day, or some other set time) to enter the previous month's receipts in your books.

You Need to be Thorough

Don't skip by your checkbook on the assumption that you collected receipts on all purchases paid for by check and already have those in your book. Don't toss aside your monthly phone bill before you've circled the long-distance business calls and totaled the charges. Don't let your mileage log languish. Add up the business miles driven for the month. If you have two separate self-employment activities, add up subtotals for each.

Why Bother Keeping Books?

People who have kept books on their businesses for a long time know that tax-return preparation is the least of the reasons they do so. Rookies may doubt this, but it's true. In my practice I tell clients that in the beginning they may keep records for me, but that within a year or two, they'll do it for themselves.

Filing a tax return, of course, does compel you to review the previous year's comings and goings. Receipts and canceled checks touch on joyous as well as heart-rending events in your life during that year, along with the mind-numbing monotony of things like insurance, mortgage, and utility payments.

Thanks to Uncle Sam, you find yourself doing a miniature "Year In Review" of your affairs, which sometimes turns out well, and sometimes turns out not so well. Joy, sorrow, and monotony are never registered on a tax return—just dollars and cents, and then only for a few government-selected items. But once you've complied with the government's seemingly insatiable appetite for information, don't collapse in exhaustion. Use that tax return as a starting point to figure out what you did that you liked and what you did that you hope doesn't happen again. In other words, use it as a planning document for the coming year and for future years. Tax return as planning document: A good reason to complete your return as soon as data is provided by external agents such as banks, mortgage companies, and brokers.

Many personal expenditures documented on your tax return can't be controlled: Mortgage interest and property taxes spring to mind. Even here there's room for tax planning. Is the mortgage interest you paid in line with last year's figure? If not, a call to your mortgage company may be in order. If you have an adjustable rate mortgage, is it being calculated correctly? If your property taxes have increased significantly, are you eligible for any special tax breaks on the state or local level?

Charitable contributions provide another obvious entry point for annual planning, but how about those miscellaneous deductions? If you're an employee, chances are your employer no longer picks up the cost of subscriptions germane to your professional development. Consider renewing a January subscription in December in order to double-up your deductions for a given year. (The advantages of doubling up are discussed later in the text.)

Perhaps you sold stock at a loss this year because your broker said it'd be good to balance off those gains. Figure out how much more tax you would have paid with no offsetting losses. Then look at the losses themselves. If you sold "dogs," those speculative stocks whose promise evaporated, then the timing of the loss was expedient. But if you sold solid stocks simply to record a loss, I think you need to evaluate your broker's trading sense, and you do that only by realistically assessing your tax situation. Ever since the government stopped taking more than half of what you make, losses (and the deductions for them) have been unfashionable.

If your tax forms offer all these possibilities for personal financial planning, imagine what you can get out of your business books. The market—and the corporations that dominate it—controls most of your personal expenditures. When it comes to your business, the control switches to you. Moreover, the data base provided by your business records is larger than that provided by your tax returns. For your business, you have monthly indicators—from income down to multiple-expense categories. The number of variables to be counted and analyzed is myriad, but your books should give you a clue to such fundamentals as:

- profits relative to cost-of-goods-sold (COGS); revenues relative to COGS (graph: profits versus COGS; revenues versus COGS)
- changes in administrative costs over time relative to revenues or relative to profits (graph: administrative costs versus revenues; administrative costs versus profits)
- wages and benefits relative to revenues or relative to profits

(graph: wages and benefits versus revenues; wages and benefits versus profits)

Your books provide a starting data base. To them can be added other, nonrevenue-specific kinds of data: hours your business is open, monthly hours worked, sales calls, slow periods (good for vacations or marketing efforts), employee productivity goals, office hours. The list goes on and on. Ultimately, you plan your business in terms of quantity (how much, when) and quality (from whom, how, at what personal cost, toward what personal end).

The minimum you want from your books is data for your annual tax return and for business analysis. Eventually your books can and should tell you how, where, and why you spend the time that makes the money that supports you. That's what bookkeeping is all about, and that's why you should bother to do it.

How Do You Know You're Doing it Right?

You won't have a balance sheet to prove that all the numbers check out. But a balance sheet sometimes only gives a false sense of security anyhow. The best indication you're doing your books right is a good night's sleep after your monthly bookkeeping session. You'll rest, assured you've done the best job you can.

The proof will come when you file your first tax return using your new bookkeeping system. Late-night cram sessions will be replaced by orderly, if still aggravating, research on how to treat some of the more complicated items on the return. Most entries will be simple transfers from your books to the lines on the forms.

If you're preparing your own tax return you'll find the IRS instructions less intimidating; if you hire an accountant you'll find his or her comments less mysterious. Options you thought far too exotic for you will now seem interesting, intriguing, or, depending on the size of your tax bill, downright life-saving. You'll experience a sense of control.

Keeping books sounds like a great idea, doesn't it? But exactly how do you do it?

□ 2 □

Receipts and Recordkeeping

Getting Started

The key to managing your business well is keeping good records. Keeping good records means keeping track of income and expenses so you know reliably what you earned and what you spent during the year.

Anyone who runs a business needs to distinguish clearly between business and personal items. Business items include:

1. Income from the sale of a product or a service on which no tax has been withheld. *Examples:* sale of a painting at a sidewalk art fair; commission you receive from a gallery; honorarium for a talk at a professional meeting; payment for typesetting a theatre program; fee for a professional installation

2. Expenditures incurred while making that income and that generate paper receipts. *Examples:* purchase of art supplies from a local dealer; fee paid for parking at a ramp

3. Expenditures incurred while making that income that do not generate paper receipts. *Examples:* coins put in a parking meter; cash payments (stay away from these!); rental payments; payments for services

4. Payments made to other individuals in the course of generating income.

The bulk of your records relate to your personal life. They are payments for health care, payments on charge accounts and installment loans, rent or mortgage payments, a paycheck from your regular job, telephone bills, and so on. Some of these items may have a bearing on your business (your rent or mortgage payment, for example, if you have an office in your home), but they are primarily personal. Good recordkeeping starts with a clear distinction between the business and personal facets of your life.

Every month you receive bills. One may be a telephone bill, another a credit card statement or a renewal notice on your health or auto insurance. You tear off part of the form and mail it with your check by a certain date. At certain times every month (usually around the first) you make payments previously scheduled by virtue of leases or mortgages or installment plans. Usually you have a coupon to send with the payment, but no invoice, as such, is sent. If you are employed, you receive one or more paychecks every month. You tear off the check stub and cash the check. These expenditures and income are personal. They are necessary to run your life but are not directly related to being in business for yourself. As a person who has a personal life in addition to a business life, you need to track income and expenses for each.

Managing Receipts and Records

For both personal and business items, start the tracking system the same way: Pick a central location where you can store receipts and records temporarily. Pay a credit card bill; put the "customer receipt" in a manila folder or an envelope or a drawer along with the rest of your personal receipts. Pick up your paycheck; put the check stub in the same folder or envelope or drawer. The key is to have a record repository in a convenient and consistent place so that records are stored there as soon as payment is made or received—that is, as soon as the transaction is complete.

Use the same system, but a separate repository, for your business expenses and income. Go to an art store and buy four brushes and some canvas; put the receipt in a separate manila folder or envelope or drawer along with the rest of your business receipts. Receive a check for seventy-five dollars for jurying a show; tear off the stub (or make a separate note if there is no stub), cash the check, and put the stub or note in that same folder or envelope or drawer.

You now have separate locations for personal and business records. What do you do then? Leave the personal records alone until the end of the year. Personal records are easier to manage. Although they may outdo business records in sheer volume, most of them are summarized annually. For a credit card, the first statement of the year tells you what you paid in interest for the previous year. Homeowners receive before January 31 a statement from their mortgage companies summarizing mortgage interest, property taxes, insurance payments, and payments to principal for the previous year. Income from a regular job is summarized on a W-2 form. If you are part of a limited partnership, you receive a Form K-1 early in the year summarizing last year's tax consequences of the partnership for you. Bank interest on checking and savings accounts is reported to you via Form 1099-INT; earnings from mutual funds are reported on Form 1099-DIV. If you sell stock during the year, you receive a Form 1099-B early the following year to remind you to report the proceeds of that sale. Other information, while not summarized for you, is readily accessible. Checks you wrote for insurance premiums are entered in your check register and the canceled check is filed in numerical order in a box of checks written that year. Your telephone and utility bills are not summarized, but there are only twelve of them to add up at the end of the year. Medical expenses for most people are easily totaled in one sitting.

Beyond the ease and convenience factor, however, it's all right to leave your personal income and expenditure records alone all year because the bulk of these items are not discretionary. You do not, generally, control your salary, nor can you stipulate what you would like to pay for rent or utilities. Someone else controls what you receive and what you pay.

A major exception is rental property. If you own rental property, you should follow the rules for business recordkeeping presented in Chapter 3, Setting Up Your Books. Rental property ownership resembles self-employment activity in both the level of control and the need for contemporaneous recordkeeping.

Using Receipts and Records

As a self-employed person owning your own business, you are in control both of what you earn and of what you spend. For this reason you need to pay closer attention to your business records than to your personal records. Paying closer attention means setting up and keeping books to track both income and expenses in your business. How often you work with your business records depends on the age and complexity of your business. If you are just starting out, setting aside four hours a month to update and analyze your records is probably sufficient. If you have a mature business or if your business requires frequent expenditures, you may need to keep books weekly or even daily. But by that point you've hired a bookkeeper!

Good records tell you how you are doing in the real world. They measure your success in terms that a materialistic society can understand and that you, as part of that society, need to address. They tell you where you spend your money and how much your art generates for you in spendable income. They help you pinpoint your resources for maximum effect so that the "starving artist" syndrome does not become your permanent lifestyle.

What's more, the IRS is placing increased emphasis on the presence of financial records as a factor in determining whether an activity is being carried on as a business or as a hobby. The absence of such records, kept on a contemporaneous basis, may lead the IRS to categorize your art activities as a hobby and disallow any loss you show from those activities.

The warnings are sufficient. Sooner or later, you will keep books on your business.

❑ 3 ❑

Setting Up
Your Books

Starting Out

The key to keeping good books is setting them up so they make sense to you. Do not go to a stationery store and buy a preprinted ledger. Usually anything preprinted is appropriate for external salespeople or store owners. Most of them will not make sense to the individual artist. What you should buy are blank ledger sheets—usually thirteen or fourteen numbered columns wide with enough to accommodate expense categories you commonly use for the transaction date and a wider column next to it to annotate your entries.

The other things you need to do your bookkeeping include:

1. Black-ink pen or black ballpoint pen. Pencil looks unprofessional, tends to smudge, is difficult to duplicate, and can be erased, which makes the IRS nervous. More to the point, the entry on a receipt doesn't change over time, so why would you ever need to change it in your books? And if you don't need to change it, why not use ink?

2. Records from your file/envelope/drawer and records from your check register for the period being entered to catch expenditures or income for which there is no receipt. (See Chapter 2 for advice on collecting receipts and other records.)
3. Your date book or appointment book for the period.
4. A calculator.
5. About four hours of uninterrupted time and a clock to keep track of it. Do not take telephone calls during this period. If you have children, find a time when they are away or when someone else is caring for them. Use any excess time to catch up on business correspondence or to plan your marketing strategy for the next week.

Never let so many records accumulate in your file or envelope or drawer that you dread the prospect of sitting down to enter the items. Limit the number of items you need to enter at one sitting so you have time to reflect on what you're doing.

Begin by dividing the records into income and expenses. Check each record for completeness. Each should bear information as to who, what, when, where, and why, as follows:

Who . . . is the payer (for income) or vendor (for expense)?
What . . . is the item for? A lecture? A sketchbook? A leotard?
When . . . was the income received or expenditure made?
Where . . . if not obvious from above information
Why . . . business purpose, project name or number

Use your date book or appointment book to refresh your memory. Identifying your records in this way will save time later in case you are audited or need to review your records.

Setting up Expense Categories

If you are setting up books for the first time, look at all your receipts for completeness, getting a sense of the categories they fall into. Make a preliminary division into income and expense. Turn first to the expense group. From your preliminary feel of what's there, separate the expense receipts into piles of like kind. You will have lots of piles until you understand how some are interconnected!

Example: You divide your expense receipts from a particular month into piles. You find yourself with these categories:

Supplies. The things that went into your artwork, such as paints/clays/raw materials, canvas, framing
Materials. The things used to fashion your artwork, such as brushes/styluses, sandpaper, varnish
Business cards. Design or printing
Hardware. Push pins, bolts, X-acto blades, light bulbs
Studio supplies. Light bulbs, grease remover
Printing. Notices of a show, recital, opening
Subscription. To a regional arts paper
Postage.
Commission. Checks to your agent
Membership. To a national arts organization
Books.
Airplane ticket.
Hotel and meal costs. In [your travel destination]
Payments to people who did odd jobs for you.
Business lunches.
Registration for a professional conference.
Gas and oil receipts.
Mixed. The largest stack of all, containing one or more of the categories listed above

What do You do Now?

The preceding categories can be combined as follows:

Final Categories	From These Piles
Supplies that went into your product	Supplies
Labor to complete that product	Payments to people who did odd jobs for you
Materials that you needed to make your product but that didn't go into it	Materials
Other Supplies (other than above)	Hardware, studio supplies
Advertising (this can be combined with Office Expense, below, if there isn't much of it)	Printing
Dues, Publications, Books	Subscriptions, memberships, books
Conferences, Continuing Education	Registration
Commissions	Commission and payments to people who did odd jobs for you, but not directly, product-related (delivery, for instance)
Office Expense	Design and printing, business cards, postage
Travel	Airplane ticket (may need to be prorated for business use)

These ten categories, augmented by a "Miscellaneous" heading, will become the expense categories you use to keep track of your business expenses. Try them out for three to six months. Drop the categories you find you don't use and add categories as you find yourself making a significant number of entries per month in the Miscellaneous column. As a rule of thumb, no more than 10 percent of your monthly entries should fall in that Miscellaneous column. If you find you have more, you probably need to refine your expense categories.

A note on Miscellaneous: This is an expense column used to lump together expense receipts that have nothing in common with one another. "Miscellaneous" is not the name of an expense. Any entry you make in the Miscellaneous category requires an explanatory note when you do your books, and separate treatment when it comes time to prepare your tax return.

Special Treatment of Automobiles, Home Office, and Travel

Do not include automobile or home-studio or office expenses in your books, since the rules on deductibility of these items vary from year to year.

For your automobile, keep a mileage log. Buy a small notebook, clip a pen to it, and leave it on the dashboard of your car so you remember to use it daily. At the end of each page, add up your business miles so that, at the end of the year, you need only add up page totals instead of individual entries. (See Chapter 8 for more information on mileage logs.)

Perhaps you've kept gasoline receipts and repair bills. Keep these in a separate envelope during the year for possible use in deducting a percentage of actual operating expenses. For most taxpayers, however, the standard IRS mileage rate results in a higher deduction. With either method, you need a mileage log of odometer readings on business use of your personal vehicle, plus an appointment book or log entry substantiating business purpose.

When you prepare your tax return, complete the part of Form 4562 where you identify business use as a portion of total miles driven during the year. If you also use your vehicle for your W-2 job, use Form 2106 for business use related to that W-2 job. If you're strictly self-employed, you'll profile your business usage on Form

4562 only. If you are self-employed and have a W-2 job where the only driving you do is to and from the office (that is, commuting), then you'll use only Form 4562 to profile the business usage of your car for your self-employment activities. If you're married and self-employed, and your spouse has a W-2 job and uses the family car for work-related driving, you need to file Form 4562 and your spouse needs to file Form 2106.

Form 4562 permits you to make an entry on the "car and truck expenses" line of Schedule C. Since auto use was not in your business books, you'll find your profit slightly lower than you thought, due to this "surprise" entry. Since you probably haven't set aside as much cash as you should have to pay your taxes, this may be a welcome surprise.

Another item that may find its way onto your tax return but that should not appear in your books is the expense related to a home office. Calculating the monthly entry for a homeowner is nearly impossible, because mortgage interest, not mortgage payments, is deductible. Beyond that, claiming a home-office deduction depends on the size of your profit. You may not know until year end whether or not you can claim that deduction.

A homeowner can deduct that portion of her housing expenses where she has a space used exclusively for business. That space is a percentage of the entire square footage of the house, and becomes the "business use percentage." That percentage is multiplied by mortgage interest, property taxes, homeowner's insurance, utilities (but not base rate on the telephone), and depreciation to come up with the home-office deduction. Keep utility bills together in one place during the year so you can use them along with the statement from your mortgage company on interest, property taxes, and in-surance paid in preparing your tax return.

Claiming a home-office deduction has always been a hot-button issue for audits, primarily when it's claimed incorrectly. Most errors in claiming home offices stem from claiming a deduction that forces you to show a loss for the year, or from not using a space exclusively for business, or from not claiming depreciation on the home you own. To reduce the number of errors taxpayers make, the IRS intro-duced Form 8829 for the 1991 tax season. Be sure to complete this form and include it in your finished tax return if you want to claim a deduction for business use of part of your home. (See Chapter 9 for more information on a home office.)

A third expense area that requires special attention is travel. Keep track of travel expenses separately. When you go out of town on a business trip, take along an envelope in which to put receipts related to that trip. At the end of the trip, total the expenses by category (lodging, transportation, local transportation, cleaning, supplies) on the front of the envelope. If the trip is 100 percent business, enter this total in the apppropriate expense category of your expense records (either "Miscellaneous" or "Travel"). Write on the outside of the envelope the dates, place, business purpose, and total expenses by individual category.

If the trip was part business and part personal, allocate the expenses accordingly. If the trip is less than half business, none of the airfare (or cost of transportation to your destination) is deductible, but you can take actual expenses for the business days. If the trip is more than half business but less than all business, multiply the percentage of business days by the total of airfare/transportation, lodging, and local transportation costs. Enter only the deductible portion in your books. Keep an envelope with travel receipts from a specific trip for each business trip you make each year. Cross-reference this envelope in your books so you can substantiate the Travel deduction you entered, if the need arises.

When you're traveling for business, keep track of meals separately. They are only 80 percent deductible. In your books, in a Business Meals/Entertainment category, enter the full amount of meal costs incurred on a business trip if the trip was 100 percent business; otherwise, enter the full amount of meal costs only on days devoted to business.

Keep in mind that the daily rate allowed by the IRS for meals may be larger than the actual receipts you have. Refer to Chapter 10 for a list of $34-per-day cities (the rest are $26 per day) and enter the larger of the two: your actual receipts or the IRS allowable daily rate. If you use the daily rate in lieu of actual receipts, document this in the "Notes" column of your ledger.

When entering meal costs in the Business Meals/Entertainment category of your expense ledger, don't worry that they're only partly deductible on Schedule C. The 20 percent meal disallowance is calculated directly on the form. (See Chapter 10 for more information on travel.)

Work with your expense categories until you're comfortable with them and they fit the way you spend money on your business. Twelve to fourteen columns should suffice for most businesses. If you have employees, however, their payroll figures should be kept in a separate set of records. See Chapter 5, Reporting Requirements, for an example of how to keep payroll records.

EXAMPLES OF EXPENSE CATEGORIES BY OCCUPATION

Table 1 contains lists of expense categories most often used by artists. Bear in mind that there will be differences within the same occupational group and that these categories are a starting point only.

Identifying Income Categories

Once you have expense categories that fit your business, turn to income. Again, begin by dividing the income receipts into like categories. Then take a moment to think how you want to use income data to tell you how your business is performing. The IRS requires only that you report all your income. When you begin distinguishing where it comes from, you're doing something for yourself.

If you're in the kind of business where you work for a handful of clients, you may choose to set up income categories that track income by client name. (See Figure 1.) Alternately, if you work for many clients, you may choose to identify income received from market sector, as shown in Figure 2. A variation on that market sector approach is setting up income categories by the type of job you do.

Selecting several income categories allows you to monitor income more closely than a simple chronological listing permits. Especially if your livelihood depends on one or two big clients, or if you need a

TABLE 1

SAMPLE EXPENSE CATEGORIES
(by Occupation)

Actor
Costumes and props
Makeup and grooming
Agent fees
Lessons
Office expense
Dues/pubs/books/plays
Union dues
Travel
Busi meals & ent
Misc

Art Teacher
Supplies*
Framing*
Pmts to ICs*
Freight*
Entry fees
Confs, cont ed
Dues/pubs/books
Travel
Busi meals & ent
Misc

Ceramicist
Clays*
Dyes, glaze*
Foundry costs*
Commissions*
Freight*
Pmts to ICs
Small tools < $200
Equip > $200
Studio supplies
Office expense
Dues/pubs/books
Travel
Busi meals & ent
Misc

Choreographer
Confs, cont ed
Pmts to ICs
Travel
Busi meals & ent
Dues/pubs/books/per-
  formances
Office expense
Misc

Dancer
Costumes and props
Makeup and grooming
Agent fees
Lessons
Office expense
Dues/pubs/books/per-
  formances
Union dues
Travel
Busi meals & ent
Misc

Designer (Generic)
Materials*
Fastenings*
Finishing work*
Freight*
Studio supplies
Advertising
Office expense
Dues/pubs/books
Travel
Busi meals & ent
Misc

Designer (interior)
Pmts to ICs*
Materials*
Commissions
Supplies
Studio supplies
Advertising
Office expense
Dues/pubs/books
Travel
Busi meals & ent
Misc

Filmmaker
Film supplies*
Editing*
Pmts to ICs*
Equipment < $200
Equipment > $200
Rental equipment
Commissions
Busi meals & ent
Cast/crew meals
Dues/pubs/books/films
Union dues
Travel
Misc

Graphic Designer
Typesetting*
Stats*
Printing*
Pmts to ICs*
Advertising
Office expense
Liability insurance
Busi meals & ent
Misc

(continued)

TABLE 1 (*Continued*)

SAMPLE EXPENSE CATEGORIES
(*by Occupation*)

Jeweler**
Precious metals*
Precious stones*
Fastenings*
Freight*
Commissions*
Advertising
Office expense
Entry fees
Pmts to ICs
Travel
Busi meals & ent
Misc

Painter
Paints*
Canvas, framing*
Brushes
Freight*
Office expense
Travel
Busi meals & ent
Misc

Poet
Office expense
Books
Dues/pubs
Readings
Confs, cont ed
Travel
Busi meals & ent
Misc

Sculptor
Materials*
Glazes, finishing
  materials*
Foundry costs*
Pmts to ICs*

Multi-media artist
Materials*
Pmts to ICs*
Small equipment < $200
Large equipment > $200
Office expense
Dues/pubs/books/per-
  formances
Liability insurance
Travel
Busi meals & ent
Misc

Papermaker
Materials*
Dyes, chemicals*
Books/dues/pubs
Confs, cont ed
Office expense
Travel
Busi meals & ent
Misc

Potter
(See ceramicist)

Stage Manager
Props*
Protective clothing
Office expense
Dues/pubs/books/plays/
  performances

Musician**
Sheet music
Strings, picks
Royalties
Small instruments
  < $200
Large instruments
  > $200
Dues/pubs/books/con-
  certs/records
Travel
Busi meals & ent
Misc

Performance Artist
Materials
Props
Pmts to ICs
Office expense
Dues/pubs/books
Travel
Busi meals & ent
Misc

Scenery Designer
Materials*
Paints, decorations*
Hardware*
Pmts to ICs
Rental equipment
Liability insurance
Dues/pubs/books
Union dues
Travel
Busi meals & ent
Misc

Surface Designer
Materials*
Dyes, decorations*
Pmts to ICs*
Freight*
Entry fees*

(*continued*)

TABLE 1 (*Continued*)

SAMPLE EXPENSE CATEGORIES
(by Occupation)

Sculptor

Freight*
Liability insurance
Office expense
Dues/pubs/books
Confs, cont ed
Travel
Busi meals & ent
Misc

Stage Manager

Confs, cont ed
Liability insurance
Travel
Busi meals & ent
Misc

Surface Designer

Studio supplies
Commissions
Office expense
Dues/pubs/books
Travel
Busi meals & ent
Misc

Video Artist

Video supplies*
Transfer, editing svcs*
Pmts to ICs*
Small equipment < $200
Large equipment > $200
Union dues
Dues/pubs
Travel
Busi meals & ent
Misc

Writer

Office expense
Dues/pubs
Books
Travel
Busi meals & ent
Misc

Key:

  * Denotes a Cost-of-Goods-Sold expense
** Likely to have an inventory

Pmts to ICs	Payments to independent contractors
Busi meals & ent	Business meals and entertainment
Dues/pubs	Professional dues and publications
<	Costing less than
>	Costing more than

---

certain number of gigs to keep the cash flowing each month, it's a good idea to track income information closely and look at the end of each month for variations that might signal trouble on the horizon. This notion of using your books to monitor the health of your business is described more fully in Chapter 4, Books as Business Tools.

You may need to adapt either of the two systems described above if you sell a product on which you are required to collect sales tax.

FIGURE 1

SAMPLE INCOME RECORD. INCOME SOURCE.

Initials Date
Prepared by
Approved by

INCOME
APRIL 1991

	DATE	NOTES	1 ABC Company	2 JB Smith	3 RC McCone	4 OTHERS	
1	4 2	INV # 10249	640 00				1
2	4 6	INV # 10250		300 00			2
3	4 7	INV # 10251 / COLLINS				250 00	3
4	4 13	INV # 10252		300 00			4
5	4 17	INV # 10253	195 00				5
6	4 20	INV # 10254		300 00			6
7	4 24	INV # 10255			1250 00		7
8	4 25	INV # 10256 / MAGUIRE				375 00	8
9	4 27	INV # 10257 — VOID —					9
10	4 27	INV # 10258		300 00			10
11	4 30	INV # 10259 / O'BRIEN				150 00	11
12	4 30	INV # 10260					12
13							13
14		TOTALS =	835 00	1,200 00	1,250 00	775 00	14
15							15
16		TOTAL APRIL INCOME					16
17		= 4060					17
18		Y-T-D INCOME = 17,400					18
19		MONTHLY %	20.6	29.6	30.8	19.1	19
20							20
21		HISTORICAL %	25.	25.	30.	20.	21
22							22
23							23
24							24
25							25
26							26
27							27
28							28
29							29
30							30
31							31
32							32
33							33

FIGURE 2
SAMPLE INCOME RECORD. MARKET SOURCE.

Initials Date
Prepared by
Approved by

INCOME
SEPTEMBER 1991

	DATE	NOTES	INDIVIDUAL COMMISSIONS (1)	NON-PROFIT ORGANIZATIONS (2)	CORPS (3)	OTHERS (4)	
1	9 3	L. C. CARROLL (DOWN PAYMENT)	150⁰⁰				1
2	9 4	G. GEORGE (BAL)	675⁰⁰				2
3	9 10	SALVATION ARMY		1600⁰⁰			3
4	9 15	ZEOS INT'L (PARTIAL)			3000⁰⁰		4
5	9 16	EDISON COMMUNITY COLLEGE (WORKSHOP)				50⁰⁰	5
6	9 20	RED CROSS		950⁰⁰			6
7	9 22	S. SMITHLEY	425⁰⁰				7
8		J. GRIFFEY	275⁰⁰				8
9		L. C. CARROLL (BAL)	300⁰⁰				9
10	9 26	D. LANPHER (DOWN PAYMENT)	280⁰⁰				10
11	9 30	EDISON COMMUNITY COLLEGE (WORKSHOP)				50⁰⁰	11
12							12
13		TOTALS =	2105⁰⁰	2550⁰⁰	3000⁰⁰	100⁰⁰	13
14							14
15		TOTAL SEPT INCOME =					15
16		7755					16
17		YTD INCOME = 49,615					17
18							18
19		MONTHLY %	27.1	32.9	38.7	1.3	19
20							20
21		HISTORICAL %	20.0	30.00	40.00	10.00	21
22							22
23							23
24							24
25							25
26							26
27							27
28							28
29							29
30							30
31							31
32							32
33							33

Figure 3 shows income ledger sheets that accommodate sales tax collections. Why put sales tax in your income books? Because sales tax is integrally tied to the price you charge for the product you sell. Sales tax generally appears on your invoices. And, if you show sales tax collection this way, you will have all the information you need at hand when it comes time to complete your sales tax reports to the government. (See Chapter 14 for more information on sales tax.)

Enter income on your income ledger sheets each month. Remember to include in your income journal only self-employment income from which no payroll tax has been withheld. If you have a part-time job that pays $6.50 an hour and Social Security or income taxes are withheld by your employer, that income should not appear in your books. It is not self-employment income. That income will be reported to you at the end of the year on a W-2 form and should be considered personal, not business, income. Remember—your books are for your business only, not for your personal income or expenses.

Entering all your business income is more important than entering all your business expenses. Failure to report income can land you in trouble with the IRS, while failure to claim a deduction will only shortchange you, not the IRS. To double-check your work, enter all income items for which you have a check stub or written record. Then go back through your business-check register and review all the deposits you made that month. Total deposits should equal the income totals you show in your ledger sheets for that month. If there's a discrepancy, track it down so you know where the difference is before you progress further into the year.

Clients frequently ask whether they should record income in their books when they bill for a job or when they're paid for the job. The question becomes more complicated for clients who receive partial payment to start a job.

If you record income as you bill for it, you're using the *accrual* system of accounting. The IRS loves this system because it means you pay tax on money before you receive it. If you do a lot of small jobs, the convenience in recording income as it's invoiced outweighs the slightly early payment of tax on the money. If, on the other hand, you do large jobs, the accrual system of accounting can have significant negative consequences.

FIGURE 3
SAMPLE INCOME RECORD. SALES TAX MODEL.

INCOME
JUNE 1991

DATE	NOTES	INVOICE #	TAXABLE	NONPROFITS	BASE CHARGE 0-0-S*	OTHER NON-TAXABLE
6/4	LAKE ST ART FAIR	(NONE)	1360⁰⁰			
6/7	ST VINCENT DE PAUL	1422		600⁰⁰		
6/7	MAIL ORDERS	1423			49⁶⁰	
		1424	118⁴⁰			
		1425	98²⁰			
		1426	72³⁰			
		1427			620⁰⁰	
6/10	GIG AT THE CC	(NONE)				50⁰⁰
6/18	SOMMERFEST	(NONE)			1424⁶⁰	
6/19	"				1732⁷⁰	
6/20	"				1612⁹⁰	
6/27	MAIL ORDERS	1428			62¹⁰	
		1429			75⁵⁰	
		1430			41⁹⁰	
		1431			102³⁰	
	TOTALS =		1648⁹⁰	600⁰⁰	5721⁶⁰	50⁰⁰

TO FIGURE GROSS SALES FOR SALES TAX PURPOSES,
USE COLUMNS 2→5 PLUS 7, THEN DEDUCT THE NONTAXABLE
PORTIONS. YOUR TAXABLE AMOUNT SHOULD EQUAL COLUMN 2.

TO REPORT INCOME ON SCHEDULE C, USE COLUMN 12. DEDUCT
FREIGHT + SALES TAX AS EXPENSES WHEN YOU PAY THEM.

YOUR RESIDENT SALES TAX SHOULD EQUAL COLUMN 9, ADJUSTED
BY TAXES COLLECTED ON-SITE BY OTHER JURISDICTIONS.

Prepared By
Approved By

MADE IN U.S.A.

FREIGHT	STATE TAX	CITY TAX		TOTAL CHARGES
	81⁶⁰	6⁸⁰		1448⁴⁰
				600⁰⁰
3⁶⁰				53²⁰
	7¹⁰			125⁵⁰
	5⁸⁹	49		104⁵⁸
8⁷⁵	4³⁴			85³⁹
47⁵⁰				67⁵⁰
				50⁰⁰
	71²³ **			1495⁸³
	86⁶⁴ **			1819³⁴
	80⁶⁵ **			1693⁵⁵
5²⁰				67³⁰
5⁹⁰				81⁴⁰
3⁴⁰				45³⁰
9⁸⁰				112¹⁰
84¹⁵	337⁴⁵	7²⁹		8449³⁹

* OUT-OF-STATE
** COLLECTED ON-SITE

Whenever possible, stick to using the *cash* method of accounting. The cash method means you report income when you receive it. Develop a set of files to keep track of invoices, including unpaid invoices, or "accounts receivable." Use your income ledger sheets to report only the cash payments you receive. You should probably use the "Notes" column of your ledger sheets for the invoice number of the job for which you've received payment. This makes reconciling accounts easier if you and your client disagree on the amount still due on a particular job.

Using the cash system is no problem as far as the IRS is concerned, unless for other reasons you're required to use the accrual system of accounting. (Situations that require taxpayers to use the accrual system of accounting are described in Chapter 15.) You'll find it easier to send out reminder notices on overdue accounts if you keep your income records separate from your invoices, and your income books are better indicators of the overall health of your business when the only information in them is cash receipts.

Putting It All Together

When you have finished entering income and expenses for the month, total each column so you know how much you spent in a particular category or received from a particular activity. Then add the totals across the page to arrive at total expense and total income for that month. Subtracting your monthly expenses from your monthly income gives you your net profit (or loss) for that month.

Monthly net profit (or loss) may make you feel good (or bad), but what you generally want to know is net profit for the year. For easy access to that information, when you do your books for the month, roll your monthly totals forward into cumulative, or year-to-date, totals. For February year-to-date expenses or income, add January's total for each category to February's, giving you a year-to-date figure for each expense and income category. For year-to-date figures through March, add the March figure in each column to the year-to-date figure on the February sheets.

Bringing these totals forward, column by column, month by month, gives you year-to-date expenses and income by category. Adding up all the year-to-date expense totals gives you year-to-date total expenses. Subtracting year-to-date total expenses from year-to-date total income figures your net profit for the year. It's your net profit that determines how much income and Social Security tax you'll pay.

Figure 4 shows excerpts from June expenses and income and the net profit the artist has year-to-date. Remember, because your books do not include automobile expense or home-office expense, they probably overstate your net profit. That's okay. That overstatement provides you with a little cushion in calculating your estimated tax payments. It also reflects reality, in that you pay for an automobile, whether or not you use it for business, and you pay for a home, whether or not you deduct part of those payments for your business. They are basically nonessential parts of your business operation that can provide some tax relief.

Storing Your Records

The last step in doing your books is to store permanently the receipts you've just entered in your books. Use large envelopes and label each with a single expense category from your books. Any receipt entered in any category should be put into the envelope designated for that category. Month after month, the receipts for supplies find their way into the envelope marked "Supplies." Canceled checks (the bulk of your other records) are filed in numerical order, probably in one of the boxes from which the checks originally came.

At the end of the year, your books show, for example, how much you spent on supplies during the year (if you've been keeping year-to-date totals). The receipts in the supplies envelope will be equal to or less than the year-to-date total in your books. Why? Because you may have written checks for some items, or you may have paid cash and made a contemporaneous record of the expense and thus have no receipt.

FIGURE 4
DETERMINING NET PROFIT YEAR-TO-DATE

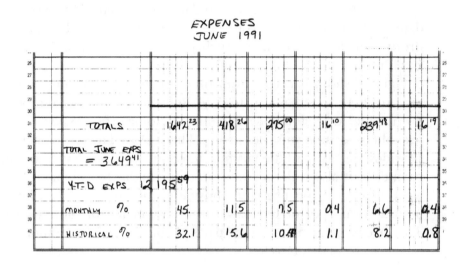

EXPENSES
JUNE 1991

TOTALS	1,642.23	418.26	275.00	16.10	239.48	16.19

TOTAL JUNE EXPS = 3,649.41

Y-T-D EXPS 12,195.59

MONTHLY %	45.	11.5	7.5	0.4	6.6	0.4
HISTORICAL %	32.1	15.6	10.4	1.1	8.2	0.8

INCOME
JUNE 1991

TOTALS =	140.00	1160.00	1700.00	1250.00

TOTAL JUNE INCOME = 4,250

Y-T-D INCOME = 28,420. *

MONTHLY %	3.3	27.3	40.0	29.4
HISTORICAL %	18.8	27.4	38.0	15.8

* NET THRU 6/91 =
28420
− 12196
= 16,224.

The figure you put down as an expense for supplies on your tax return is the figure from your books. If you're audited, you'll use the supplies envelope plus a stack of canceled checks and a listing of the nonreceipted expenses to substantiate your right to claim that expense total. You can easily pull the canceled checks from their numerical order because of the identifying entry you made in the Notes column of your ledger sheet. Your nonreceipted expenses have a similar identifying note showing where the expense was incurred. At an audit, the sum of the receipts in a specific envelope plus canceled checks plus listing of nonreceipted expenses must equal the total you entered on the tax return for that specific item.

□ 4 □

Books
as Business Tools

Background

Keeping books regularly gives business people the data they need to assess the health of their businesses. What about artists? Do they need to assess the health of their businesses? Consider a sculptor whose medium is bronze. Does it make sense for this artist to use information from his books on the cost of producing a particular piece to assist him in pricing his product? Or take a painter. Does it make sense for her to understand what hourly rate underlies her fee schedule? How about you? Are you curious about how much you make per hour at your art?

For some artists, making money is one of those things they do at other jobs. For them, art is an endeavor unsullied by the profit motive. If they make money from it, fine, but making money isn't really an important consideration in their art activities.

The IRS couldn't agree less. In fact, the IRS has gone a step beyond the "making money" idea to say that a business must be profitable. If a business does not show a profit in three out of any five consecutive years, the IRS may reclassify it as a hobby and disallow any losses claimed.

Artists are particularly susceptible to the hobbyist label because art usually involves a significant degree of pleasure in its creation. The IRS looks at these two features—lack of profitability and degree of pleasure—in assessing whether or not a person is conducting a business or engaging in a hobby. The difference is that, with a business, expenses that exceed income are allowed to give a taxpayer a loss to use in offsetting other income (earned, as through a W-2 job, or unearned, as through dividends, interest, and capital gains). With a hobby, expenses can be deducted only up to the amount of income received.

Consider Earl E. Rizer, an emerging poet. In 1990, he spent nearly $2,000 on postage, copying, office supplies, meetings with agents, and one trip to New Haven for a reading of his works. He had no income from his poetry. Can he deduct his expenses to offset his other income and thereby reduce his tax liability?

Rizer's is a tough, but not uncommon, case. His ability to deduct expenses hinges on how he's conducted his affairs. Has he attempted to market his work? Does he keep books regularly? Does he have an agent? What is his experience in running a business? How long has he been doing it?

The answers to these questions will be weighed by an IRS auditor in the larger context of Rizer's financial life in arriving at a final decision on whether he can deduct his poetry expenses. Is he using the poetry business as a dodge to avoid taxes, or is he serious about pursuing a second career? That obviously subjective choice colors the way an auditor will rule on Rizer. Is this blatant class bias? Perhaps. What's true is that upper-income taxpayers enjoyed a plethora of tax shelters prior to 1987, which in many cases saved them from paying what reasonably could be considered their fair share of the general tax burden. Those shelters were eliminated by the Tax Reform Act of 1986. Some "creative" upper-income folk switched their devotion from limited partnerships to small businesses, frequently in the arts. The result has been tougher criteria for auditing taxpayers with significant income from earned or unearned sources. For the individuals caught in the IRS inquisition, the situation undoubtedly seems unfair. In the larger context of tax collections, the increased audit attention eliminates most would-be cheaters, to the benefit of artists who operate as legitimate businesses.

To see how the subjectivity of an auditor works, consider two scenarios. Assume, first, that Rizer was bitten by the poetry bug in 1990. His poetic instincts had been aroused his sophomore year in college, but were repressed during his subsequent career as a corporate attorney. Overwhelmed by midlife crisis, Rizer went out and spent money on writing supplies and sent his three best poems to poetry magazines all over the United States and Europe. He didn't keep a separate checkbook, hadn't made time to join any local poets' societies, and paid cash for a lot of the items he bought.

An IRS auditor would have a field day with Rizer. No one can guarantee that any business will make a profit, but the way Rizer went about running his poetry business was chaotic. He ignored local support networks that could have furnished potential leads, and was haphazard in keeping records. Clearly he enjoyed himself, but it's more likely he wanted to shelter some of his corporate income than launch a second career as a Brooks Brothers bard.

Now change the scene only slightly: Rizer is still a corporate attorney, but he's been active in a local poets' group for the past four years. Reading his works to peers has enabled him to polish three poems, which he submits to *Vanity Fair, Harper's,* and *Sojourners.* The first two were chosen on recommendations from a mentor, the last on the basis of a personal contact at the magazine.

While Rizer still doesn't have a separate checkbook for his poetry business, he has marked poetry expenses in his regular checkbook register and also has receipts for most items. His plans for the coming year include attending an emerging poets workshop at a local university, and he has set a goal of turning out five more poems of publication quality. He plans to maintain his current schedule of two hours per day devoted to writing.

These two scenarios are as different as night and day, although the financial facts remain the same: Income = $0; Outgo = $2,000. In the first case, Rizer is clearly a hobbyist and should tuck away his poetry expense receipts with his memories and American Express bills. In the second case, Rizer is clearly in the poetry business and his expenses are deductible on Schedule C. What if Rizer shows a loss in 1991, and then again in 1992? Can he continue to deduct his losses? The answer is yes, provided he's conducting his affairs in a businesslike fashion, with the aim of making a profit. Probably in that time he has started to make *some* money, even though his expenses continue to outweigh his income.

If he has no income at all in that three-year period, then perhaps he should seriously consider reverting to hobby status. He would no longer need to keep books, and his poetry readings could be undertaken more informally. In other words, it's not always worth it to claim a loss on a tax return. While you save some money on income taxes, you also spend significant time and effort in developing the records you need to substantiate your activities and your profit motive. In some cases, this is time better spent on your creative endeavors.

In the real world, it's improbable Rizer would work at a business for three years and settle for no income at all. Just because the business that's showing no income is art doesn't mitigate fiscal realities. Living costs money and business is what makes the money that pays the bills so you can live. This seemingly endless cycle is part of life.

True, the United States tax code is nothing like Ireland's, where poets roam, and live, without fear of the tax collector. But it's also not like Italy, Germany, or even Singapore, where the tax bite off the top (that is, before expenses) makes expatriate Americans eager to see the Jersey shore or the wharves of San Francisco.

The reality is that most businesses, including art businesses, bring in money their first or second year, and show a profit no later than the fifth year.

An Editorial Perspective

Over the years I've seen a cycle develop in my artist-clients' businesses. I believe it is predictable for most businesses, art included. Figure 5 shows those revenue growth periods and plateaus. Here is what you see in that figure:

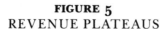

FIGURE 5
REVENUE PLATEAUS

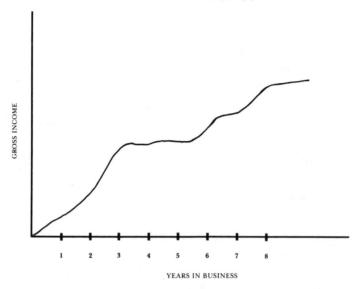

- The first year you "go professional" and file a Schedule C, you show certain gross revenues. Probably your revenues increase monthly as you move through the year. Gross revenues increase, sometimes dramatically, the second year.
- By your third year "out" as a declared business, you hit a revenue peak—you plateau. I call this a "shoulder year," where the monthly revenues you achieve in the last half of that third year are a reliable predictor of what you'll gross during the next two years.
- The fourth and fifth years are plateau years. You're not grossing more than you did by the end of your third year. It's hoped you've managed to cut overhead costs a little. As that fifth year draws to a close, you're probably aware that your business could serve your customers better through more timely delivery of product or staff to handle incoming telephone calls and correspondence. You find yourself wanting more time for the things you do best—create, communicate, plan, investigate new materials, dream dreams. You become somewhat restless at the thought that you aren't getting ahead, or getting ahead as fast as you think you should. You're tired of working 80-plus hours a week.

Some of the stuff you've always done yourself you now understand you can delegate to a subordinate (employee usually, but sometimes an independent contractor). This costs money. Providing better service to your customers means adding some kind of administrative staff. This costs money. Giving yourself some time off while others do the "grunt work" (the repetitive, easily directed tasks that are part of any manufacturing process) means adding production staff. This costs money. Organizing your work area more efficiently means adding space. Once again, this costs money. Deciding to add more physical space means more infrastructure, including higher phone bills and utility payments. More money.

Scared to death over all this money? Look at your prices. It's time to make a change. I've found over the years that I want my business consulting fees to keep pace with the hourly rate my plumber charges me. (You'll get a laugh from this. But it's simple, and it works.) As your cost of living increases, why not join the movement and institute changes of your own?

Artists as a group are fearful that asking higher prices may dry up their markets. I think they underestimate what they do. No price stays the same in a capitalist economy. Don't gouge, but don't be afraid to ask what you need to get for a particular work. Price changes come with the maturing of the business in that fifth year.

The sixth year shows a revenue increase. (It had better. You have more staff and more space.) That revenue increase tides you through the seventh year, as your time for more creative pursuits, including marketing to more "powerful" markets, expands. You become "pickier and choosier" about your clients and begin to define the market segment you want to serve.

Another shoulder year occurs at the end of that seventh year, going into the eighth. You may expand along lines you identified and wanted to pursue at the third-year shoulder but couldn't afford or risk at the time. Then you plateau for another two or three years, or even more.

At some point, you should call a halt to expansion. You may want to maintain personal control of the business, even at the expense of greater profits. Or you may believe that bigger is not always better—

especially in terms of quality but also, equally, in terms of profitability.

While I've seen certain cycles in the businesses my clients conduct, I've also heard clients say: "If anyone had told me how long this would take . . . " The comment usually remains unfinished. I have the impression they wouldn't forsake their chosen course but, at the same time, they are amazed at the suffering, discomfort, and deprivation they have endured to reach some level of financial security.

Using Your Books to Manage Your Business

Keeping records is important to a business that's losing money every year. They're the primary key tool in evaluating how money is being spent—what was a good use for the money, what was a waste—and in tracking cash flow. Keeping records becomes even more important as a business begins to make money. Once a business becomes profitable, issues of physical expansion, adding staff, and increasing compensation become pressing. For many businesses, profitability brings with it more dangers than losses did.

Set the stage for your future success by becoming familiar now with how your books can help you. The first step is using them to help set prices. Pricing your work is difficult because it involves saying publicly what you think you're worth. Pricing art is particularly difficult because people don't need to buy it. They'll buy art for reasons of prestige or social standing, for decoration, or perhaps because they like or relate to the piece. But they don't need it in the same way they need food or shelter.

Because the purchase of art is discretionary, its value is subjective. At a minimum, however, you as the artist-creator need to cover your costs. Sometimes this is not possible, but then you face a host of other problems, not the least of which is the IRS assuming you are running a hobby instead of a business.

If you cover only your costs, you have said your time is worth nothing. Do you seriously think this is true? How much is your time worth? A plumber earns $65 an hour in Saint Paul. A plumber keeps water inside the pipes. When you call a plumber, it usually means the water in your house has found an unauthorized way out of the pipes. Buying a plumber's time, then, is usually not discretionary. On the other hand, people usually enjoy a vase or a painting on the wall more than they enjoy a pipe that no longer leaks. So how do you price your work? Start with your books. They allow you to identify the costs of production and the costs of the environment in which the goods are produced (that is, overhead costs). Production costs plus your time plus a percentage of the overhead costs equal the cost to you of the item produced.

You know the production costs from your books. A time log, taken over a period of two weeks, will tell you how many hours on average you spend to produce a piece of work. Use a spiral notebook, one page a day. Jot down in quarter-hour increments how you use the full twenty-four-hour period. Distinguish between production time and overhead, administrative, and other nonincome-producing time. After two weeks, you should arrive at some accurate measure of how many hours you spend in productive, income-producing work.

Your books also tell you how much money you spend on overhead. You can calculate in one of two ways. If you produce twenty works in a year, divide total overhead by twenty. If your work comes in fits and starts, divide total overhead by twelve to arrive at a monthly overhead figure. Then apply that figure against the length of time it took to complete a particular project.

What's left after you subtract production costs and overhead from your gross income is your net income. From it you can calculate what you earn on an hourly basis. This equation works best for projects that are already completed. But it can also be the basis on which you bid a project. As a professional, you know what the raw materials will cost. You know how long it will take you to complete the project, so you can factor in your overhead. If you need to hire assistants, you know how much you will pay them. You calculate time spent in design and execution, put an hourly factor on it, and come up with a preliminary total. Don't forget taxes, retirement plan contributions, and profit. Finally, add a 10 percent "slush factor" and *voila!*— the bid.

Of course, it helps to temper that bid with reality. You can bid the project and get it on the basis of your presentation or your reputation or the extras you add. And it helps to know whether you really want the job or not. If you don't, you can bid up the price until the commission awarded exceeds your physical or artistic pain threshold.

If you win the bid, your planning abilities are called into play. Can you bring in the project on the budget you set, knowing that if you can't, the only slush factor is the money earmarked for you?

Part of the beauty of working for yourself is setting your own hours. The larger beauty, however, is testing yourself against your own standards. No one else calls the shots, and no one else sets limits on your performance. The business you create is one that you mold to meet your objectives. To an extent, you respond to the external market, but you have the final say on how fast your business grows and how far it goes. Does this make the idea of artist as entrepreneur more understandable?

Once you accept the need to be paid for your time, you've lost some of your innocence. You've also understood the need to keep books and use them to explain your business. Although it may be true that some people do not keep books out of fear of making mistakes, other people do not keep books because they have the luxury of running their art as a sideline, a hobby; money does not matter to them. In the arts community, they are probably a minority.

So your books can tell you about pricing. What else can they do? They can tell you:

1. Which client segment provides the most revenue. This knowledge allows you to plan marketing to this segment, to be sensitive to changes in this segment, or to redirect your business if a lucrative but intellectually unfulfilling segment occupies too much of your time.
2. How to cut costs, especially on overhead. Mature businesses focus on cutting production costs, newer businesses on overhead costs.
3. How to protect market segments you want to retain and discourage those you don't.
4. How to keep uncollectible accounts at a minimum.

What do you need to do with your books to gain greater insight into your business? Not much more than what has already been discussed. For the dollar total in each column, calculate a percentage of total expenditures or total income; for each year-to-date total, do the same. Percentages are easier to manipulate than raw figures; differences, called "variances" in statistics, are easier to detect.

The most elementary form of business evaluation checks for variances of more than 5 percent in any monthly expense or income category from the average for that expense or income category, determined by at least eighteen months' experience.

During the first six months of a business, expenses and income will fluctuate wildly as you spend money on whatever seems to be needed and take in money from any source offering it. As your business matures, you begin to channel expenses, pinpointing areas where spending is essential, and controlling income so it is more predictable, both as to source and frequency.

After the first year or two, you have an intuitive grasp of how much you need to lay out to produce at a certain level. Both expenses and income become somewhat predictable. This makes deviations from the norm measurable, using average costs per expense category from your experience or from the figures you enter on your tax return. Using these norms as a baseline, you are then able to tell whether an expense total for a particular column in a particular month is reasonable. In general, if it deviates from the norm more than 5 percent, you should review that month's expenditures to see if they were all necessary or if you are becoming somewhat slack in your fiscal management.

Similarly, if you can predict that 30 percent of your monthly income comes from a certain corporation, and in August that percentage dips to 18 percent, you may have cause for alarm. Perhaps someone with whom you schedule business is simply on vacation; that's okay. But maybe they didn't like your last project; that's not okay. Your books can alert you to changes in your business atmosphere before it's too late.

A third way your books can be used to evaluate your business is by determining trends. To identify trends you need to have kept statistics over a two- or three-year period. Likely areas for trend analysis are:

1. Cost of goods sold as a percentage of income (line graph, with different years shown in different colors or lines). See Figure 6.
2. Income by quarter, comparing several years (bar graph, with different years identified by color or pattern). See Figure 7.
3. Expenses as a percentage of income by month (line graph, with different years shown in different colors or lines). See Figure 8.
4. Overhead expenses as a percentage of gross revenues, by month, over several years (line graph, with different years shown in different colors or lines). See Figure 9.

Some Hints

Converting raw data to percentages facilitates month-to-month or year-to-year comparisons. Setting up your books to show year-to-date totals per expense (or income) category as well as monthly totals per expense (or income) category lays the groundwork for easy comparisons.

Graphing isn't hard to do. We all learned it in the third or fourth grade and figured we never would use it as long as we lived. Surprise! Graphs, because they're visual, can show us trends before we're able to digest the raw data and draw any conclusions. Figures 6 through 9, which graph the four scenarios above, using fictitious but not implausible numbers, show how such graphs might look.

What's difficult is finding the meaningful data to compare and graph. Graphing how much you spend for office expenses over the years against revenues generated doesn't tell you much, if anything at all, about your business. Graphing what you spend for advertising against revenues generated might tell you a lot. Graphing cost-of-goods-sold totals against revenues should give you a handle on why your profit is larger or smaller from one year to the next.

Over time you'll find the data that's important to your business. Some of it will appear in your books: cost of goods sold, gross reve-

FIGURE 6
EVALUATION TOOL: COGS AS PERCENTAGE OF INCOME.

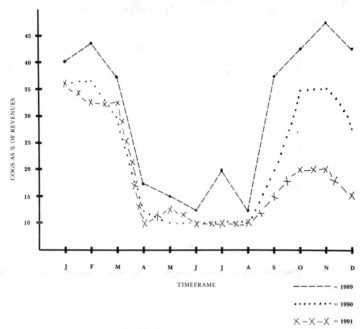

FIGURE 7
EVALUATION TOOL: REVENUES BY QUARTER, ACROSS TIME.

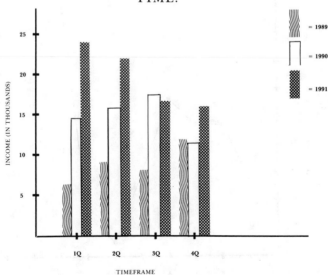

FIGURE 8

EVALUATION TOOL: EXPENSES AS PERCENTAGE OF INCOME.

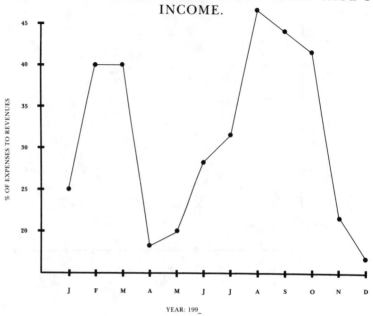

YEAR: 199_

FIGURE 9

EVALUATION TOOL: OVERHEAD EXPENSES AS PERCENTAGE OF GROSS REVENUES.

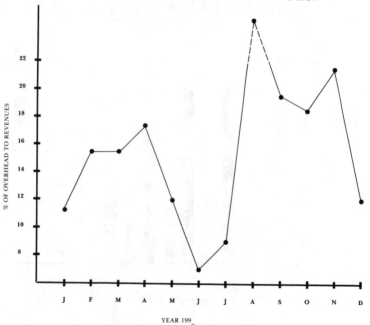

YEAR 199_

nues, advertising, net profit. Some of it will come from records you keep periodically, such as time logs, the number of calls you receive as a result of a particular ad, phone calls coming into your studio.

Some of it you'll cull from your records, organizing the material in a different way to achieve greater insight into how your business has changed. For example, you may at some point want to figure out which jobs provide the best profit for you by putting together a bar graph plotting number of jobs against income categories (less than $200; $200 to $500; $500 to $1,000; $1,000 to $2,500; over $2,500).

Experiment. Don't be shy about taking pencil to paper and reorganizing the data you find in your books to help you manage your business. Keep track, perhaps in a separate notebook, of the questions that pop up in your mind from time to time. Believe it or not, we all have some intuitive sense of the way business operates. The idle question, such as "I wonder how much time I really put into doing this project," is fertile ground for data analysis.

That question tells me you need to start logging your time on projects. But maybe you can't do that, because you often move from project to project in your studio, working a bit on this one and a bit on that one. Then log your time as split between the two (or three or more) projects you work on that day. This isn't great data but it's better than nothing. Knowing how much time you put into a project that produces a certain fee helps refine your bidding or pricing skills.

Remember: When you first start keeping books on your business, you aren't in a position to identify what you want to graph or when or for what time period. Keeping books is the first step. Knowing how to use them for your own purposes, instead of as a defensive measure to keep the IRS off your back, will come with time.

The objective as you start out is to set up books that, first, are easy to maintain. You don't want to spend more than four hours per month on bookkeeping, including business planning.

Second, they should provide a data base for future use in evaluating facets of your business. The key is to add bits each month: the year-to-date totals for each expense or income category; the up-to-date monthly reports on employee wages. You won't have more time to spend on this two years from now, so begin by building a base that will serve the future needs of a growing business.

Third, maintain some consistency in your recordkeeping. Changing expense categories every year means the data for a particular category is in a different place on your ledger sheets every year. Set up your categories, test them for six months, and then settle on a system that will serve you for several years at least.

Computerization

I'm often asked about the benefits of keeping books on a computer. You may chuckle to find that I myself use ledger sheets for my business and enter the data manually each month. I don't like computers for bookkeeping because each data item is isolated. Even when I view a particular expense category—office expense, for example, which is a huge item in the tax-preparation business—I don't get as much information as I do from my ledger sheets. This is largely due to the limits of computer screens. Someday they will serve us as well as ledger sheets do now in their ability to show volumes of information at a glance.

Some of my clients use and like the Quicken software program. It's easy to set up since you make the same kind of expense and income category identification as if you were keeping books manually. It's cheap (no small objective these days), especially in light of its power to combine data. Year-end reports for tax-preparation purposes are as easy to generate as pushing a button. One drawback for me is that Quicken is tied to the way you use your checkbook.

Having a computerized bookkeeping system allows you to spin out graphs at will. To me that's positive and negative. Quicken can run circles around a pencil-and-paper routine and produce a superior-looking graph. But my brain needs to be more thoughtful or reflective when combining data, which the old pencil-and-paper method forces me to be.

Sometimes I start graphing information and then realize early on that it will give me no insights or, worse yet, won't make any sense at all. That paper goes to the recycling pile. A computerized system would graph the data and give me the best-looking report possible—

even if it was, in computerese, "garbage out." I don't want to see you churning out so many graphs, charts, and analyses that you drown in a sea of paper. Doing your books manually, archaic as it is, has the advantage of holding down the amount of superfluous information you track.

What's the bottom line? Use a computerized bookkeeping system as it makes sense for you to convert to it. Don't be shamed by charges that your manual ledgers are hopelessly behind the times. I see the day when computer entries will be as easy to make as pushing a button to download a particular thought. Until then, I'll keep my little notebook and pencil to jot down ideas as they occur to me. Feel free to join me.

□ 5 □

Reporting Requirements

Overview

When you are in business for yourself, there are several reporting requirements you must meet. Some reports you must file on behalf of other people; others you must file to keep yourself one step ahead of the tax collector.

Reports to File for Independent Contractors

Whenever you pay an independent contractor more than $600 in a calendar year, you must file a Form 1099-MISC by January 31 of the following year. Enter the amount you paid the independent contractor in the box labeled "Nonemployee compensation." If you rent your studio from an individual (as opposed to a partnership or corporation), and you pay that individual more than $600 in the calendar year, you must issue that person a Form 1099-MISC, entering the amount paid for the studio rent in the "Rents" box of the form.

The original Form 1099-MISC is filed with the federal government. One copy is filed with the payee and one copy remains in your records as proof you complied with the law. You may need to send one copy to your state tax department. Form 1099-MISC must be filed by January 31 of the year following the year the services were performed. Failure to file the report, or filing it late, will result in a late-filing penalty or fine, and may lead, in case of audit, to the disallowance of the claimed deduction for services rendered.

Form 1099-MISC must be sent to the government with a cover sheet, Form 1096. Examples of these forms appear in Figures 10 and 11. States that require you to send them a copy of Form 1099-MISC usually have their own cover sheet. Call your state income tax department for filing instructions.

Whether an individual is an employee or an independent contractor hinges on the nature of the work assigned. Although states are more concerned than the federal government about the status of a worker, it is best to follow certain guidelines in determining whether an individual is an independent contractor or an employee.

In general, if a person works for you, on your premises, more than half-time, for more than seventeen weeks per year, he is an employee. A person who works for you only a few hours per week on a regular basis is your employee.

An employee is entitled to have you pay half his Social Security payments and all his Workers' Compensation and unemployment insurance premiums. If you also provide group medical or retirement plan coverage, he must be included if he meets the plan's requirements. Since these benefits amount to a considerable outlay annually, it's important to determine early on whether the person you hire will be an independent contractor or employee.

An independent contractor controls his hours of work and usually works on his own premises. All you do is control the quality of the work performed. Work assigned an independent contractor is intermittent and project-oriented. Work may be seasonal.

Given the additional expense of having an employee, it's probably

FIGURE 10
FORM 1096 (1991 VERSION)

DO NOT STAPLE	6969	☐ CORRECTED		

Form 1096
Department of the Treasury
Internal Revenue Service

Annual Summary and Transmittal of U.S. Information Returns

OMB No. 1545-0108

1991

ATTACH IRS LABEL HERE

Type or machine print FILER'S name (or attach label)

Street address (room or suite number)

City, state, and ZIP code

If you are not using a preprinted label, enter in Box 1 or 2 below the identification number you used as the filer on the information returns being transmitted. Do not fill in both Boxes 1 and 2.

Name of person to contact if IRS needs more information

Telephone number
( )

For Official Use Only

1 Employer identification number	2 Social security number	3 Total number of documents	4 Federal income tax withheld $	5 Total amount reported with this Form 1096 $

Check only one box below to indicate the type of form being transmitted.

If this is your FINAL return, check here . . . . ▶ ☐

W-2G 32	1098 81	1099-A 80	1099-B 79	1099-DIV 91	1099-G 86	1099-INT 92	1099-MISC 95	1099-OID 96	1099-PATR 97	1099-R 98	1099-S 75	5498 28
☐	☐	☐	☐	☐	☐	☐	☐	☐	☐	☐	☐	☐

Under penalties of perjury, I declare that I have examined this return and accompanying documents, and, to the best of my knowledge and belief, they are true, correct, and complete.

Signature ▶ .... Title ▶ .... Date ▶ ....

Please return this entire page to the Internal Revenue Service. Photocopies are NOT acceptable.

Instructions

Purpose of Form.—Use this form to transmit paper Forms 1099, 1098, 5498, and W-2G to the Internal Revenue Service. DO NOT USE FORM 1096 TO TRANSMIT MAGNETIC MEDIA. See **Form 4804,** Transmittal of Information Returns Reported on Magnetic Media.

Use of Preprinted Label.—If you received a preprinted label from IRS with Package 1099, place the label in the name and address area of this form inside the brackets. Make any necessary changes to your name and address on the label. However, do not use the label if the taxpayer identification number (TIN) shown is incorrect. **Do not prepare your own label. Use only the IRS-prepared label that came with your Package 1099.**

If you are not using a preprinted label, enter the filer's name, address (including room, suite, or other unit number), and TIN in the spaces provided on the form.

Filer.—The name, address, and TIN of the filer on this form must be the same as those you enter in the upper left area of Form 1099, 1098, 5498, or W-2G. A filer includes a payer, a recipient of mortgage interest payments, a broker, a barter exchange, a person reporting real estate transactions, a trustee or issuer of an individual retirement arrangement (including an IRA or SEP), and a lender who acquires an interest in secured property or who has reason to know that the property has been abandoned.

Transmitting to IRS.—Group the forms by form number and transmit each group with a **separate** Form 1096. For example, if you must file both Forms 1098 and Forms 1099-A, complete one Form 1096 to transmit your Forms 1098 and another Form 1096 to transmit your Forms 1099-A. Also submit a separate Form 1096 for each type of corrected form.

Box 1 or 2.—Complete only if you are not using a preprinted IRS label. Individuals not in a trade or business must enter their social security number in Box 2; sole proprietors and all others must enter their employer identification number in Box 1. However, sole proprietors who are not required to have an employer identification number must enter their social security number in Box 2.

Box 3.—Enter the number of forms you are transmitting with this Form 1096. Do not include blank or voided forms or the Form 1096 in your total. Enter the number of correctly completed forms, not the number of pages, being transmitted. For example, if you send one page of three-to-a-page Forms 5498 with a Form 1096 and you have correctly completed two Forms 5498 on that page, enter 2 in Box 3 of Form 1096.

Box 4.—Enter the total Federal income tax withheld shown on the forms being transmitted with this Form 1096.

Box 5.—No entry is required if you are filing Form 1099-A or 1099-G. For all other forms, enter the total of the amounts from the specific boxes of the forms listed below:

Form W-2G	Box 1
Form 1098	Boxes 1 and 2
Form 1099-B	Boxes 2 and 3
Form 1099-DIV	Boxes 1a, 5, and 6
Form 1099-INT	Boxes 1 and 3
Form 1099-MISC	Boxes 1, 2, 3, 5, 6, 7, 8, and 10
Form 1099-OID	Boxes 1 and 2
Form 1099-PATR	Boxes 1, 2, 3, and 5
Form 1099-R	Box 1
Form 1099-S	Box 2
Form 5498	Boxes 1 and 2

For Paperwork Reduction Act Notice, see the separate Instructions for Forms 1099, 1098, 5498, and W-2G.

Form **1096** (1991)

FIGURE 11
FORM 1099-MISC (1991 VERSION)

Form 1099-MISC (1991 Version) — three sample forms showing Miscellaneous Income reporting with boxes for Rents, Royalties, Prizes/awards, Federal income tax withheld, Fishing boat proceeds, Medical and health care payments, Nonemployee compensation, Substitute payments in lieu of dividends or interest, Payer made direct sales of $5,000 or more of consumer products to a buyer (recipient) for resale, Crop insurance proceeds, State income tax withheld, and State/Payer's state number. OMB No. 1545-0115. Copy A For Internal Revenue Service Center. File with Form 1096. Department of the Treasury - Internal Revenue Service. Do NOT Cut or Separate Forms on This Page.

best to try the person out temporarily as an independent contractor before offering regular employment. It is only fair to explain before you hire him, however, that an independent contractor is responsible for payments of quarterly taxes and any and all insurance premiums, so that rude surprises do not await him at tax time or if he is injured on the job.

Honesty up front is the best policy and will make for a better employee, should you find that your business requires a part-time or full-time employee who is on your business premises, under your control, for definable work times for an indefinite period.

Reports to File for Employees

Once you have an employee, your reporting requirements increase along with your financial requirements. First, open a separate payroll account at the bank. Make sure the checks come with two detachable check stubs to record withholding information. One stub goes to the employee with the check, the other remains in your payroll book.

Second, apply for a Federal Employer Identification Number (FEIN). Do so by filing Form SS-4 with your IRS district office. A number will be issued in approximately four weeks and will trigger the sending of quarterly reporting forms to you.

Alternatively, you can call your regional IRS service center, which will issue a number over the telephone. To use this abbreviated method, you need to have a completed Form SS-4 in front of you so you can read the information to an IRS agent. Your number is assigned immediately; within five days you must submit the SS-4 form, with your signature and the newly issued FEIN, to your IRS district office. Using this abbreviated method is helpful if your bank won't open a business or payroll account without an FEIN. Otherwise the regular mail application is fine.

If you live in a state or city that levies a separate payroll or sales tax, you also need to apply for a state and/or city tax identification number.

The last employer identification number you need is a number for your unemployment insurance account. Contact the local office of your state department of jobs and training to apply for that number.

In order to write out a payroll, you need to know some things about your workers. Everything you need to know is on Form W-4, where each employee records his Social Security number and the number of withholding allowances he wishes to claim. Make sure you have a signed Form W-4 for each employee.

In fact, have employees complete and sign a new W-4 at the beginning of each calendar year. Why? Let's say a worker finds she owes $1,500 in federal tax when she files her tax return. In some cases she'll be shocked and suspect you don't know diddly about how to withhold taxes. The first thing she'll want is proof that you complied with her written instructions, which appear on her Form W-4. Between what she wrote on Form W-4 and the withholding tables for that year (Circular E for federal withholding; each state has its own withholding tables), you should be able to demonstrate you fulfilled your responsibilities. Now your employee must sort out the underpayment with the IRS.

A reminder while we're on the subject of W-4s. Two possible responses to the question of how many withholding allowances an employee claims require you, the employer, to send a copy of that Form W-4 to your regional IRS office. The first is a claim of eight or more withholding allowances. The other is a claim of being exempt from federal taxes. Each of these situations is so rare that the IRS wants to know about it. As someone who's there to make employment as smooth as possible, double-check with your employee to make sure she knows what she's doing. No withholding allowances means the maximum amount is withheld; "exempt" means she had no tax liability in the prior year (all her withholding tax was refunded to her), and expects none in the current year.

If your employee erroneously checks the "exempt" box, she'll be hit with a $500 punitive penalty. This hurts her and, in turn, you, because you have a highly dissatisfied employee on your hands. An ounce of prevention is called for.

Now you're ready to write your first payroll.

Figure 12 is a reproduction of the payroll record I recommend to

FIGURE 12
PAYROLL REPORT FORM.

INDIVIDUAL PAYROLL RECORD

Name_____ Clock No._____

Address_____

Social Security No.	Position	Date Born	Telephone No.

Regular Rate	Overtime Rate	Withholding Status

PAY PERIOD ENDING 19	TOTAL HOURS Regu-lar	Over-time	GROSS PAY	Social Security	Federal With.	State With.		NET PAY	OVERTIME PREMIUM	CUMULATIVE GROSS PAY
					DEDUCTIONS					
1 Jan.										
2										
3										
4										
5										
Total Jan.										
1 Feb.										
2										
3										
4										
5										
Total Feb.										
1 Mar.										
2										
3										
4										
5										
Total Mar.										
Total 1st Quarter										
1 April										
2										
3										
4										
5										
Total April										
1 May										
2										
3										
4										
5										
Total May										
1 June										
2										
3										
4										
5										
Total June										
Total 2nd Quarter										
Total Year To Date										

Form 100   Nelco Forms, P.O. Box 10208, Green Bay, WI 54307-0208   **100**   NTF 0183A   Copyright 1980 by Nelco, Inc.

my clients. Nelco, in Green Bay, Wisconsin, sells it. It's a convenient way to keep up-to-date information on employee gross earnings, federal withholding tax (FWT) and state withholding tax (SWT), Social Security tax withholding (FICA), and net pay. It also has room to track additional withholding, such as city taxes or charges you make against the employee: parking in the city lot you pay for, or the employee's part of the health insurance premium, for instance. Customize the form to meet your individual requirements.

It's important to make sure the columns and lines balance by the end of each month. Add down the columns for gross pay, FWT, SWT, and FICA. From the gross pay total, subtract (FWT + SWT + FICA). From that total, subtract the net pay from each pay period.

You should come up with zero. If you don't, go back to that month's individual withholding to make sure you didn't make an error in addition or subtraction. Correcting an error after a month is relatively simple. Issue a check for a withholding error in your employee's favor or provide a note with the next paycheck to explain any additional withholding. If the amount of error you made in your employee's favor is small, it's good advice to absorb the additional cost and not add that note to your employee's paycheck.

Waiting until the end of a quarter to correct inconsistencies has obvious pitfalls. Any adjustment is too large, probably, for you or your employee to absorb. And errors left undetected from month to month take longer to find.

As a tax accountant, I charge my clients a flat rate to prepare their quarterly tax reports. That flat rate depends on the number of employees they have and so is predictable. Any "reconciliations" (read "corrections") I need to make costs them extra. I find few errors (or the errors are easily detectable) when clients keep monthly totals. Hunting for discrepancies proceeds this way:

1. Check that the monthly figures add up to the quarterly totals shown. Make sure the gross pay times 7.65 percent equals the quarterly FICA total shown.

2. Check that the quarterly totals shown balance, that gross pay less FWT, less SWT, less FICA equals net pay.

If a discrepancy arises at the quarterly level, check first to see that the Social Security withholding is correct. Next, see if the "gross less FWT, less SWT, less FICA" net is correct. Your inconsistency has likely occurred in one of these two areas. Correct and proceed.

Keeping reconcilable monthly and quarterly totals facilitates preparing quarterly employer tax reports. It's just another example of how computing information in small segments leads to greater overall accuracy and ease in reporting.

The withholding information you enter on the payroll stubs are the federal, state and city, and Social Security taxes withheld from each paycheck you write. The check you pay each worker equals the gross amount earned less federal and state and city withholding and Social Security tax withheld. The amounts of federal, state, and city tax are determined by marital status and number of withholding allowances and can be looked up in a catalog sent to you after you apply for your federal, state, and city identification numbers. The Social Security tax is 7.65 percent of gross earnings in 1991 and in 1992.

These amounts, plus your portion of Social Security tax (the same 7.65 percent your employees pay), must be deposited at a federal reserve bank in your area. Most banks that handle business accounts are federal depositories. Use your federal deposit coupon (Form 8109) when you receive it (it's one of those items you automatically receive after you apply for an FEIN) to make a deposit each time you write out a payroll. Calculate the amount to deposit as follows. Add up the Social Security withholding from each employee. Multiply that total by two, so you have a figure that equals the employees' share plus your share as the employer. To that total add the total federal withholding tax from each employee. This equals your Form 8109 deposit.

Deposit payroll taxes as you go. That way you won't be tempted to use the withheld funds for operating expenses, which can leave you in a financial bind and trigger punitive penalties if you are caught borrowing your workers' money.

Because writing out a payroll is time-consuming, set up a monthly payroll system. If monthly payrolls aren't standard, or if your workers seem unhappy with them, set up a semimonthly system, paying on the fifteenth day and the last day of the month. Establish the practice that paychecks are available on the first business day after the close of the payroll period.

Thirty days after the end of each quarter (March, June, September, December) you are required to file Form 941 (Employer's Quarterly Federal Tax Return) with the IRS. This report reconciles the amounts withheld and deposited with the amounts that should have been withheld and deposited, and allows you to make up any small discrepancies.

Any state or city with its own payroll tax has its own reporting form. Local due dates generally conform to federal due dates. Materials are sent to you from state or city tax departments after you apply for state or city identification numbers. You'll probably need one number for the state and another for the city.

Another state quarterly report you need to file is for unemployment insurance premiums. After you apply for an unemployment insurance account number, your state department of jobs and training should send you the forms to complete quarterly reports. Unemployment insurance is an employer-paid tax; that is, nothing is withheld from employees' paychecks to contribute to the account. It is based on wages paid, up to a certain threshold set by each state.

Annually, you are required to file a Form W-2 for each employee by January 31 of the following year. Form W-2 is a five- or six-part form with room for two employees on each sheet. The top (colored) copy is sent to the Social Security Administration in your district with Form W-3 as a cover sheet. The last copy is yours to keep. The middle three or four copies go to the employee to file with her individual income tax return(s).

The other annual federal report is Form 940 (FUTA—the federal unemployment tax form), also due by January 31. In addition to these quarterly and annual employer reporting requirements, most states also require employers to carry Workers' Compensation insurance as well. Check state requirements to make sure you are following the law.

If possible, complete Form 941 (fourth quarter), Forms W-2 and W-3, Form 940, and all the state or city forms during the first week of January, while business is still slow due to the holiday lull. That way, a large part of the book work will be out of the way and you can focus on your own tax return.

Table 2 summarizes federal employer reporting requirements. Check with your state and city tax departments to see what reports and payments they require.

TABLE 2

FEDERAL EMPLOYER REPORTS

QUARTERLY REPORT

Form 941
Purpose: to calculate quarterly liability for amounts withheld from employees for federal income tax; for employer and employee share of FICA; to record deposits made to employer's account during the quarter.

Due dates: Reports are due on the last day of the month following the end of the quarter (that is, April 30, July 31, October 31, and January 31).

Employers having a fiscal year other than the calendar year must still file quarterly reports using the due dates listed above.

(Note: States and municipalities that collect income tax may also have reports due at the same time as Form 941. State unemployment tax reports are due at the same time as Form 941.)

ANNUAL REPORTS

Form W-2
Purpose: to summarize employee earnings and withholding information for employee, employer, and Social Security Administration.

Due date: January 31 to employees; February 28 to Social Security Administration.

Form W-3
Purpose: to transmit W-2 forms to Social Security Administration and to summarize total earnings and withholding information from all employees.

Due date: January 31 to employees; February 28 to Social Security Administration.

Form 940
Purpose: to calculate federal unemployment tax liability.

Due date: January 31

Liability less deposits equals the amount you need to send with Form 941 or, if deposits exceed the liability, the refund you have coming. Sending more than $500 with Form 941 results in a penalty, which is explained below.

Additional forms: Most employers need to make periodic deposits of amounts withheld from employees. Use Form 8109 to make deposits to your employer tax account by writing checks to your local bank. Make deposits whenever the total withheld (federal income tax plus the employer's and employee's share of FICA) exceeds $500. Preferred method: each time you write a payroll, add up the FICA withheld from all employees and double that amount. Add to that total the total federal income tax withheld from all employees. That total is the amount you should deposit with Form 8109. You may be paying tax slightly ahead of time but you've eliminated the potential of using money belonging to your employees for your own operating expenses and you've eliminated the potential for penalty for using your employees' money.

Reports to File for Yourself

If you are self-employed, you are earning income from which no tax has been withheld. Because there is no withholding at the source and no employer is making periodic payments of your money on your behalf, you must make those payments yourself. You make periodic estimated tax payments using Form 1040-ES. Chances are good that if you need to make federal quarterly payments, you also need to make state payments. Check with your state tax office for the appropriate forms for making estimated state tax payments.

Self-employed people pay estimated taxes quarterly, on the fifteenth days of April, June, September, and January. (State deadlines usually conform to federal deadlines.) If the fifteenth falls on a Sunday or holiday, the deadline is moved to the following business day. Failure to make payments on time results in interest penalties. A postmark is considered proof of filing on time. A detailed discussion of paying estimated taxes is included in Chapter 20.

The other report you may need to file for yourself is a sales tax report. Even if your state has no income tax, it almost certainly has a sales tax payable on goods sold in that state. If you sell goods directly, you are probably responsible for collecting sales tax on those goods and then passing the amount collected to the state revenue department at intervals the state determines. See Chapter 14.

A last note: Many metropolitan areas levy separate sales taxes on goods sold within their jurisdictions. Be sure to ask your state department of revenue for information on sales tax collection and reporting requirements for metropolitan areas in which you live or in which you operate your business.

□ 6 □

Capitalization

Overview

Capitalization has been part of the tax code for decades. Prior to 1987, however, its provisions applied only to companies whose revenues exceeded $10 million annually. Small business wasn't affected.

The Tax Reform Act of 1986 changed all that by eliminating the dollar threshold for applicability. Tax code section 263A made capitalization provisions applicable to any manufacturing business with an inventory. Initially, all artists were subject to capitalization provisions. The ensuing hubbub resulted in an exemption, passed in the summer of 1988, removing the creative arts from the capitalization requirements. Not exempted were video artists and filmmakers.

The exemption, issued through Internal Revenue Bulletin 88-62, was retroactive to the start of 1987 and offered a compromise to video artists and filmmakers. If they elected a "safe-harbor provision," they could deduct half of their expenses in the current year, 25 percent the following year, and the last 25 percent the third year, regardless of their profit. Filmmakers and video artists who chose not to elect the safe-harbor provision could deduct expenses for their work only as they sold it. In other words, standard capitalization rules applied.

Definition

Capitalization means making an operating expense part of the capital asset it supports or prepares for sale. A clear example is a construction company, where certain overhead expenses such as electricity, rent on property, and wages, are tied to the amount of inventory the builder holds. Capitalization means that operating expenses are not written off in the year they're incurred, but rather as buildings are completed and sold.

How It Works

If you're required to capitalize expenses, you need to develop a work sheet, once you know what your annual expense totals are, by expense category. The first column is the total amount you spent for a particular expense category. The second column might be the part of the total spent on general overhead, while the third would then be the part attributable to your inventory.

You need to allocate operating expenses between general overhead (the amount you'd have to spend regardless of the size of your inventory) and overhead attributable to your inventory. Each expense category may have different percentages applied. Bank charges might be split 25 percent/75 percent, while rent on business property would likely be split 10 percent/90 percent. On audit, you would have to demonstrate how you arrived at the allocation you used.

Once the allocation is complete, the general overhead figures (column 2) are entered directly on the tax form, while the inventory-related figures are entered in the cost-of-goods-sold section as part of current-year purchases. These capitalized expenses are written off only as inventory is sold.

Advertising is one operating expense you can always write off in full in the year you incur the expense. There are several others, all generally associated with moving your product out the door. They include marketing and distribution expenses, bidding expenses, depreciation on capital assets acquired in previous years and already on a depreciation schedule (Form 4562), and articles purchased for resale. For further information, check with your accountant or read the IRS code (section 263A), available in most public libraries.

To calculate how much of the capitalized expenses need to be included in year-end inventory, you need to use three figures: beginning inventory, purchases, and ending inventory. If your year-end inventory is the same as your beginning inventory, and if your purchases amounted to twice your beginning inventory, one-third of your capitalized expenses become part of your ending inventory.

I won't go into more detail, because if you're subject to capitalization provisions, you shouldn't be doing your own tax return. This discussion is offered only to begin to explain what your accountant is doing on your tax return.

Filmmakers and Video Artists

If you're in the industry as a creator, producer, grip, camera operator, director, or any of the many other roles, you're subject to capitalization provisions.

You belong in one of two groups. The first is the creative artist who initiates a project that will be of limited market appeal. It's a good idea and a contribution to the culture, but under the best of circumstances it'll lose money. Maybe you have a couple of grants to finance it. If this description fits, the safe-harbor election is tailor-made for you. Choose it now and write off your expenses in the 50-25-25 proportions outlined above.

If that description doesn't fit, chances are you're what I call a hired gun. You're hired for a specific film project. You start work when called, and when you leave at the end of the day or the end of the project, your involvement in the film or video ends. You should use standard capitalization.

FIGURE 13

MINI BOOKS FOR A FILM MAKER OR VIDEO ARTIST

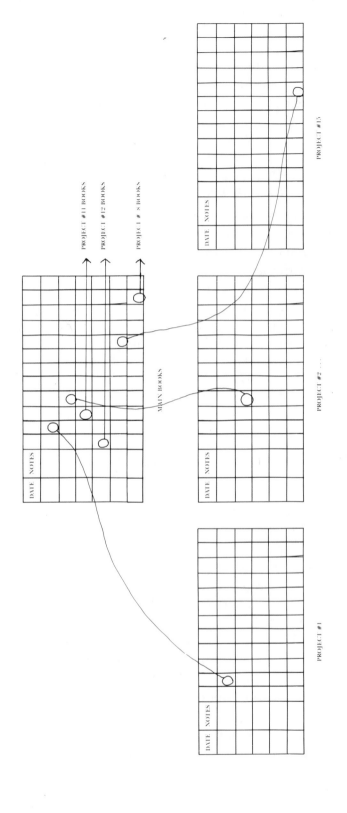

What? And do all that allocating? Not really. Stop and think for a minute. If you work on and complete fifteen film or video projects during the year, you're being paid for all of them close to the time you finish shooting. Technically, you aren't writing off expenses before you've "sold" the "project."

If push came to shove with the IRS, you could divide your regular books into fifteen mini books, each with the expenses attributable to one project. Then you'd take your overhead expenses and allocate them to each of the fifteen projects based on its proportion of your total income for the year. Figure 13 shows how this might look, *if* push came to shove and you were audited!

An example may help. Let's say filmmaker Baker earned $50,000 this past year from her video work in four separate projects for which she was paid as an independent contractor. Project A paid $15,000, B $10,000, C $20,000, and D $5,000. Direct expenses were $2,000 for A, $1,000 for B, $5,000 for C, and nothing for D. Indirect expenses for the year totaled $18,000, itemized as follows:

> studio rent = $3,600
> telephone and business long distance = $1,200
> equipment = $3,000
> dues, publications, memberships, films = $1,500
> payments to independent contractors = $2,000
> business interest = $400
> travel and entertainment = $1,200
> bank charges = $100
> office expense = $1,900
> small equipment = $1,500
> insurance on equipment = $600
> auto expense = $1,000

(To be sure, nothing in real life is this simple. Expense figures are rarely round numbers. The example is for illustration only.)

Indirect expenses would be allocated to each project in proportion to the income it brought to Baker: 30 percent to A, 20 percent to B, 40 percent to C, and 10 percent to D. Since Baker was paid for all projects in the current year, all costs would be deductible in the current year.

What about the other kind of filmmaker or video artist? What if you're shooting your own films and perhaps hiring "guns" to work for you? You're stuck with the safe-harbor provision. Set up and keep books as described elsewhere in this section. At tax time, make the kinds of changes required to meet capitalization requirements.

Remember that the safe-harbor election is irrevocable. You cannot choose to use safe-harbor rules for one or two years and then switch to regular capitalization rules in a subsequent year because you're working for another filmmaker on a project basis.

Outcomes

I have yet to have a client audited to whom capitalization requirements might apply. I don't look forward to the day. Each year I caution these clients that an audit might occur, and that they might be a test case of how far down on the business scale the IRS wants to enforce these requirements.

The same holds true for my film and video clients. Since the law is comparatively much clearer for them, I don't worry as much about possible audits. My concern comes from having seen one client burned by electing the safe-harbor option. His art films found an audience and he began making money. Expenses, even with the carry-over amounts from prior years, haven't kept pace with his income. Thus he finds himself with huge tax liabilities and not that much left over to pay them off, since his allowable deductions are only half of what he actually spent out of pocket. Eventually he'll stabilize, but for now he's in a tight spot.

For More Information

Join a professional association and monitor national lobbying efforts to change the law. As you file your tax returns, consult a tax accountant who's familiar with capitalization. Maybe bring along a copy of this book. Consult Internal Revenue Code Section 263A for basic information, and read Internal Revenue Service Bulletin 88-62 for information on the safe-harbor option.

PART

II

SPECIAL

TAX

TOPICS

□ 7 □

Depreciation

Overview

Depreciation is a major reason taxpayers hire accountants to complete their tax returns. The myriad rules, seemingly endless exceptions to those rules, tables with apparently conflicting information, and multiple options for handling depreciable property can strike terror in the heart of the most devoted reader of IRS publications. A good clue that even the IRS considers depreciation one of the trickiest parts of tax-return preparation is the length of its own publication on the topic. Publication 534, "Depreciation," is almost one hundred pages long, where the average length of IRS publications is usually sixteen to twenty-four pages. That said, is there any hope that you'll ever understand this topic?

Of course. Like most things in the tax world, depreciation is a bunch of little pieces of information, none of which, by itself, is difficult to understand. It's when you put all the little pieces together that you have something so complicated that it appears intimidating.

This is certainly true of depreciation. Keep your attention focused on those little pieces of information until you have enough little pieces to be able to put them together and make up the big picture.

The key to understanding depreciation is to remember that each depreciable item has only one set of rules that apply to it. For example, if you buy a camera this year, you select the set of rules to use in calculating the deduction you'll take on this year's tax return. For the length of time you own that camera the rules never change, though the dollar amount you deduct is different from year to year.

Use this list of questions to assign the correct rules to each piece of equipment you buy in a given year:

1.   Is it listed or unlisted property?
2.   What is its life?
3.   Are there any drawbacks to using MACRS?
4.   How much did I spend on capital assets this year? Was more than 40 percent of this spent in the last three months of the year?

For this camera purchase, the answers are:

1.   Listed, so information needs to be reported in a special place on Form 4562.
2.   Five years.
3.   No.
4. $6,200. (The camera cost $800). Less than 40 percent of the $6,200 was spent in the last three months of the year, so the midyear convention will apply to the camera (and to all other capital assets).

"Whoa!" I hear you saying. What are all these terms? What's a midyear convention? Is it held in Miami? Have patience: My intention is to give you a quick introduction; I have the rest of this section to provide details, refinements, and options. By the time you've finished reading through this part, you will know what kind of property—in IRS lingo—you're buying and how you can deduct its cost on your tax return. You'll also begin to understand how to time your purchases for maximum advantage.

Do I have your attention? Good. On to the "little pieces."

Definition

Depreciation is a decrease, over time, in the value of a capital asset with a determinable life that is used to produce income, where the decrease in value is caused by wear and tear, decay, or obsolescence. A capital asset must meet all three criteria (determinable life, income-producing activity, decreased value over time) in order to be depreciated. Some items never depreciate: land, because it has no determinable life; most string instruments, since they do not decay or decrease in value over time; and start-up costs, since they are not income-producing. (If start-up costs lead to an income-producing activity, however, they can be *amortized,* a different concept).

DETERMINING THE LIFE OF AN ASSET

Since 1987, the IRS has assigned a five-year life to automobiles, computers, and film and video equipment. Office furnishings have a seven-year life. Residential rental property has a life of 27.5 years, while commercial rental property (including home office space) has a life of 31.5 years. IRS Publication 534, "Depreciation," gives the life of every class of depreciable property.

CHOOSING A DEPRECIATION METHOD

The depreciation method to be used for items purchased after 1986 is called the modified accelerated cost recovery system (modified ACRS, known by the acronym MACRS), which uses a double-declining balance (DDB) method of calculating allowable annual depreciation.

One notable exception is assets purchased after 1986 that are used less than 50 percent for business. They must be depreciated using the asset depreciation range (ADR) life system with alternate MACRS, also spelled out in Publication 534. Generally, if you use an asset less than 50 percent for business, you depreciate it over a longer period of time. Office furniture, for example, must be depreciated over ten years, using alternate MACRS, if it's used less than

50 percent for business. In the case of automobiles or other listed property, the number of years over which the asset is depreciated remains the same, but alternate MACRS (a slightly slower method) must be used. ("Listed property" is explained later in this chapter.)

For assets placed into service prior to 1987, continue using the depreciation method and life you originally used until the asset is fully depreciated. For assets purchased prior to 1981 but placed into service in a subsequent year, use the depreciation method least favorable to you. For example, a harp purchased in 1983 for $3,000 and placed in income-producing service last year would be depreciated under MACRS rules.

I'm not tricking you with the harp example, by the way, nor am I testing to see how closely you've been following this discussion. A harp is the one string instrument you can depreciate because its valves wear out over time. (Ah, the things you learn in preparing artists' tax returns . . .)

How MACRS Works

In theory, the double-declining balance method of depreciation divides the cost of the business asset by its expected life and then, in the first year, doubles that amount of allowable depreciation. In the second year, the cost of the asset less the first year's depreciation, divided by the assigned life, gives regular depreciation. Again, multiplying regular depreciation times two gives the double-declining balance amount you can deduct in that second year.

The double-declining method breaks down at a certain point, as you'll see. (Also, in the example below, you'll see a new term—midyear convention. It is explained later in this chapter.) Example: A $2,000 computer yields this much depreciation in the first year: ($2,000 ÷ 5) × 2 = $800 × 1/2 (midyear convention) = $400. And this much depreciation in the second year: [($2,000 − $400) ÷ 5] × 2 = $640.

In the third year, subtract depreciation of the first two years from the cost, then divide by the life, and double the figure that results.

In theory, you continue this way until there is no balance left. If you start calculating, however, you soon find you can continue calculating smaller and smaller deductions, well into infinity. The IRS has set a limit on the life of an asset, which means its value is used up over that assigned life. That means you need to deduct the purchase price over that assigned life, not over the potential life created by using the double-declining balance method of calculating allowable depreciation. That's where you need to leave the theory behind MACRS and turn to the tables the IRS recommends you use to calculate allowable depreciation on a particular asset in a particular year.

For this computer with its five-year life, turn to Table 3 at the end of this chapter where you see that the fourth and fifth year deductions equal 11.52 percent of cost (or $230 per year), with the sixth year deduction equal to 5.76 percent of cost (or $115). Total depreciation on the computer, then, for the six years is $400 + $640 + $384 + $230 + $230 + $115 = $1,999 (you lose one dollar because of rounding).

Any asset is fully depreciated over the number of years in its assigned life plus one year. You never claim depreciation expense that exceeds your cost or basis in the asset.

Now let's go back to the midyear convention used in the first-year calculation. With the midyear convention, the IRS forces you to add a year of life to any asset you depreciate. The IRS assumes that you purchased the asset in the middle of the year, regardless of when you actually purchased it. The midyear convention requires you to use only a half-year of depreciation the first year and the last year you own the asset; the other years are full years.

Use the midyear convention for all assets purchased after 1986, unless you purchase a lot of capital assets in the last three months of the year. If 40 percent of the total value of the assets purchased in the current year falls in the last quarter of the year, you must use the midquarter convention.

Assume you purchased that computer in October, and it was the only capital asset you purchased during the year. First-year depreciation would be figured this way: ($2,000 ÷ 5) × 2 = $800 × .125 (midquarter convention for fourth quarter) = $100. And second-year depreciation this way: [($2,000 − $100) ÷ 5] × 2 = $760.

With multiple purchases, you have separate calculations to perform. Assume you bought the $2,000 computer in October and a $1,000 desk in June. Since more than 40 percent of the total expenditure for capital assets occurred in the last quarter of the calendar year, you know you need to use the midquarter convention. For the computer, you know you use the fourth quarter of the midquarter convention. For the office furniture, you can use the second quarter of the midquarter convention (since June falls in the second quarter of the year): ($1,000 ÷ 7) × 2 = $286 × .625 (midquarter convention for second quarter) = $179. (Note: The midquarter convention for the third quarter is .375; for the first quarter, .875.) Second-year depreciation on the office furniture, then, would be: [($1,000 − $179) ÷ 7] × 2 = $235.

To simplify your life, there are tables at the end of this chapter that reduce these steps to a simple percentage for each class of property (three-year, five-year, seven-year) for the first year of service through the last, with one column of percentages using the midyear convention and four columns, one for each quarter, using the midquarter conventions. Using Table 4 (seven-year property) for the office furniture purchased above, you'd calculate first-year depreciation this way: $1,000 × .1786 = $179. And, for the second year: $1,000 × .2348 = $235.

Expensing

Expensing is a form of depreciation by which you write off the entire cost of an asset in the year you buy it. Expensing is limited to $10,000 per year for individuals (not corporations or partnerships), provided you purchased less than $100,000 in capital assets during the year. Expensing is further limited by your net profit for the year; you cannot use expensing to create a net loss in your business.

Any asset you cannot or choose not to expense must be depreciated. Take, for example, a computer design center costing $15,000. If you have a large-enough net profit, you can expense $10,000 of that system but must depreciate the $5,000 balance over five years.

Expensing is also known as Section 179 expense, because Internal Revenue Code Section 179 lays out the guidelines on writing off a capital asset in the year of purchase.

Listed Property

Automobiles, computers, and film and video equipment (including cameras) are special in that they are considered by the IRS to be "listed property," which has its own special section on the back of Form 4562. The IRS tracks listed property carefully.

Depreciation on listed property is always calculated in the "listed property" section of Form 4562, whether it involves a current-year purchase or prior-year purchase. Totals from the listed property section are then carried to the general depreciation section for a final total that, in turn, is carried to Schedule C for sole proprietors, to Form 1065 for partnerships, or to Form 1120 or 1120-S for corporations.

Depreciation Recapture

If you use an asset in business and then retire it to personal use, or its use falls to less than 50 percent in the current year, you need to "pay back" some of the depreciation claimed. This is called depreciation recapture.

The amount recaptured is the difference between the MACRS amount of depreciation you claimed and the straight-line depreciation you are allowed for the asset depreciation range (ADR life) of an asset. (This is a second use for ADR life. The other you've already seen is using the ADR life from the start, to depreciate a capital asset you use less than 50 percent for business. In depreciation recapture, you need to revert to the ADR life when business use drops to less than 50 percent.)

Table 7 shows allowable straight-line depreciation percentages for capital assets that were depreciated using the midyear convention; Tables 8 through 11 show allowable straight-line depreciation percentages for those depreciated using midquarter conventions. These tables cover only assets with a maximum ADR life of ten years. For other assets, consult the tables in Publication 534.

To see how recapture works, let's assume that thousand-dollar desk you bought in the example above was retired in its third year of service. (Maybe you gave it to your cousin who was starting her own business.) As a business asset, it had a seven-year life, and depreciation taken in the first two years was $179 plus $235, or $414. Allowable depreciation, had straight-line depreciation with ADR life of ten years been used, would have been (from Table 9, since the midquarter convention for the second quarter was used): $1000 × (.0625 + .10) = $163. The recapture amount is the difference between the claimed depreciation ($414) and the allowed depreciation ($163), or $251. This becomes "other income" in the income section of Schedule C.

Note that converting this desk to personal use results in a double whammy; beyond the usual depreciation addback, the life of the furniture went from seven to ten years.

Special Rules for Luxury Automobiles

Part of the rationale behind the 1986 Tax Reform Act was to clamp down on upper-income taxpayers and their use of tax loopholes to support an affluent lifestyle. One such loophole was the luxury automobile written off over three years at the expense of the middle- and lower-income taxpayer.

Perhaps lawmakers went too far when they defined a luxury automobile as any automobile costing more than $12,800, but that's what they did. In addition to extending the life of any vehicle (five years, up from three under ACRS), the act limited annual deductions. The limit on the combined total of depreciation and Section 179 expense for 1991 is $2,660 for the first year of service, $4,300 for the second,

$2,550 for the third, and then $1,575 for each succeeding year, until the vehicle is fully depreciated. Lower limits apply for vehicles placed into service before 1991.

If you use your luxury vehicle less than 100 percent for business, that limit is $2,660 times your percentage business use. The percentage business use you claim in any given year must be substantiated by your daily mileage log. If your business use falls below 50 percent in any year, you must switch to the ADR life (the same five years) and recapture the excess depreciation taken in prior years (since the straight-line depreciation used with ADR life is less than the accelerated depreciation used with MACRS).

Special Rules for Partial Business Use of a Capital Asset

Any depreciable asset used less than 100 percent in business requires you to keep a daily log book of usage. This applies to automobiles, computers, and film and video equipment.

Special Rules on Home Office Use

If you own your home, have an office in it, and deduct expenses for operating your home on Schedule C (for example, a percent of mortgage interest, property taxes, insurance, and utility payments), you must depreciate the same percentage of your home using the 31.5 year real property table in the Form 4562 instructions (reprinted at the end of this chapter as Table 5).

Beginning with the 1991 tax forms, claiming a home-office deduction requires you to file Form 8829 with your tax return.

Claiming a home office or studio has tax consequences when you sell your residence, since the tax on capital gains attributable to the percentage of business use falls due and cannot be deferred, as can

TABLE 3

DEPRECIATION OF FIVE-YEAR PROPERTY
(Automobiles, Computers, Cameras, Film/Video Equipment)

| Year | Half-Year Convention | Midquarter Convention | | | |
		First Quarter	Second Quarter	Third Quarter	Fourth Quarter
1	20 %	35 %	25 %	15 %	5 %
2	32	26	30	34	38
3	19.2	15.6	18	20.4	22.8
4	11.52	11.01	11.37	12.24	13.68
5	11.52	11.01	11.37	11.30	10.94
6	5.76	1.38	4.26	7.06	9.58

the capital gain attributable to the residential portion. One way around this: Do not claim a home-office deduction for two full calendar years before you sell your home. The depreciation taken in prior years still reduces the basis of your house, but at least the entire gain can be rolled over into the new (and more expensive) residence.

TABLE 4

DEPRECIATION OF SEVEN-YEAR PROPERTY
(Office Furnishings, Tripods, Kilns, TV Cameras)

| Year | Half-Year Convention | Midquarter Convention | | | |
		First Quarter	Second Quarter	Third Quarter	Fourth Quarter
1	14.29%	25.01%	17.86%	10.72%	3.57%
2	24.50	21.43	23.48	25.52	27.56
3	17.49	15.31	16.77	18.22	19.68
4	12.50	10.93	11.97	13.02	14.06
5	8.92	8.74	8.87	9.29	10.04
6	8.92	8.74	8.87	8.85	8.73
7	8.92	8.74	8.87	8.85	8.73
8	4.46	1.10	3.31	5.53	7.63

TABLE 5

DEPRECIATION OF 31.5-YEAR PROPERTY
(Commercial Office Space, Office in Your Home)

Accelerated depreciation tables for computing first-year depreciation for 31.5-year property placed in service in each month:

	1st year	Years 2–7
January	3.0423%	3.175%
February	2.7778%	3.175%
March	2.5132%	3.175%
April	2.2487%	3.175%
May	1.9841%	3.175%
June	1.7196%	3.175%
July	1.4550%	3.175%
August	1.1905%	3.175%
September	0.9259%	3.175%
October	0.6614%	3.175%
November	0.3968%	3.175%
December	0.1323%	3.175%

If you own your own home and claim home-office deductions, don't neglect to claim the depreciation deduction. Depreciation is an "allowed" or "allowable" expense, which means it'll be counted against you if you were entitled to take it but chose not to take it. Choosing not to claim depreciation on a home office so as not to hassle with capital gains calculations when you sell your home is not permitted. The only time you do not claim depreciation on a home-office situation is when the depreciation deduction pushes you into a net-loss situation.

Some Practical Advice

The threshold on what constitutes a capital asset has dropped steadily over the past few years. Currently a good rule of thumb is that any asset costing more than $200 should be depreciated; more

---

TABLE 6

DEPRECIATION FOR 27.5-YEAR PROPERTY
(Residential Rental Property)

Accelerated depreciation tables for computing first-year depreciation for 27.5-year property placed in service in each month:

	1st year	Years 2–8
January	3.4848%	3.636%
February	3.1818%	3.636%
March	2.8788%	3.636%
April	2.5758%	3.636%
May	2.2727%	3.636%
June	1.9697%	3.636%
July	1.6667%	3.636%
August	1.3636%	3.636%
September	1.0606%	3.636%
October	0.7576%	3.636%
November	0.4545%	3.636%
December	0.1515%	3.636%

---

precisely, it should be depreciated or expensed. Try to expense as many small capital assets as you can; depreciating a $225 lens over five years is a pretty tedious exercise.

If you keep your books with a category labeled "Small Equipment," and in that category you have several individual items costing $100 to $200 each, you may have a sizeable expense total for that category. Instead of entering the total on the "other expenses" line of Schedule C, enter the total as five-year property and expense it on Form 4562. This prevents an auditor from forcing you to depreciate it, should your return pop up for review.

Your automobile log should, at a minimum, reflect mileage totals for each job site you visit or, alternatively, odometer readings backed up by an appointment log for the day. Keep a mileage log on the dashboard of your car, with a pen or pencil clipped to it, for easy use. If you don't keep a log, forget about claiming a deduction for business use of your personal automobile.

TABLE 7

DEPRECIATION RECAPTURE
Midyear Convention

ADR Life

Year	2.5	3	3.5	4	5	6	6.5	7
1	20	16.67	14.29	12.5	10	8.33	7.69	7.14 %
2	40	33.33	28.57	25	20	16.67	15.39	14.29
3	40	33.33	28.57	25	20	16.67	15.38	14.29
4		16.67	28.57	25	20	16.67	15.39	14.28
5				12.50	20	16.66	15.38	14.29
6					10	16.67	15.39	14.28
7						8.33	15.38	14.29
8								7.14

Year	7.5	8	8.5	9	9.5	10
1	6.67	6.25	5.88	5.56	5.26	5 %
2	13.33	12.5	11.77	11.11	10.53	10
3	13.33	12.5	11.76	11.11	10.53	10
4	13.33	12.5	11.77	11.11	10.53	10
5	13.34	12.5	11.76	11.11	10.52	10
6	13.33	12.5	11.77	11.11	10.53	10
7	13.34	12.5	11.76	11.11	10.52	10
8	13.33	12.5	11.77	11.11	10.53	10
9		6.25	11.76	11.11	10.52	10
10				5.56	10.53	10
11						5

While depreciating a vehicle is discussed in some detail in this section, you should know that the steady increase in the standard mileage rate has made it the preferred method of deducting auto expenses. If you like, you can gather your receipts during the year and figure your deduction using the actual expense method adjusted by business percentage use of the vehicle. But in nine cases out of ten you'll find the standard mileage rate produces a larger deduction. (More on autos is included in Chapter 8.)

TABLE 8

DEPRECIATION RECAPTURE
Midquarter Convention: First Quarter

ADR Life

Year	2.5	3	3.5	4	5	6	6.5	7
1	35	29.17	25	21.88	17.5	14.58	13.46	12.5 %
2	40	33.33	28.57	25	20	16.67	15.38	14.29
3	25	33.33	28.57	25	20	16.67	15.39	14.28
4		4.17	17.86	25	20	16.67	15.38	14.29
5				3.12	20	16.66	15.39	14.28
6					2.5	16.67	15.38	14.29
7						2.08	9.62	14.28
8								1.79

Year	7.5	8	8.5	9	9.5	10
1	11.67	10.94	10.29	9.72	9.21	8.75 %
2	13.33	12.5	11.77	11.11	10.53	10
3	13.33	12.5	11.76	11.11	10.53	10
4	13.33	12.5	11.77	11.11	10.53	10
5	13.34	12.5	11.76	11.11	10.52	10
6	13.33	12.5	11.77	11.11	10.53	10
7	13.34	12.5	11.76	11.11	10.52	10
8	8.33	12.5	11.77	11.12	10.53	10
9		1.56	7.35	11.11	10.52	10
10				1.39	6.58	10
11						1.25

For More Information

IRS Publication 534, "Depreciation," contains all you want or need to know about the subject.

TABLE 9

DEPRECIATION RECAPTURE
Midquarter Convention: Second Quarter

ADR Life

Year	2.5	3	3.5	4	5	6	6.5	7
1	25	20.83	17.86	15.63	12.5	10.42	9.62	8.92 %
2	40	33.33	28.57	25	20	16.67	15.38	14.29
3	35	33.34	28.57	25	20	16.67	15.38	14.28
4		12.5	25	25	20	16.66	15.39	14.29
5				9.37	20	16.67	15.38	14.28
6					7.5	16.66	15.39	14.29
7						6.25	13.46	14.28
8								5.36

Year	7.5	8	8.5	9	9.5	10
1	8.33	7.81	7.35	6.94	6.58	6.25 %
2	13.33	12.5	11.77	11.11	10.53	10
3	13.33	12.5	11.76	11.11	10.53	10
4	13.34	12.5	11.77	11.11	10.53	10
5	13.33	12.5	11.76	11.11	10.52	10
6	13.34	12.5	11.77	11.11	10.53	10
7	13.33	12.5	11.76	11.11	10.52	10
8	11.67	12.5	11.77	11.12	10.53	10
9		4.69	10.29	11.11	10.52	10
10				4.17	9.21	10
11						3.75

TABLE 10

DEPRECIATION RECAPTURE
Midquarter Convention: Third Quarter

ADR Life

Year	2.5	3	3.5	4	5	6	6.5	7
1	15	12.5	10.71	9.38	7.5	6.25	5.77	5.36 %
2	40	33.33	28.57	25	20	16.67	15.38	14.29
3	40	33.34	28.57	25	20	16.67	15.39	14.28
4	5	20.83	28.58	25	20	16.66	15.38	14.29
5			3.57	15.62	20	16.67	15.39	14.28
6					12.5	16.66	15.38	14.29
7						10.42	15.39	14.28
8							1.92	8.93

Year	7.5	8	8.5	9	9.5	10
1	5	4.69	4.41	4.17	3.95	3.75 %
2	13.33	12.5	11.76	11.11	10.53	10
3	13.33	12.5	11.77	11.11	10.53	10
4	13.33	12.5	11.76	11.11	10.52	10
5	13.34	12.5	11.77	11.11	10.53	10
6	13.33	12.5	11.76	11.11	10.52	10
7	13.34	12.5	11.77	11.11	10.53	10
8	13.33	12.5	11.76	11.12	10.52	10
9	1.67	7.81	11.77	11.11	10.53	10
10			1.47	6.95	10.53	10
11					1.32	6.25

TABLE 11

DEPRECIATION RECAPTURE
Midquarter Convention: Fourth Quarter

ADR Life

Year	2.5	3	3.5	4	5	6	6.5	7	
1	5	4.17	3.57	3.13	2.5	2.08	1.92	1.79	%
2	40	33.33	28.57	25	20	16.67	15.39	14.29	
3	40	33.33	28.57	25	20	16.67	15.38	14.28	
4	15	29.17	28.57	25	20	16.67	15.39	14.29	
5			10.72	21.87	20	16.66	15.38	14.28	
6					17.5	16.67	15.39	14.29	
7						14.58	15.38	14.28	
8							5.77	12.5	

Year	7.5	8	8.5	9	9.5	10	
1	1.67	1.56	1.47	1.39	1.32	1.25	%
2	13.33	12.5	11.76	11.11	10.53	10	
3	13.33	12.5	11.77	11.11	10.53	10	
4	13.33	12.5	11.76	11.11	10.52	10	
5	13.33	12.5	11.77	11.11	10.53	10	
6	13.34	12.5	11.76	11.11	10.52	10	
7	13.33	12.5	11.77	11.11	10.53	10	
8	13.34	12.5	11.76	11.12	10.52	10	
9	5	10.94	11.77	11.11	10.53	10	
10			4.41	9.73	10.52	10	
11						8.75	

❑ _8_ ❑

Using Your Personal Automobile for Business

Overview

Using your car for business represents a potentially valuable deduction. To make the most of it, know the rules on documenting usage and calculating the deduction.

Mileage Log

Claiming a deduction for the business use of your automobile starts with an accurate, verifiable record of overall usage. Generally this means a daily log of beginning and ending odometer readings for each type of driving: commuting, personal, W-2 job (beyond commuting; may include driving to a second W-2 job), and business (self-employment). Of these four types of driving, only personal miles are not essential for you to track.

There is no deduction for commuting mileage, so the IRS is particularly interested in having you declare an accurate number of commuting miles. Commuting is defined as the first business trip each day and the last business trip each day.

Example 1. You leave home to drive to your W-2 job, spend the entire day there, and drive home in the evening. What you have: all commuting miles.

Example 2. You leave home to drop your child at the daycare provider. From there you proceed to your W-2 job, where you spend the day. After work you drive to the daycare center to pick up your child. You stop at the grocery store and dry cleaner before returning home. What you have: commuting miles (daycare center to work and work to daycare center) and personal miles (all the rest).

Example 3. You leave home to drive to a W-2 job. From that job you drive to a second W-2 job. After completing your shift, you drive home. What you have: commuting mileage plus W-2 mileage from the first W-2 job to the second.

Example 4. You leave home to drive to a W-2 job. You stop home for dinner before driving to an evening W-2 job, from which you eventually drive home. What you have: all commuting miles (because you've divided your business day into sections).

Example 5. You leave home for your studio. From your studio you pick up supplies at an art store, stop to visit with a gallery owner, and meet a colleague for lunch. After lunch you return home. What you have: commuting (home to studio and lunch location to home) and business (all the rest).

Example 6. You leave home for your job where you're treated as an independent contractor, even though that's the only place you work. At the end of the day, you return home. What you have: all commuting miles.

Example 7. Your studio is in your home. You leave home to see a client about a bid, stop to look at a new piece of equipment, drop off a finished product, and meet an agent for lunch. After lunch you stop to pick up new supplies and return to your studio to work. Later in the evening you attend a work-related conference. What you have: all business miles.

To summarize: Everyone has commuting mileage except self-employed people who work for multiple customers, and employees who travel to multiple sites as part of their regular job responsibilities. Be aware, however, that home-to-studio or studio-to-home trips for a self-employed artist are considered commuting, regardless of the number of outside contracts the artist has.

Once you're comfortable with these distinctions, buy a notebook you won't be afraid to use to record the different kinds of miles you drive. Clip a pen or pencil to it and leave it on the dashboard of your car. There you'll see it and be more inclined to use it than if it were hidden in the glove compartment. Traffic delays and stop lights are particularly suited to documenting your trips.

In the log, besides starting and ending odometer readings, use a code to track the different types of driving you do. Use C for commuting, P for personal, W for W-2 (out of the office or second job), and B for business miles. If you're exclusively self-employed with multiple customers, forget about P or W or C (unless you have an external studio) and focus instead on shorthand notations of your itinerary so you're able to substantiate the business purpose for the readings you enter. Gaps in odometer readings occur whenever you drive for personal reasons. Figure 14 shows how your log might look.

As you reach the end of a page, add up the miles driven for each category. This increases accuracy and reduces year-end work.

There's no single correct way to document automobile use. You can identify business trips with B and jot down some (or all) destinations each day in the mileage log, or you can keep your itinerary in an appointment book. But you must be able to justify to a stranger (an IRS auditor) two years after the fact where you went on July 12 or September 19 that resulted in your claiming a deduction for twenty-six miles or thirty-eight miles, respectively. Develop a system that fits your style and then use it!

At the end of the year, subtract the January 1 odometer reading from the December 31 odometer reading. This is the total number of miles driven in the year. Add up your subtotals for the C, P, W, and B categories. You'll need this information when you complete tax forms to claim a deduction for business use of your vehicle, regardless of the deduction method you select: standard mileage rate or actual expenses.

FIGURE 14
ODOMETER LOG

DATE	ODOMETER Beg. of Trip	End of Trip	MILES	TOLLS	PARKING	DESTINATION	BUSINESS PURPOSE	NAME OF USER
6-14	17452	17457	D-M (supplies)					
6-15	17457	17499	Mimeshade Galley					
6-19	17601	17616	PO; Supplies					
6-20	17619	17633	conf					
6-21	17633	17647	"					
6-24	17688	17707	D-M /Supplies					
6-25	17707	17711	Install White					
	17711	17718	Supplies					
	17718	17744	installation					
6-26	17799	17833	"					

Standard Mileage Rate Method

The standard mileage rate is a federally calculated figure designed to include the average costs of operating a vehicle per mile of use. The figure is announced late in November or December for use the following year. Watch your local newspaper or call the IRS in December for the new rate. Always be sure to specify the year you're asking about, because the IRS is not accustomed to taxpayers being a step ahead of the game.

Because it's intended to cover the average costs of operating the average vehicle, the standard mileage rate includes such things as average gas and oil costs, repairs and maintenance, cost of the average vehicle, and insurance. If you use the standard mileage rate to deduct the business use of the vehicle you own, the only additional items you can deduct are business parking costs and a percentage of interest paid on your car loan (total interest paid multiplied by the percentage of business use).

The standard mileage rate deduction is available only to those who own their cars. If you lease a car, you must use the actual expense method of deducting expenses. Also, if you have ever used the actual expense method of deducting auto expenses on a certain car, you may not be eligible to use the standard mileage rate deduction on that car. Generally, once you switch from using the standard mileage rate as a basis for deducting expenses on a car, you can't use the method again until you buy a different car. The only exception is if you used the actual expense method with a straight-line (instead of accelerated) method of depreciation.

Using the standard mileage rate is specific to each car you own. In other words, you may use the actual expense method for one car and the standard mileage rate for the other. Just be sure to have adequate documentation (in the form of auto logbooks) for each vehicle to substantiate the deduction you take for each.

Because the standard mileage rate is designed to include the average costs of operating an average vehicle, including purchase price, part of the standard mileage rate is an allowance for depreciation. This bit of information doesn't factor into your tax-return preparation until you sell your car. Then it becomes a factor in calculating gain or loss on the vehicle. See Chapter 16 for an example of how the depreciation implicit in the standard mileage rate is figured into the gain/loss equation.

Since 1990 there has been no limit on the miles you can drive using the standard mileage rate deduction. This tax simplification has greatly benefited the average taxpayer through reduced paperwork and increased write-offs.

Actual Expense Method

The actual expense method of deducting expenses for business use of your automobile requires documenting all operating expenses (gas and oil, repairs and maintenance, insurance, license) and multiplying by the total percentage of business use. To this total can be added business-related parking expenses. If you are self-employed, you can also take the self-employment percentage of your business mileage and multiply it by interest paid on your car loan as an "other interest" deduction on Schedule C.

The actual expense method also provides for a certain percentage of the cost of the vehicle to be depreciated (or expensed), subject to the limitations described in Chapter 7. Briefly, the depreciation method is determined by whether or not you use your car more than 50 percent for business. If you do, use accelerated depreciation

(MACRS); if not, use straight-line depreciation. The maximum allowable depreciation is determined by the cost of the vehicle and the percentage of business use.

You must depreciate your vehicle on Form 4562. Be sure to use the "listed property" section of that form. Vehicles are always entered first on the form, regardless of the year placed in service.

Using the actual expense method of deducting expenses for business use of your car requires you to keep not only a mileage log, but also receipts for all automobile expenses.

Remember that the depreciation you deduct as part of the actual expense method figures into your calculations of capital gain or loss when you sell the vehicle. Although you can never have a capital gain from overdepreciating a vehicle using the standard mileage rate method, you *can* have a taxable gain from overdepreciating a vehicle using the actual expense method.

Leased Vehicles

If you lease a vehicle, you must use the actual expense method of deducting expenses for business use of the car. You may not use the standard mileage rate deduction.

To calculate your annual deduction, add up all the expenses you incurred in operating the car for the year. Include gas and oil, repairs and maintenance, insurance, license plate tags, and lease payments. Then multiply that total by the percentage of business use (from your automobile log) to arrive at your business deduction.

If you use your leased vehicle for both W-2 purposes and self-employment purposes, report business use for the former on Form 2106 and business use for the latter on Form 4562 (for subsequent transfer to Schedule C).

If your employer reimburses you for business use of the vehicle you drive, whether you own it or lease it, and if that reimbursement is higher or lower than the standard mileage rate deduction, the reimbursement is included in taxable wages (Box 10 of Form W-2). Your allowable deduction may be higher or lower than the amount your employer paid you. If it's higher, you have an additional deduction on Form 2106, which subsequently is taken as a miscellaneous deduction subject to the 2 percent of adjusted gross income threshold on Schedule A. If your allowable deduction is less than the amount your employer paid you (and it may well be), then you have excess income, calculated on Form 2106 and transferred to the "wages" line of Form 1040.

If your employer reimbursed you for business use of your leased vehicle at the standard mileage rate for the year, that reimbursement doesn't show up on your W-2 form. But you still need to include it in your calculations on Form 2106, since the standard mileage rate probably exceeds the amount you're able to deduct, because you have to use the actual expense method on a leased vehicle.

Leasing a Luxury Vehicle

Since 1987, a luxury vehicle has been defined as any vehicle costing more than $12,800. This threshold has implications for the person who leases a luxury vehicle. There's no way, since the 1986 Tax Reform Act, the government will allow you to lease a Jaguar convertible and write it off at taxpayer expense.

To deduct expenses on a leased luxury vehicle, use the actual expense method described above (operating and lease expenses times percentage of business use). That gives you your deduction. The next step is to add a certain amount to income to adjust for the fact that the lease payments on a Jaguar are significantly higher than they are on a Ford. This is called the inclusion amount.

You need to look at the tables in IRS Publication 917 to determine the inclusion amount for the specific vehicle you are leasing, since the inclusion amount depends on what year of the lease you're in, as well as the fair market value of the car at the time of leasing. (Your dealer should have included it in your lease contract.)

The inclusion amount from the tables in Publication 917 is adjusted by your overall percentage of business use. If you've had the car for only part of the tax year, adjust for that, too. Enter this inclusion amount on the "other income" line of Form 1040 if you use the car for your W-2 job, or on the "other income" line in the revenues section of Schedule C if you use the car for self-employment activities. Label the entry clearly as "inclusion amount for leased vehicle."

Special rules apply to vehicles leased between April 2, 1985 and January 1, 1987. See Publication 917 for instructions on how to calculate the "additional inclusion amount" for cars leased during this time.

Lease or Buy?

Leasing has become an affordable way of moving into a nice car. I still prefer ownership, however, with certain exceptions.

It's better to lease than to own if you drive an above-average number of miles each year (upwards of 20,000, say, and most of those for business) and can negotiate a lease agreement with a three- or four-year term but without maximum miles. What you're doing, then, is pounding the heck out of a car you won't ever have to see again, while providing yourself with a new vehicle every three years or so and all the accompanying safety features you need if you drive for a living.

It's better to lease than to own if you can't afford a new car and need a reliable vehicle to get you around the country—to art fairs, for example. Breakdowns with a full load of work are costly, aggravating, and potentially dangerous.

Finance or Pay Cash?

Even though interest on an auto loan is partially deductible on Schedule C (in an amount equivalent to the percentage of business use times interest paid), I prefer paying for a car outright, unless you can get a financing deal that costs less than you can earn in a safe investment.

A car is a waste of money, just about any way you look at it. It's not like a house, which generally appreciates over time and gives you a roof over your head long after it's paid for. In many instances you finish paying off the car loan and trade in for another car and another loan. I've heard automobile dealers argue that a car payment is as integral a part of your monthly budget as a house payment. Phooey!

You get the best value by buying a solid, reasonably priced car new, and driving it for ten years or 90,000 miles, whichever comes first. Especially with the standard mileage rate deduction, you'll find this the best business investment you can make.

Commercial Vehicles

If you drive a commercial vehicle (taxicab, snowplow, or a truck with commercial plates), you do not need to keep a mileage log of business use. Instead, keep a log of personal use. Mileage on a commercial vehicle is defined as primarily business mileage, and the same rules apply that govern employee use of a company-owned car.

Miscellaneous

When you sell or otherwise dispose of your automobile (even if you have someone haul it away for scrap), you have a potentially taxable transaction. See Chapter 16 for reporting requirements.

You must own the automobile for which you're taking a deduction. A borrowed vehicle doesn't qualify. If you use a friend's car, draw up a rental agreement under which you pay specified amounts depending on usage. With such an agreement in place, you can write off those payments as rental equipment. Remember: If payments to that friend exceed $600 in the year, you need to issue a Form 1099-MISC to that friend by January 31.

Store your mileage log with your other business receipts for the year. The log is an important document; take care of it!

Some Practical Advice

In 90 percent of the cases I see in my tax practice, the standard mileage rate method results in a bigger deduction for low-business-use drivers as well as for high-business-use drivers. The same is true for high-volume drivers and luxury car owners. The IRS wants to simplify auto deductions, both for itself and for the taxpayer. It made the pot sweet enough to convince most taxpayers to go the standard mileage deduction route.

If you're audited and you didn't keep a mileage log contemporaneously, reconstruct one from your date book prior to going into the audit. No mileage log generally means total disallowance of any automobile deduction claimed.

Never rewrite your mileage log to make it look neater. If you're stopped in traffic or jotting notes on the freeway, your entries will vary in clarity and evenness. That's good; it shows you kept the log as you went along during the year, and did not construct it after the fact.

For More Information

IRS Publication 917, "Business Use of a Car," describes in detail all issues related to using your car for work.

□ 9 □

Home Office

Definition

When your studio is in your home, you have a home office. Whether or not you're able to deduct as a business expense a part of the costs associated with your home depends on two factors: the exclusive use of a definable space for business purposes, and the profitability of your business; specifically, having a large enough profit so that home office deductions don't create a business loss.

If you don't meet both criteria you may have a home office, but it's not a tax-deductible expense for you.

Exclusive Use

The part of your home where you have your office or studio must be a separate room or a definable space that you use only for business. You can create a definable space by partitioning a room into separate areas.

If you use an area for both business and personal reasons—a living room, for example, where you practice your dance moves or meet with clients during the day—you fail the exclusive-use test and have no allowable deduction. Perhaps you have a second bedroom you use for business. Maybe it has a folding bed you use if company comes. To protect your deduction, get that bed out of the room and have your company sleep in the living room. Same with children's toys, same with your aunt's luggage, and so on.

The major exception to the exclusive-use test affects daycare providers.

PROVING EXCLUSIVE USE

If you're audited, the issue of home-office space will almost certainly arise. In preparation for the audit, you need to graph your home, showing the location and dimensions of rooms, hallways, and entries. The auditor then examines the drawing to see that the percentage of your home used as office space, which you claimed on your return, is supported by the calculations she can make from your graph. It's good to graph your living and work areas before you deduct home-office space, because it will highlight possible pitfalls. An auditor is looking not only for the correct percentage of business use, but also for violations of the exclusive-use requirement.

Assume, for example, that you use your front room solely for business. You have your easels and painting supplies in one corner, your file cabinets in another, your portfolio in a third, and so on. The front entry door to your house is also there, *but,* you tell the auditor triumphantly, all guests are instructed by a sign over the front doorbell to use the rear entry. "Where's your mailbox?" the auditor innocently inquires. "Why, in the front of the house," you reply. "Gotcha!" says the auditor. As you sit there dazed and bewildered, the auditor catches you on a technicality. Since you use the front door to pick up your mail, your front room has some personal use and hence doesn't qualify as business space. (Lest you think I sat up nights concocting an implausible scenario, let me tell you this really happened in a 1990 audit. Truth is frequently stranger than fiction, especially with the IRS.)

Use the graph to double-check your assumptions. Be especially careful to use accurate measurements and watch out for passage-ways! If the only route to a personal-space room is through a business-space room, you've lost the business use of that room.

Profitability

You must show a profit in order to deduct home-office expenses. This regulation has been on the books since 1983 and enforced since 1986. Checking the "yes" box for home-office deduction and show-ing a loss on Schedule C often results in an audit. Instructions dis-allowing a home-office deduction in case of loss were ignored so often that, for 1991 and beyond, a separate schedule (Form 8829) must be attached to your tax return to claim a home-office deduc-tion. (As always, a new form signals intensified IRS scrutiny.)

The Principal-Place-of-Business Issue

IRS publications state that, to qualify as a deduction, your home office must be your primary place of business. I have taken a more lenient position due to several recent court cases. None of them is enough by itself to prove loosened IRS guidelines, but together they point to some gray areas affecting artists.

If you teach art at a local college, are you entitled to a home-office deduction? I would argue that you are. While your primary place of business is the college, most colleges do not provide adequate studio space to create artwork—the artist's equivalent product in the publish-or-perish atmosphere of academia.

If you have an external studio, can you also have a home office? Again, I would argue yes. At a minimum you need a clean place for your records and administrative work. Auditors frequently don't understand how dirty your work is. You may need a separate studio (which happens to be located in your home) for a different kind of artwork—maybe the finishing stages of the dirty stuff you're doing in a warehouse, maybe entirely distinct work incompatible with a warehouse. Maybe you need that second (home) studio because you work with toxic chemicals in your external studio and want to remove yourself to a cleaner environment as soon as practical. In any of these instances, I think you can argue successfully before the IRS that a home-office deduction is legitimate.

What you *can't* defend is a second studio/office you maintain for your own convenience. If you're an academician with studio facilities on campus in addition to your cubicle office where you consult with students, but you live fifty miles from campus and want a studio in your home so you can work weekends and late into the night, that home office is not going to be deductible to you. And, if it's not deductible to someone who lives fifty miles from campus, it's certainly not deductible to someone who lives in the same town and rents external studio space.

Editorial Comment

Just because something isn't deductible doesn't mean you shouldn't do it. If you want a second studio-office for your convenience and you can afford it (without a tax support), go ahead and do it. Spending money is a wonderful exercise in choice. If the second studio is important to you but Uncle Sam says he can't help you pay for it, too bad—go for it anyway. Then, when it comes time to prepare your tax return, deduct for whichever studio gives you the larger write-off (usually the external office).

Deductible Expenses for the Homeowner

If you own your home and meet the criteria for deducting home-office space, you may deduct the percentage of business use of the following expenses associated with your home: mortgage interest, property taxes, homeowners' insurance (but not FHA or PMI charges), utilities (heating gas or oil, electricity, water, and trash, but not the base rate on your home telephone), depreciation (home only, not the land on which it is situated). You may also deduct a percentage of the repairs and maintenance you put into your home annually, provided it is your primary place of business and clients regularly come to your home office.

A word of warning: The five deductions listed above are a package deal. You can't choose to use some and not others. Most people would, for instance, prefer to forgo a depreciation deduction because of the complications a home office causes when you sell your house. But the rules are clear: If you're allowed the deduction (that is, if you meet the exclusive rule test and have a large enough profit), you must take them all.

If your profit allows you to take some home-office deductions before you fall into the loss area, you must take them in the order presented. Remember that whatever you deduct on Form 8829 can't be deducted on Schedule A, so adjust your home-mortgage interest deduction on Schedule A by the amount taken on Form 8829 and your property-tax deduction on Schedule A by the amount taken on Form 8829.

Also note that if you purchased your home on a land contract or contract for deed, you do not receive a Form 1098 in January telling you how much interest you paid on your mortgage during the previous year. Only 1098 interest goes on the "mortgage interest" line of Schedule A or Form 8829; land-contract or contract-for-deed interest is entered on the "home mortgage interest not reported to you on Form 1098" line of Schedule A and on the "other interest" line of Form 8829.

Practical Hints

A rule of thumb for figuring how much of your purchase price is attributed to land: If you're on a standard city lot, 10 to 15 percent of the purchase price is attributed to land. If you're on a larger lot (a quarter-acre), then attribute at least 20 percent to land. If your parcel is larger, ask the agent who sold you the property to provide a breakdown between land and house. Remember that only the house is a depreciable asset.

If you live in a condominium, your depreciable basis is the same as the purchase price, since your stake in the land on which the complex is built is negligible.

If you made significant capital improvements to your house after you bought it but before you placed it into service as business property, and the improvements don't directly affect the business area, use the purchase price (less land allowance) as the depreciable basis for your office. For improvements to the area used exclusively for your business that you made subsequent to purchase, depreciate these as a separate item on Form 4562.

Building a Separate Studio

If you build a studio, which is separate from your living area, on land you own, you are eligible to deduct a portion of the building costs over the life of that construction (31.5 years). If you run separate utilities to the building when you construct it, you can also deduct those utility expenses. Do not file Form 8829 (for home-office deduction), because your office is then not in your home. This deduction is available to you even if you do not show a profit from your art business. An important consideration is whether or not you can afford this kind of separate space. Not having much income from your art business while building a separate space in which to house it may open you to charges that you have a hobby, not a business. (See Chapter 13, Business or Hobby?)

Deductible Expenses for the Renter

If you rent an apartment and meet the criteria for deducting home-office space, you are able to deduct the percentage of business use of the following expenses associated with your home: rent, and utilities (but not the base rate for your telephone).

You cannot deduct any part of your renters' insurance premium. If you have a separate policy or rider for business coverage, you can deduct the extra cost of that policy or rider as an insurance cost.

Many states provide a rebate to renters based on gross income. Whatever you claim as a home-office deduction counts against that rebate. After you've completed Schedule C and before you move to Form 8829, take a quick look at what that state rebate might be if you don't claim home-office space. Then choose the option that gives you the better dollar return.

Moving Expenses

If you move your studio from one location to another, the expenses of making that move are deductible on your Schedule C. (Form 3903 is used for deducting expenses to move personal property, not business property.) If you have a home office and change residences, then a part of the moving costs are deductible on Schedule C as an "other expense" entry. Generally, you'll calculate the percentage of business use by volume: business goods and equipment as a percentage of everything moved.

For More Information

See IRS Publication 587, "Business Use of Your Home."

□ 10 □

Travel

Overview

Travel is one of the most watched expense categories on a tax return. The potential for abuse is astronomical. We've all heard joking comments about somebody (usually an upper-income professional) who pulled a fast one on the IRS. Even in the media, throwaway lines allude to the vacation-turned-business-expense. Don't be fooled by the appearance of common cheating: People often talk bigger than they deduct. They may even think their accountants took big deductions, when in reality the accountants did the right thing and protected the clients.

Definition

Travel expenses include transportation to the site, lodging, and local transportation. Meal expenses must be tracked separately, because they're only partly deductible. Incidentals (tips, cart rental at airports) are deductible only if you are deducting actual meal expenses.

Deductibility

Business travel is deductible on Schedule C for a sole proprietor and on Form 2106 for a W-2 employee. Personal travel is not deductible. For a trip to be considered a business trip, a majority of the days on the road must be devoted to business, and a preponderance of the workday must be devoted to business, specifically, to income-producing activities.

For a trip that mixes both business and personal days, a deduction can be taken only for the business days. If business days count for less than 50 percent of the total days out of town, then none of the transportation to the site is deductible and only the actual expenses (lodging, meals, local transportation) incurred on the business days are deductible. If more than 50 percent but less than 100 percent of the days out of town are business days, then the deduction equals a prorated share of transportation to the site (business days divided by total days out of town) plus actual expenses on the business days. If 100 percent of the days out of town are business days, then total costs of transportation to the site, plus expenses, are deductible.

Special Rules

For trips of seven days or less, only the day you return is automatically counted a business day. For trips of more than seven days, the first and last days are automatically counted as business days.

Meal expenses for business days are deductible using either the actual expense method (actual meal receipts for each business day) or the per diem rate for the city where you're conducting business. If you eat in cheap places or with friends, you're better off using the per diem rate in most places. It's twenty-six dollars per day, except for some major metropolitan areas where it's thirty-four dollars per day. The best strategy is to keep actual expense receipts and then, when you enter the deduction in your books, enter the larger of the two: your actual receipts total or the allowable per diem expense. A listing of $34-per-day cities is printed at the end of this chapter. The per diem for meals in foreign locations is generally more.

The primary purpose of travel must be business if the expenses are to qualify as business expenses. Do not try to hook some business function onto a primarily personal trip and expect to deduct it.

Total expenditure on travel is an item watched carefully by the IRS. Your travel deduction is weighed against that claimed by other professionals in your field. If travel costs you $2,000 and your gross income is only $6,000, the IRS will wonder what prudent businessperson spends one-third of his total income on travel.

Protecting Your Deduction

Because travel is a "hot button" item for the IRS, make sure you have good documentation on any deduction you take. Keep copies of all correspondence and phone calls setting up the visit. When you're in business and set off on a business trip, you don't drop in or show up on someone's doorstep unannounced. You preschedule appointments and stick to a tight timeline to allow yourself to get in and out of town in the shortest possible time.

Automatically eliminated is the deduction for travel when you're in town for a wedding or family get-together and decide to do some marketing to local galleries. You're entitled to take actual expenses for the day or two you spend primarily on business, but nothing else—not a portion of the transportation costs there, and no lodging or meal or local transportation costs for any of the nonbusiness days.

Examples

Examples of deductible travel:

1. Trip to Chicago museums as part of required activities for a fellowship you have received.

2. Professional convention.

3. Four scheduled meetings in a three-day period with art gallery directors in New York to set up showings of your works.

Examples of nondeductible travel:

1. Trip to see museums in Chicago (or New York or Rome) for firsthand experience of the art. The IRS will argue, successfully, that you could study it from catalogues or books, or that this is part of your basic education and cannot be deducted as necessary to produce income.

2. Travel to Honolulu in December or January to gather material for collages. Even if your only sources are in Hawaii, you could order the material by mail or pick it up on a family vacation. Not deductible because of absence of specific business schedule and because of overlap with personal vacation.

3. Casual visits to several galleries while you're in town for your brother's bar mitzvah. Primary purpose for visit is personal.

4. Four scheduled meetings with art gallery directors in a ten-day period. In business, no one hangs around a place ten days because one or two individuals are not available. A tight business trip would accomplish this work in two or three days, maximum.

Editorial Comment

Don't try to mix business and vacation or family business on the same trip. First, the two aren't compatible. Second, the deduction you'll have for business expenses is probably not large enough to merit the distraction. Business has a way of eating into your personal time, so don't ruin a vacation by mixing the two.

When in doubt, follow your conscience. If you're traveling out of town primarily for a personal event, forget about deducting any part of the trip. Example: You live in Wisconsin and take your tuba to Sarasota to play for your brother's wedding. Don't try to take any business deductions, even if you found four stores willing to carry your latest tape. An auditor would make mincemeat of your story!

For More Information

IRS Publication 1542, "Per Diem Rates," is updated annually. For per diem rates in foreign locations, consult the monthly U.S. State Department bulletins on allowable expenses. Generally, the rate quoted for foreign locations is a combined rate for lodging and for meals and incidentals. Lodging constitutes 60 percent of the combined quote; meals and incidentals, the other 40 percent. A good rule of thumb for foreign locations is $124 per day, translating to $49 per day for a meal allowance.

Locations Eligible for $34-a-day Standard Meal Allowance

State	City	County
California	Death Valley	Inyo
	Los Angeles	Los Angeles, Kern, Orange, Ventura, Edwards AFB, China Lake Naval Center
	Oakland	Alameda, Marin, Contra Costa
	Palm Springs	Riverside
	Sacramento	Sacramento
	San Diego	San Diego

State	City	County
	San Francisco	San Francisco
	San Jose	Santa Clara
	San Luis Obispo	San Luis Obispo
	San Mateo	San Mateo
	Santa Barbara	Santa Barbara
	Santa Cruz	Santa Cruz
	South Lake Tahoe	Dorado
	Tahoe City	Placer
	Yosemite National Park	Mariposa
Colorado	Aspen	Pitkin
	Boulder	Boulder
	Denver	Denver, Adams, Arapahoe, Jefferson
	Keystone/Silverthorne	Summit
	Vail	Eagle
Connecticut	Hartford	Hartford, Middlesex
	Salisbury	Litchfield
District of Columbia	Washington, D.C.	Virginia counties of Arlington, Loudoun, and Fairfax; Maryland counties of Montgomery and Prince George's
Florida	Miami	Dade, Monroe
	West Palm Beach	Palm Beach
Georgia	Atlanta	Clayton, De Kalb, Cobb, Fulton
Illinois	Chicago	Cook, Lake, DuPage
Louisiana	New Orleans	Jefferson, St. Bernard, Orleans, Plaquemines
Maryland (see also District of Columbia)	Annapolis	Anne Arundel

State	City	County
	Baltimore	Baltimore, Harford
	Columbia	Howard
	Ocean City	Worcester
Massachusetts	Andover	Essex
	Boston	Middlesex, Norfolk, Suffolk
	Martha's Vineyard/ Nantucket	Nantucket, Dukes
Michigan	Detroit	Wayne
Nevada	Las Vegas	Clarke, Nellis AFB
New Jersey	Atlantic City	Atlantic
	Eatontown	Monmouth, Fort Monmouth
	Edison	Middlesex
	Newark	Bergen, Essex, Hudson, Passaic, Union
	Ocean City/Cape May	Cape May
	Princeton/Trenton	Mercer
New Mexico	Cloudcroft	Otero
	Santa Fe	Santa Fe
New York	Monticello	Sullivan
	New York City	Bronx, Kings, Manhattan, Richmond, Queens, Nassau, Suffolk
	Saratoga Springs	Saratoga
	White Plains	Westchester
Ohio	Cleveland	Cuyahoga
Pennsylvania	Chester	Delaware
	King of Prussia/ Fort Washington	Montgomery
	Philadelphia	Philadelphia
	Valley Forge	Chester
Rhode Island	Newport	Newport
South Carolina	Hilton Head	Beaufort

State	City	County
Texas	Dallas/Fort Worth Houston	Dallas, Tarrant Harris, LBJ Space Center, Ellington AFB
Virginia (see also District of Columbia)	Williamsburg	Williamsburg
Washington	Seattle	King

□ 11 □

Business Structure

Overview

How you organize yourself to operate as a business has personal as well as tax implications. Knowing the options available to you—and their respective advantages and disadvantages—can save you money, time, and aggravation.

The three basic business organizations are:

1. Sole Proprietorship. One person operating a business. May have a business name (dba, or "doing business as") but has no other legal structure.

2. Partnership. Two or more people operating a business. Usually has a business name and a partnership agreement. Files its own tax return (Form 1065).

3. Corporation. A business owned by shareholders and run by employees. Has been incorporated under the laws of a state (not necessarily the state where it has its headquarters). Files its own tax return (Form 1120 or Form 1120-A if it's a small corporation) and

pays its own taxes. May also elect to divert profits through share-holders, in which case it files Form 2553 to elect Subchapter-S status and files Form 1120-S.

Advantages and Disadvantages of a Sole Proprietorship

A sole proprietorship is the easiest business structure to operate, the easiest to file reports on, the easiest to draw money from, and the easiest to shut down.

There are virtually no formal requirements for operating a sole proprietorship. You should keep books on your business, but there's no law that says you have to. You may need a license to operate in some states, but that requirement relates to what you do, not to your choice of a sole proprietorship as your business structure.

Generally, you use your own Social Security number as your business identification number. If you have employees or an SEP or Keogh retirement plan, you need a Federal Employer Identification Number. If you sell a product subject to your state's sales-tax laws, you may need a state sales-tax number.

You aren't required to have employees, and if you don't, payroll taxes isn't an issue. You can take money (called a "personal draw") from your business account at will, subject only to availability, without violating any laws, because you're taxed on your net profit (income less expenses) whether or not you take a cent from the business. Finally, when you stop doing business, all you need to do is stop filing a Schedule C with your personal tax return. There are no other steps to take to dissolve your business.

The disadvantages of the sole proprietorship lie primarily in the ease with which you can operate it. Because you and the business are virtually one and the same, there's no liability protection should a customer sue you. You are personally responsible for any debts incurred in the course of running your business. Remember to issue a Form 1099-MISC to anyone to whom you pay more than $600 in the calendar year, but that's not a major hardship.

Finally, you're all alone. Sole proprietorship means one proprietor, one owner. There's no one to share the decision-making, responsibility, or work, and there's no one to share the joys, triumphs, and thrills that inevitably come with owning your own business. Of course, your management meetings tend to be short . . .

Advantages and Disadvantages of a Partnership

A partnership is a working business entity comprised of at least two people. At least one of them must have an active role in running the business. A partnership exists when there is a written or working agreement between at least two people and when that partnership files an informational return (Form 1065) with the federal government.

A partnership is midway between a sole proprietorship and a corporation. It's almost as easy to operate as a sole proprietorship because you can draw money from the partnership at will, and, like a sole proprietorship, you aren't required to have employees.

On the other hand, where the sole proprietorship shines as an example of bureaucratic disengagement, a partnership is more regulated. It must have its own federal and state identification numbers. It should have a double-entry form of bookkeeping for the partners' protection. Licensing and sales-tax requirements depend on the nature of the business, not on the fact that you chose a partnership as your business structure.

A partnership is required to file its own tax return (Form 1065), although the partnership itself pays no taxes. Profit or loss from a partnership, plus the draw taken by each partner, is passed through to the partners via Form K-1, a part of Form 1065, to report on their individual tax returns (using Schedule E for profit or loss plus draw, and Schedule SE for the self-employment tax imposed on profit and draw).

A partner cannot claim home-office use.

When you cease operating your partnership, you need to settle with your partners. Presumably, the means of arriving at an equitable split of assets is spelled out in the partnership agreement. You must also file a final Form 1065. Dissolving a partnership is easy compared to a corporate dissolution, but more cumbersome than dissolving a sole proprietorship.

The major disadvantage of a partnership is the absence of liability protection. This is similar to a sole proprietorship with a major difference: In a partnership you have more than one person incurring debt on behalf of the others. If the partnership goes belly-up, any partner can be held personally liable for the debts of the partnership.

Having someone there to share in decision-making, responsibility, and work is a double-edged sword. Group dynamics enter the picture. You'll learn things about your partners you may wish you never knew. The partnership will assume the importance of a marriage or other primary relationship and will take as much work to maintain. Management meetings, though still not required by law, will be longer.

Editorial Comment

I've seen partnerships run successfully for years on end by brother-brother, sister-sister, and husband-wife combinations. Nonrelated individuals may use the partnership structure as a transition to corporate status. In general, don't consider partnership a long-term structure for your business. Either move up to a corporation after you've worked out some operating procedures and established a cash flow, or go your separate ways.

The key to successful partnership is a good partnership agreement. You should hammer out an agreement with your prospective partners before you become immersed in the daily details of running a business—within the first three months of operation. Let me stress that *you* should hammer out the details, then take a rough draft of your agreement to an attorney for review and fine-tuning. Don't sit in an attorney's office, at $85 to $125 an hour, and go back and forth about who's going to keep the books.

Unclear as to what belongs in a partnership agreement? Samples can be found in legal reference books in the business section of your library or in community college courses on starting your own business. Briefly, any good partnership agreement consists of three parts: how it starts (who puts in what), how it operates (who decides what, who has responsibility over what, who does what), and how it ends (in the case of mutual agreement, someone walking out mad, disability/incapacity, or death). Make sure you cover all the bases and decide on buy-out terms that won't ruin the business, even if the personal relationship on which the business was built goes down the tubes.

A partnership will end, as does every organic thing, so plan for it while you're still wearing rose-colored glasses at the birth of your business. Gentleness, especially toward the partners with whom you're sharing something as intimate as a business relationship, is recommended in coming up with settlement or buy-out terms. Just as in a marriage, no partner is not going to turn into an SOB overnight, so craft terms all of you can live with. (Maybe not happily, but live with.)

In my role as Dr. Doom, I always remind clients who are setting up a partnership to have wills. Wills become extremely important for partners, because partners, unlike shareholders, usually operate the business. Even if you're on excellent terms with your partner's spouse or parents (the most common heirs if someone dies intestate), you may not want the same kind of long-term, intimate, day-to-day relationship you had with the dear departed.

Practically, the will and who gets the partner's share of the business in case of death should be spelled out in the partnership agreement, so everybody knows what to expect and everybody's playing by the same rules. Must you automatically leave your share of the business to the surviving partners? Of course not. Your part of the business is an asset. Establish a purchase price and method in the partnership agreement; in your will, give the surviving partners the right of first refusal on the partnership share, and reiterate the buy-out terms (price and method) you set up in the partnership agreement. That way your surviving blood relatives have the value of your labor, and your surviving partners have the peace and quiet they'll crave in the wake of your demise.

On the heels of my will talk, I remind clients to have limited powers of attorney in place in case of the incapacity of any partner. Early in the partnership, the partnership must agree on who can decide when someone is incapacitated. The power of attorney is limited to conducting business until the incapacitated individual is restored to health or is no longer able to function.

Enough cheery thoughts! These precautions will provide a good base for discussion among the partners about the documents they should sketch out—in some detail—prior to visiting an attorney who can critique and formalize them. Putting these documents together is much like laying the foundation for a house; the better job you do now, the fewer hassles you'll have when the big storms hit.

SPECIAL RULES FOR A RENTAL-PROPERTY PARTNERSHIP

A major exception to the description of a partnership set forth above is the property partnership, where two or more people buy, and then run, rental property together. In the first year of operation, the landlords should file Form 1065 as an information return only, indicating they will, in subsequent years, split out income and expenses for each property according to the ownership interest each has. This is an obvious shortcut, designed to eliminate some of the paperwork for people who own rental property together. Where the relationship is at arm's length, however, it's probably preferable to continue filing Form 1065, even though it's an additional administrative expense, in order to keep the relationship as clear as possible.

Advantages and Disadvantages of a Corporation

When you enter the realm of corporations, you've abandoned all flexibility and simplicity, trading them for structure, respect, and liability protection.

There are two kinds of corporations: the Standard (C-) Corporation, and the Subchapter S (S-) Corporation. Both begin the same way: incorporation at the state level as a standard corporation. If all shareholders elect to have profits or losses passed through the corporation to them, and if they file their election on Form 2553, the Standard (C-) Corporation becomes an S-corporation. Subchapter S refers to a specific subchapter in Section 1361 of the Internal Revenue Code, which governs the operation of corporations.

The advantages to incorporating include some liability protection (less with an S-corporation than with a standard or C-corporation), the ability to fund group health insurance plans, larger contribution potential for pension plans, and the deductibility of payroll taxes (FICA, Workers' Compensation, federal and state unemployment insurance).

The disadvantages for most one-person corporations include:

- The requirement that you have a payroll, even if you are the only employee. A corporate employee can't just draw funds from the corporation, as the sole proprietor can from her business.
- Quarterly filing of payroll taxes, plus unemployment taxes in most states.
- Annual meeting of the board of directors.
- Separate corporate bank accounts.
- Use of the double-entry bookkeeping system.
- No deduction for home-office space.
- The fact that failure to operate your incorporated business like a regular corporation can result in IRS denial of your corporate status. Such a ruling could be retroactive. Losses from an S-corporation, then, which you claimed on your individual income tax return to offset other income, could be denied.

A corporation requires you to have the same kinds of agreements in place that you have in a partnership. In the corporate structure, however, the partnership agreement is replaced by the articles of incorporation and bylaws. Powers of attorney to cover the incapacity of principals in the corporation are still recommended, as are wills. With a corporation, however, you're less likely to end up working next to your deceased partner's spouse, because there is a board of directors to pick successors. The more closely held the corporation is, the more important these safeguards are.

Comparison Chart

Table 12 identifies the relative advantages and disadvantages of each business structure.

Nonprofits

A nonprofit—shorthand for Nonprofit Corporation—is a Standard (C-) Corporation and should be operated in the same way. It needs to have employees and use double-entry bookkeeping. Generally, it needs to file its own tax return. Form 990 and 990T are due May 15 for calendar-year nonprofits, or four and one-half months following the close of the fiscal year for nonprofits that have a fiscal year.

If total revenues for a nonprofit are less than $25,000 in its accounting year, no return is required. But bear in mind that failure to file Form 990 results in a late fee of $10 per day, up to $5,000.

EDITORIAL COMMENT

Establish a Nonprofit Corporation only if you have donors lined up or the likelihood of receiving a steady flow of grant money. Otherwise you've created an expensive monster—one that requires all the paperwork of a Standard Corporation without the underlying saleable product to keep the cash flow flowing. The only difference between a nonprofit and a Standard Corporation is the former's ability to apply to the IRS for tax-exempt status, and the eligibility

	Sole proprietorship	Partnership	C-Corporation	S-Corporation
Owner/principal can draw out funds at will	Yes	Yes	No	No
Files its own tax return	No	Yes	Yes	Yes
Pays income taxes	No	No	Yes	No
Double-entry bookkeeping	No	Yes	Yes	Yes
Uses reimbursement forms	No	Recommended	Yes	Yes
Separate bank account	Recommended	Yes	Yes	Yes
Balance sheet	No	Yes	Yes	Yes
By-laws	No	Partnership agreement	Yes	Yes
Articles of incorporation	No	No	Yes	Yes
May have employees	Yes	Yes	Yes	Yes
Must have employees	No	No	Yes	Yes
Annual meeting to set objectives	Recommended	Recommended	Required	Required
Liability protection	No	No	Full	Conditional
Formal dissolution procedure	None	Final return	Final return, dissolution documents, and state notice	Final return, dissolution documents, and state notice

for tax-deductible contributions that status confers. While this is no small thing in our tax-happy society, don't be blinded by it to the other things you'll need to do to keep the corporation in good working order.

For More Information

The IRS publishes several publications dealing with this topic: Publication 583, "Taxpayers Starting a Business"; Publication 541, "Tax Information on Partnerships"; Publication 542, "Tax Information on Corporations"; Publication 589, "Tax Information on S-Corporations"; Publication 334, "Tax Guide for Small Business"; Publication 937, "Business Reporting."

□ 12 □

Employee or Independent Contractor?

Overview

Whether a person is an employee or an independent contractor is a two-sided issue. First, are the people you hire to work for you in your business employees or independent contractors? Second, when someone hires you to work in their business, are you an employee or an independent contractor?

In general, you have little control over whether you're hired as an employee or an independent contractor. You're usually given a "this-is-the-way-things-are, take-it-or-leave-it" offer you can't (or won't) refuse. Sometimes you're asked to sign a form agreeing to work as an independent contractor and to take care of your own taxes and insurance. Occasionally you're asked to provide evidence of Workers' Compensation coverage before you're allowed to start work.

If you're truly an independent contractor, working on a variety of projects for a range of people, being hired as such poses no problem. But if you work for one person (or company) on an exclusive basis, you're not an independent contractor. Can you force that person (or company) to hire you as an employee? Practically, no. Theoretically you have the right to file a complaint with your state's jobs department or labor department, but that may well result in your termination (no doubt for "lack of work").

When You Do the Hiring

While there's little you can do to correct your own misclassification as an independent contractor, when you are hiring you should not ignore the distinctions between independent contractor and employee. A person who works for you is your employee if he or she works on your premises, is substantially under your control, and works hours you set. A person who works for you is an independent contractor if she is able to come and go as she pleases, controls the work she agrees to do for you, is available for hire by others, and controls her own work environment.

With such simple guidelines, what's the big deal? The big deal is cost. Employees cost more. Employer-paid taxes include Social Security (currently 7.65 percent of a worker's gross pay) and unemployment tax, along with Workers' Compensation insurance. Depending on the state in which you live, these can add 10 to 15 percent or more to the cost of having someone work for you in your business.

Add to that the bureaucratic hassle of writing paychecks with withholding, filing quarterly federal and state payroll reports, and completing the annual paperwork employees require, and you start to see why it's easier to hire workers as independent contractors. The effort needed to complete a 1099-MISC form pales in comparison with the effort it takes to complete a W-2, quarterly 941s, 940, and quarterly state withholding and unemployment reports.

Who's Forcing You to Hire Employees?

Almost no one, really. But you may conclude, on the basis of your own experience, that there's something unethical about hiring someone as an independent contractor when he's really your employee. There's the extra tax the independent contractor pays (the full 15.3 percent for Social Security instead of the 7.65 percent an employee pays to match the equivalent amount paid by the employer). His tax return is significantly more complicated: Form 1040 with Schedules C and SE where a short form (Form 1040EZ or 1040A) might otherwise have sufficed. Finally, there are no benefits—no safety net in case of illness or injury.

Disputes over a worker's status usually surface when something goes wrong. Perhaps the worker is injured and files to collect Workers' Compensation benefits. Or the work ends and the worker files a claim for unemployment benefits. At that point the state may begin to investigate your employment practices. Unpaid employee taxes can be assessed retroactively; penalties are frequently added.

Even if nothing goes wrong, you may find yourself on the receiving end of a state-initiated inquiry about your use of independent contractors. These are generally random investigations, though sometimes they're aimed at a particular industry or employment sector. Again, taxes and penalties can be assessed retroactively.

Update on Enforcement

Based on evidence supplied by the states, the IRS has begun an enforcement campaign some characterize as a move to eliminate independent contractors. This overstates what's really happening. Some people are—legitimately—independent contractors. Most artists certainly are. They aren't threatened by the latest IRS moves.

Those threatened by the IRS action are the employers (many of them small companies) who have full-time workers on their premises but call them independent contractors to avoid paying the employer's share of federal and state taxes. I've seen this in my tax practice; a client will say she's been offered a position as an employee or independent contractor and wants to know which she should choose. My advice to her is pretty straightforward: If the pay is the same, choose employee status. To be an independent contractor, she needs to be paid at least 20 percent more, in exchange for the benefits she's forfeiting.

It's becoming less and less common for hiring authorities to offer a worker the choice between employee or independent contractor. I strongly recommend you play it conservatively and go the employee route when there's any margin for doubt.

I do sometimes recommend hiring someone as an independent contactor for the first few months, as a kind of probationary period. The time-frame should be very limited, but it gives you an additional opportunity to test a person's capabilities before making him part of your organization. Ideally, you've gone through the hiring process so carefully you won't be unpleasantly surprised once the person is on the job, but it's certainly true that it's harder to fire an employee than it is to discontinue work assignments to an independent contractor. Taking on a person as an independent contractor for the first few months of what might develop into a long-term relationship also provides a margin of safety for your business in case you're not able to afford that extra employee.

But exercise some good judgment here. Whenever you offer a job, you owe it to the people you interview to be clear about your intentions for them. People make plans around promises, express or implied, so you don't want to lead someone to think great things are just around the corner unless they truly are. If you're afraid you can't afford to keep someone beyond three months, you owe it to him to let him know that and, perhaps, to hire him at a premium for the period, to make it worth his extra effort for an organization he'll never see again.

Editorial Comment

Treating others as you want to be treated is a good rule of thumb in business. Especially in small business, where you'll be in daily contact with individuals you hire, honesty and ethics set a tone of mutual respect. They create an atmosphere in which productivity and civility can flourish. They lead to the aura of gentleness, which carries over to your customers and builds goodwill for your business.

For More Information

See IRS Publication 937, "Business Reporting." One section lists twenty factors the IRS uses to determine a worker's proper classification.

▫ 13 ▫

Business or Hobby?

Introduction

The term "hobby" raises the hackles of most artists. They equate the term with unprofessionalism, lack of commitment, and frivolous, paint-by-number kinds of endeavors. Adding fuel to the fire is public incredulity that any artist can actually make a living selling art. When your daughter brings home her intended, "artist" is the next-to-last thing you want to hear when you ask what he does for a living. ("Biker" is worse.) And don't forget the patronizing "You're an artist, dear? How nice." Paraphrasing Rodney Dangerfield, "Artists don't get no respect."

The hobby-word needs to be defused. What the world considers a hobby—an activity engaged in an hour or two each week, aimed at restoring or preserving mental and/or physical health—is not at all what the IRS considers a hobby. Remember, the IRS is never interested in your mental or physical health. It's interested only in your money and the tax it can collect on it. That gives us some perspective for the following discussion.

How the IRS Defines Hobby

To the IRS, a hobby is any activity undertaken without a profit motive.

The business-or-hobby issue is not confined to artists. Consider Olin One, the weekend golfer. His handicap is 5, so you know he's pretty good. On weekend getaways to his condo in a lakeside resort complex, he gives pointers freely to other urban refugees. Sometimes they give him a $5 or $10 tip; sometimes they buy him drinks at the end of the day. He's a hobbyist, according to the IRS.

Let's change the scenario slightly. Olin's now put up a sign at the lakeside resort country club, announcing that he's available to give lessons. Perhaps he has a sharp accountant, who's suggested he can pull in a few more bucks while writing off his club dues and greens fees for a net loss on his taxes—a nifty tax shelter. To the IRS, Olin One remains a hobbyist. His seeking clients in such a limited setting belies a profit motive.

Let's change the scenario again. Olin is advertising in the local paper, he's negotiated a deal to serve as the golf pro at the country club, and he's now at the resort four days a week. Given these circumstances, the IRS would consider Olin's undertaking a business. Even though he may not show a profit his first or second year out, eventually his fees will outstrip the expenses he incurs in club membership and greens fees, and his business will be profitable. He may, in a year or two, begin selling woods and graphite clubs. He's in a great position to allow clients to sample the difference and then provide clubs customized to their strengths. Should Olin make money in this business? Sure. The opportunities are legion.

Return, for a moment, to that second scenario. What's so wrong with Olin reporting the money he makes and then deducting his club membership dues and greens fees and showing a loss on his taxes? Isn't that his right, as an American taxpayer?

Olin probably makes big bucks the rest of the week, which allows him the privilege of belonging to the country club and enjoying the amenities of a lakeside condo. Maybe he has a high-paying W-2 job or substantial interest and dividend income. An activity that can help pay for his membership dues, amounting to thousands of dollars

per year, plus his greens fees, which equal that or more, would itself
be a godsend. If it also produces a loss to offset the tax on his other
income, it's nigh onto a miracle. Given that context, an IRS auditor
would almost certainly call Olin One's activities a hobby and disallow
any loss he claimed on his tax returns.

But what if Olin One were retired, living on a fixed income, and
wanted to use the golf thing to pick up a few extra bucks? First of all,
this impoverished Olin wouldn't need a business loss to offset the
paltry income he receives. Second, if he were operating his business
in the rarefied social air of a country club, he wouldn't be able to
afford the annual dues, or he'd of necessity negotiate them as part
of his agreement to serve as a golf pro. Finally, if he were living on a
fixed income and needed some extra money to make ends meet,
he'd make sure his business generated a profit.

Olin One is mythical, though real-life counterparts no doubt exist.
The IRS has been set on alert ever since the Tax Reform Act of 1986
for taxpayers who earn the bulk of their income from sources other
than their Schedule C activities, especially when those activities produce a tax loss that offsets the income from those other sources.
This focused enforcement is the result of public discontent that
boiled up in anger against wealthy Americans. People charged that
the rich used their fancy loopholes and high-priced accountants to
escape taxation while middle-class Americans were being taxed beyond endurance. The Tax Reform Act of 1986, initiated by and
passed under President Reagan, addressed those equity issues by
closing off tax shelters the wealthy had grown accustomed to and by
tightening existing policies so prohibited tax shelters weren't traded
in for sham business schemes providing the same degree of tax
relief.

The Reagan reforms set politics on its head. Here, after all, was a
Republican president turning the screws on what is traditionally a
Republican constituency. Nevertheless, it happened. The Tax Reform Act of 1986 is a startling piece of legislation to have emerged
from a Republican regime.

This issue of whether an activity is a business or hobby will receive
increased attention in the next few years as a result of a compliance
review by a special IRS contingent at the Ogden service center. That
review, the results of which were released in 1991, found some six-

teen areas where taxpayers were out of sync with the IRS. In the area labeled "Hobby Losses," the compliance team wrote:

> Taxpayers are continuing to claim losses on Schedules C and F for activities that are not business ventures. These losses continue for a number of years and all indications are the venture will never realize a profit. Examples include show horses, raising various kinds of pets, prospecting, automobile racing, and creation of artistic works (sculptures, paintings), writing, etc.

(Source: Internal Revenue Service, Public Affairs Office, Ogden IRS Center, P.O. Box 9941, Ogden, Utah 84409, pp 11–12.)

This is an early warning that closer scrutiny will be given to the profitability of Schedule C activities.

The Three-of-Five-Consecutive-Years Rule on Profitability

The easiest way to defuse IRS suspicion that you're a hobby and not a business is to show a profit in three of any five consecutive years the IRS reviews.

A caveat is appropriate. This profit shouldn't be one dollar, or one hundred dollars, or any other manufactured figure. Manufactured figures are easy to spot in computer checks of tax returns. Make sure the figures in your business books correspond to the figures you enter on your Schedule C and that your profit is real, regardless of its size.

Do not, of course, try to deduct anything for home-office use if you have a loss for the year. Deductions for home-office use are limited to your profit for the year. Also, do not try to expense the cost of any capital asset purchased during the year. Expensing, known in the tax world as electing the Internal Revenue Code Section 179 provision, is limited to your profit for the year.

Suppose you understand the rules on deductibility of home-office expenses and how to treat capital assets, but you still don't show a profit in your business? Do you skip filing Schedule C? Do you declare yourself a hobbyist? Do you decide to postpone filing a tax return until answers appear to you in a dream? No, no, and no.

OTHER CRITERIA THE IRS USES TO DECIDE THE ISSUE

Once a business has shown losses for three consecutive years, the IRS computers may indeed be scratching their electronic brains, wondering what you're about. Whether you're audited depends more on whether you've reported all your income than on losses shown in three successive years. If, for example, you forget to report fifty dollars in interest income on the bank account your Aunt Emma opened for you in Billings, Montana, that deficiency will show up on the IRS computers. Coupled with the fact that you filed a Schedule C showing a loss, it may be enough to trigger an audit. At the audit, the issue of whether you're a hobbyist or businessperson will almost certainly be raised.

What kinds of things will the auditor ask you? What follows is a sampling, based on actual audit inquiries.

You'll be asked if you keep books on your business and how often you do your books. You'll be asked if you have a separate checkbook for your business. Probably the audit notice asked you to bring a current résumé with you. That will show how long you've been engaged in the activity, as well as the level of expertise you bring to the business. You'll be asked about your work schedule, including how much time you spend in your studio producing your art, how you market your art, and the kinds of market research you undertake to enhance your marketability.

If you're assigned an auditor who knows anything about the art world (this is not likely, but it's possible), you'll also be asked questions about what kind of things you're producing and how you intend to market them. Having an agent, a gallery, or some other external representative working on your behalf to get your art out there is a great help in convincing an auditor you mean business.

If you're assigned an auditor who knows nothing about art, you should probably downshift to second gear in the hope of being able to explain to this person what you do, why you do it, and why you expect to make a livelihood doing it. Use language your parents might understand. Instead of calling yourself a "multimedia artist," explain that your art form involves bringing together various communications media, including television/video, performance, literary, and fine-art pieces. Keep things simple.

Instead of saying that you've wanted to be an artist all your life, tell the auditor about your artistic focus and how you're working to bring your interpretation of reality to the marketplace. Be specific. Be succinct. If you wander, his eyes will begin glazing over as his brain begins formulating his next question.

Stay with it. You're not on the offensive, but tell him in rapid order how you've researched galleries in Tucson, St. Paul, Boston, and Atlanta, and the kind of gallery you want to see exhibiting your works. Show him letters and telephone correspondence from you to galleries and from galleries to you; show him the contract you have with a representative to market your works. Let him know about the professional societies to which you belong. If you don't have any of these, you're left to rely on your résumé. The longer you've been active in the profession, the more likely it is your activities will be classified a business and not a hobby, but a strong résumé is not enough by itself to prove you operate your activities as a business.

Elsewhere in this book I've characterized audits as "IRS inquisitions." But they won't seem painful. This is partly the result of the changes enacted under Commissioner Goldberg. Yes, we now have a kinder and gentler IRS. But caught unawares, the taxpayer may be lulled into a false sense of security, ending up surprised that the "conversation" he had with an auditor resulted in significant tax levies against him.

See Chapter 18 for more information on how to conduct yourself at an audit. On the specific issue of protecting yourself against the hobbyist label, suffice it to say you should prepare yourself to educate your auditor in the simplest, most basic terms about: what you do, how you do it, why you do it, how you market it, and what you've done right in your business and what you've done wrong and how you're correcting those errors.

How Hobby Status Affects You

A hobbyist reports income and expenses on the "other income" line on the front of Form 1040. The deduction for expenses incurred in operating a hobby activity is limited to hobby income. A hobbyist does not use Schedule C.

Some Practical Advice

Don't be so intimidated by the possibility of facing an IRS audit that you roll over and play dead if you have a loss in your business for the third straight year. Clients sometimes suggest to me that I file their business activities as hobby activities in that third year. While I usually take that opportunity to ask them what they're doing to market their works and to provide guidance and suggestions wherever possible, the conversation usually ends up convincing both of us that filing as a business on Schedule C is the proper course of action.

The IRS can't guarantee you a profit. It will not automatically classify your activities as hobby activities if you continue to show losses. But some prudence is in order. It makes sense that you cannot continue to absorb losses year after year. Sooner or later you want and need to hit a market niche where you'll find a financial outlet for your work. Continuing losses are tantamount to running around with a hole in your pocket. Sooner or later, you mend the hole and stop losing money.

Operating any business is much the same, even when the business is art. You may find cash falling out of your pockets the first several years but eventually, through experience and a keener awareness of the financial opportunities existing for your work, you'll find your way. That, in turn, takes care of the IRS.

A final comment: It's rare for someone who's shown profits on Schedule C to find an auditor reclassifying the activity as a hobby. Generally those most vulnerable to the charge of being hobbyists are those new to the profession. Remember the box in Part I of Schedule C, which asks if this is the first Schedule C being filed on this business? That's what tips off the IRS computers to new activities and provides data that may result in the business-or-hobby issue being raised at a later date.

Your best defense is to conduct yourself as a prudent business owner would. Keep your expenses in line with your income, make sure you can document any and all deductions you claim on Schedule C, market yourself efficiently, and let your books show what's really going on in your business.

For More Information

Internal Revenue Code Section 183 describes the kinds of criteria the IRS uses to evaluate an activity and classify it as a business or hobby.

□ 14 □

Sales and Use Tax

Definitions

Sales tax is a tax imposed at the point of sale on goods, products, or services by a state or local taxing authority. If you don't sell products directly to an end-user, don't worry about it.

A use tax is a tax you volunteer to pay to your state of residence on goods, products, or services you purchased from an out-of-state vendor that, had you purchased the same from an in-state vendor, would have been taxable in your state of residence.

Sound simple? We've only just begun.

Overview

As of March 1991, forty-five states and the District of Columbia impose a sales tax. (Only Alaska, Delaware, Montana, New Hampshire, and Oregon have no state sales taxes. Alaska municipalities have the right to levy municipal sales taxes.) Every state that has a state sales tax (and we're including the District of Columbia for the purpose of this discussion) also levies a use tax—either from the vendor as a required periodic sales tax report, or from the consumer as part of an annual tax return.

That's a lot of tax. In some states, sales-tax collections dwarf income-tax collections. And the taxes have increased since the 1986 Tax Reform Act. Remember that one? The one that cut federal tax rates? That act also reordered the relationship between the federal and state governments, shifting fiscal responsibility for health and social welfare programs to the state or county level.

When fiscal responsibility is shifted, expect to see a change in the way the money is raised. Since 1987 we've seen enormous increases in state sales-tax rates, municipalities vying with one another to impose city sales taxes, special taxes on visitors (ranging from surtaxes on rental cars to special tax rates on hotels and restaurants), and pressure for a national sales tax (similar to the value-added tax you see in other countries).

Some states have experienced a total breakdown in state services, while legislators debated over how and whom to put the bite on, in order to balance the state budget. (Most states constitutionally require a balanced budget. This is not true of the federal government, which, when faced with a deficit, issues bonds to finance the shortfall. The bonds are payable sometime in the future, which is what all the crying that we are "mortgaging our children's future" is about.)

Who Pays?

Some states distinguish between who's responsible for paying sales tax—the consumer or the vendor. The distinction has some bearing on who can sue whom if the tax isn't collected, but that goes beyond this basic discussion. Usually it's the consumer who pays the sales tax. (That's why a lot of people say that the sales tax is the most regressive tax, because it doesn't take into account the consumer's ability to pay, unlike income tax.)

The consumer may pay it, but it's the vendor who collects it and passes it along to the taxing authority. How often collected sales taxes are passed along depends on local regulations; in many locales, the threshold is $500. If your state has a sales tax, check with your state revenue or tax department to obtain a copy of the regulations affecting your particular situation.

If you're a small-business owner reading this, you already know the punchline. If you're new to the game, you're about to receive a rude introduction to the paperwork-is-killing-the-small-business-owner routine. Having somebody collect money for you is a pretty slick idea. Wouldn't it be great to have "Vito" visit the galleries that sold your works six months ago but still haven't managed to deliver your part of the sale to you? And wouldn't it be even better if you never needed to pay Vito for his services?

In this scenario, you—the small-business owner—are Vito, the "enforcer," the guy who insures with Mr. Smith and Mr. Wesson. (Actually, the size of the business has nothing to do with it. Any business subject to sales-tax laws has to collect them. It's just that, for small businesses, the additional paperwork is sometimes the straw breaking the camel's back.) Do you have to go to somebody's home to shake 'em down? Nah. Your collection is prepaid on credit card or cash orders. If somebody welshes on ya, ya just pay it out of your profits. Get the pitcha?

Perhaps I exaggerate. But not much. Sales tax is a system imposed by states on businesses operating within their jurisdictions to collect taxes on behalf of those states. Make that states and municipalities. They're both in on the take.

What do you get for it? Nothing. Nothing good, at least. You may be fined or have your license suspended or, in extreme cases, be driven out of business if you don't do the collection job properly, but you'll never get a reward for doing it right.

How to Protect Yourself

Sales-tax laws, like every other law, are written down somewhere. Someone knows the answers to every question. How do you find the answers to the questions affecting your business? Start with your state revenue or tax department. Ask for a copy of the guidelines on what's subject to sales tax in your state. Then ask what cities also have a municipal sales tax. It's okay to give them your name and address; they're much too busy to follow up on every phone call requesting information. If you hear the name of the city where you live or do business, call the city tax office or license bureau and ask that information on the city sales tax be sent to you.

You want the guidelines sent to you because what's taxable and what's not varies widely. Some states, generally those with a lower sales-tax rate, tax everything—goods, services, clothing, food. Others, generally those with a high sales-tax rate, tax only some items— goods and services but not clothing and food in one place, goods but not services or clothing or food in another place, or some other mix. There are as many different ways to tax goods and services as there are states in the union. A graphic designer's work might be taxable in one state, but not in another. What's important is that the graphic designer who lives in one state and operates in other states knows the sales-tax regulations in all of them, and has access to an information pipeline so he's aware of changing regulations.

Beyond initiating inquiries with your state or local tax authority, keep your ears open at professional conferences and read your local group's newsletter. They know, or have heard of, tax changes affecting your business group because they have probably been lobbying on your behalf to protect you from sales-tax requirements.

Do not, as a rule, listen to your peers, unless you know one or two who generally comply with federal and state regulations. "Nobody I know in the (fill in the blank) field charges sales tax on their (name of product). So why should I?" Just because all the folks you associate with don't follow the law doesn't make it okay for you. Just imagine an auditor's face when you tell her that your friend Julie doesn't charge sales tax, so why should you. The point is, you charge sales tax because state and/or local law requires it, not because your colleagues do.

If you doubt your accountant, check with your state or local sales-tax department; describe what you do and ask if it's subject to sales tax. (Do not leave your name on this kind of call.) They'll give you the right answer. If it differs from your accountant's advice, get a name, phone number, and reference to a state tax-code section to educate her about the nuances of your profession and to keep your relationship clean.

Does or should your accountant know about sales tax law? Not necessarily. It's as distinct from income tax preparation as are retirement planning and employer taxes. It's nice if she does, but don't expect it. Ultimately, it's best for you to know everything you need to know as a business owner in the field. That way you can check on the kind of job your accountant is doing for you.

A bad scenario: You employ an accountant to prepare income tax returns. You sell goods at regional art fairs and the accountant knows that because she is asking about travel expenses for each fair site. You can reasonably expect the accountant to ask about sales-tax payments if you haven't already included them on the interview worksheet. If the accountant doesn't ask about sales tax, it may mean she is simply "number-crunching" the tax return. That is, she is putting the numbers you provided in the correct places on the correct forms, instead of knowing something about your business. Generally you pay more for an accountant who knows something about your field than you do for a mere number-cruncher. Keep this in mind as you shop for a new accountant.

Reporting Requirements

It is incumbent on you, the tax collector, to know the correct state and local sales-tax rates. Failure to charge or collect tax becomes your financial responsibility, so you want to do it right.

You enter the sales-tax pipeline in most states by applying for a state sales-tax number. Generally, each state has its own application form. It may be the same form you use to obtain a state identification number when you hire employees or apply for a license. States and cities tailor their applications to avoid issuing multiple numbers, so, in general, expect to have only one state identification number, and one city identification number if your municipality charges sales tax.

Complete and mail the application before you make a taxable sale. Some states are extremely punitive and levy penalties as high as one hundred dollars if you sell something subject to sales tax before you've completed the paperwork to obtain a sales-tax number. States undoubtedly have good reasons for wanting uniform compliance, but such tight regulations sometimes catch the honest but unsuspecting artist unawares.

Suppose you've been selling your work for years through a gallery. Then the vice president at the corporation where your Aunt Sarah works sees the bronze golfer statuette you gave her on her birthday. He likes it. He wants one. Pretty soon, with modifications, your golfer is in high demand—the VP's country-club buddies, a special trophy for corporate high-achievers, and so on. The minute you sell a finished piece to an end-user, you're required to collect the sales tax on that item. But maybe you want a month or two after selling the first piece to start the state paperwork because you're pretty busy and the tax doesn't amount to a whole lot, anyway. But your delay can result in a penalty situation when you file your first sales-tax report, because you didn't have a sales-tax number when you made that first sale.

How to Fix This Situation

It's sad but true: You should have known the sales-tax laws before you got into the position of making a taxable sale. That way, when an opportunity came along, you could anticipate the legal requirements. Maybe they should teach this as Prognostication 401, a senior seminar at all arts colleges, or maybe they should include this as Chapter 33 in the *Book of Life for Artists Who Never Went to Art School*. Wherever they should teach it, this lesson is often lost. It's not that people want to escape the law; it's more that they just don't know they are subject to its often-strange provisions.

I tell my clients to do the right thing. Collect the tax. Then, in an attempt to reach some kind of moral position:

1. File the application for a sales-tax number. Where it requests information on the "date of first taxable sale," enter a date after the day you're making the application—whatever gives you a few days between what was your actual taxable sale (which, presumably, is

what's sparked your applying for the number) and your application date. You want this "slush" time *only* to avoid state penalties for being caught short on the paperwork, not to avoid taxes.

2. Send the sales tax payable on that sale to the taxing authority by the due date for the regular tax filing. Generally, the deadline is the end of the month after the quarter ends, although in some states it's the twentieth day after the quarter ends. If you collect a lot of sales tax, say more than $500 in a quarter, you'll find yourself facing monthly filing deadlines.

You've complied with the spirit of the law, if not the letter. Now that you know the rules, collect the tax and file the report in a timely fashion.

A Note on Use Tax

You may be liable for use tax even if you aren't required to pay sales tax. If you buy a significant portion of the raw materials you use in your art from out-of-state vendors, sales tax isn't part of the bill you pay. That doesn't mean you've escaped it. Your state of residence wants you to pay sales tax in the form of a use tax to your state of residence on all those untaxed purchases. Check with your state tax department for further information.

Special Rules for Art Fairs

If your business takes you to art fairs throughout the country, you've grown accustomed to seeing state sales-tax collectors with their hands out, waiting for your donation to the cause before you leave the premises. The sales tax you pay in another state, when paid directly to a revenue agent, is an easy way of complying with that state's laws, unless you weren't aware the state had a sales tax and hence didn't charge your customers accordingly.

It's easy because, in most instances, there is no follow-up paperwork to complete. To avoid getting caught short by not charging sales tax, check with fair officials when you secure your space. It's certain they'll know the local laws.

HERE'S ONE THAT STILL GETS AWAY

Musicians frequently sell their records, cassettes, and CDs from the stage after a concert. Revenuers do not, as a rule, appear at their dressing-room doors following the concert to demand the state's share of the sales. Maybe they don't like music.

Sale of a Business

Squeezed by falling revenues and facing a citizenry fed up with tax increases, many state legislatures have turned to taxing the sale of your business (or part of your business, in the case of a partnership). Double-check possible sales-tax consequences with the person who's helping you establish a sales price for your business. Dividing the price between inventory and real property, on the one hand, and intangibles on the other, now may have sales-tax implications.

Ensuring Your Proper Deduction

Sales taxes appear on your income tax return as part of your income because they are part of the payment you receive for the jobs you complete. Your gross receipts equal the sum of all the payments you receive for all the jobs you do each year. Refer to Figure 3 in Chapter 3 to see how you should keep track of sales tax in your income ledgers.

When you take a deduction for sales tax depends on when you

pay the state (and city, if applicable) revenue department, not when you collect the tax. Regardless of the frequency with which the state or local taxing unit requires you to forward the taxes you collect, you want to be sure to file the December (or, in some cases, the fourth quarter or annual) report no later than December 31. Again, a postmark is ample proof of date paid. So, on New Year's Eve, add your sales-tax report to the stack of bills and independent contractors you're paying. A December 31 sales-tax report may make for a lousy celebration, but you'll have more money to spend in the new year, thanks to these extra deductions.

For More Information

Contact your state revenue or taxation department for guidelines on what's subject to sales and use tax in your state of residence.

□ 15 □

Inventories

Definition

A business has an inventory whenever it has raw materials or unfinished goods it uses to produce its product or provide its services. With inventory defined so broadly, it's not surprising that every business has an inventory of some size. Perhaps it's a stock of paper earmarked for a design project, or perhaps it's a collection of partially used containers of dye, or perhaps it's the photographs in a print portfolio.

Tax Implications

Having goods in an inventory means you can't write off the expenses of purchasing the goods that go into your product until you sell the finished product into which the goods have gone. It also means you can't write off the expenses of purchasing goods you intend to resell until you actually sell them.

A car dealer, for example, cannot automatically deduct the cost of all the cars he has on the lot in the year he buys them. Let's say he purchases a hundred new cars at an average cost of $15,000, for a total outlay of $1,500,000. He can't write off any part of that total until he begins selling cars, and then he can write off only the actual cost of each vehicle he sells. Let's assume his average selling price is $20,000. If he sells all 100 cars in the same year he buys them, then he reports income of $2,000,000 and expenses of $1,500,000 (plus salaries, overhead, advertising, and all the other expenses required to run a business).

Remember how Schedule C looks? Part III, on the back of the schedule, is entitled "Cost of Goods Sold." It's the part designed for people who have inventories. There's a line to enter the inventory you have at the beginning of the year, and then there's a line to add the figure for purchases you make during the year. Let's assume for the sake of simplicity that this car dealer is just setting up his business. In the current year he lays out the $1,500,000 for the first 100 cars he'll have on his lot. His entry on Schedule C for beginning-of-the-year inventory is zero; his entry on Schedule C for purchases is $1,500,000. That entry might be less than the amount he actually spent if he gave one of the cars to his wife. Such a transfer of assets from business to personal use is what's meant by "items withdrawn for personal use." If he gave her a top-of-the-line model, that car might have come with a wholesale price tag of $30,000. His entry on the "purchases" line would be $1,500,000 less $30,000, or $1,470,000.

Let's further assume he sells sixty of the cars. His gross revenue is the total price he received for the sixty cars. To determine how much he can write off against that revenue total, he must add up the purchase price of the other forty vehicles left on the lot at close of business on December 31. That total becomes his "inventory at end of year." Let's say it's $625,000. Subtracting year-end inventory from his total inventory gives him his cost-of-goods-sold figure for the current year. This is the amount he can deduct against his current-year income: $845,000.

Figure 15 shows how Part III of his Schedule C might look.

FIGURE 15
SCHEDULE C COST OF GOODS SOLD

Schedule C (Form 1040) 1991   Page **2**

Part III Cost of Goods Sold (See instructions.)		
33 Inventory at beginning of year. (If different from last year's closing inventory, attach explanation.).	33	O
34 Purchases less cost of items withdrawn for personal use .	34	1,470,000 —
35 Cost of labor. (Do not include salary paid to yourself.).	35	—
36 Materials and supplies .	36	—
37 Other costs .	37	—
38 Add lines 33 through 37.	38	1,470,000 —
39 Inventory at end of year.	39	625,000 —
40 Cost of goods sold. Subtract line 39 from line 38. Enter the result here and on page 1, line 4	40	845,000 —

Part IV Principal Business or Professional Activity Codes
Locate the major category that best describes your activity. Within the major category, select the activity code that most closely identifies the business or profession that is the principal source of your sales or receipts. **Enter this 4-digit code on page 1, line B.** For example, real estate

Advantages and Disadvantages

The primary advantage of declaring an inventory is that your expenses line up more accurately with your revenues. In the case of the car dealer, he won't be able to write off the other $625,000 until he sells those cars. Had he been legally able to write off the entire $1,470,000 in the year he spent the money, he would have shown a huge loss for that year and an unusually large profit the following year, as he sold cars the cost of which he'd already deducted. This would wreak havoc in most people's budgets.

A secondary advantage of declaring an inventory is that you take stock of what you have. Since most taxpayers file tax returns based on calendar-year figures, inventory is taken the final day of the year. This December 31 (or, better yet, January 1) exercise reacquaints you with your stock and may prompt decisions to throw out obsolete or outdated materials or to begin a project that will use up the stuff.

The major disadvantage of declaring an inventory is the flip side of its primary advantage. You've spent the $1,500,000 but can't see the tax benefits of it now. This situation is analogous to depreciation; you've spent money on equipment but can't immediately realize a tax advantage commensurate with the expenditure. The money's gone, but you don't have the tax break to show for it.

The reason the IRS wants business owners to keep an inventory is clear. If people wrote off total expenditures for capital assets as they purchased them, federal revenue planning would be out the window and the government would always be in for a surprise when the tax filing season ended. The long and the short of it is that our government simply can't operate in such an unpredictable fashion.

For perspective, look at other nations. Japanese businesses, for example, have a much easier time fully deducting current-year expenditures than their American counterparts. That's why some people charge that American businesses are increasingly run by accountants. It's not that the accountants are so all-fired bright, it's that American tax laws force businesses to operate within certain strictures so that the federal government has a predictable flow of income.

It may be helpful to remember how large the American economy is. Between our gross national product and a population topping 250 million, it's by far the largest economy in the world, three to four times the size of Japan's or Germany's. This economic behemoth requires stability, not only for internal order but also because the American economy sets the tone for the international economy. If we're in chaos, everyone else will be sucked into it.

Who's Required to Keep Track of Inventory

Even though most businesses have some level of raw materials or unfinished goods sitting around at the end of the year, not every business needs to keep track of inventory. There are two major categories of business owners required to keep track of inventory. You must keep track of inventory if the amount of raw materials or unfinished goods is a material factor in the way you calculate your profit for the year, or if you purchase goods you intend to resell.

To understand how purchases of materials could become a material factor in calculating your annual profit, take the situation facing an artist who discovers, in December, that her profit for the year is likely to be $35,000. With a stroke of accounting genius, she lays out $10,000 for raw materials: clay if she's a potter, film if she's a photographer, a prepaid account at the typesetter's if she's a graphic designer. Flourishing her pen, she writes a check that reduces her profit to $25,000. An intriguing maneuver, but the IRS would slap it down as a willful attempt to manipulate her profit for the year. She'd be required to put the materials into an inventory, forced to use the accrual system of accounting, and closely monitored for years.

Take the same example with some changes. Another artist regularly spends $10,000 per month for materials that go into his work. (Obviously he has a much larger annual profit than $35,000!) Would that same December expenditure trigger IRS action? No. It would be considered normal in the context of that artist's spending habits. In other words, there's no obvious attempt to manipulate annual profit and tax liability. In assessing whether or not you fall into the "material factor" category, consider not how much you spend, but rather the timing of the expenditure and your overall pattern of spending money to operate your business.

But can't you buy a computer system or a camera or a fax machine to cut your profit without running afoul of the rules on inventory? Sure, for the simple reason that these are capital assets, subject to different tax rules and different tax treatment. (See the earlier section on depreciation.) Inventory items are not capital assets. Clay has no tax life, nor does film or prepaid accounts. Buying equipment at the end of the year is a great way to cut your tax bill, provided you need the equipment. Buying raw materials to cut your profit is not.

The other major category of business owner required to keep an inventory is the owner who purchases goods for resale, such as the car dealer. That's an easy example to understand but may seem pretty far removed from the art world. In fact, many artists find themselves in that category. Painters or designers who produce limited-edition prints, musicians who record their works on cassettes and CDs, jewelers who acquire precious and semiprecious stones— all are purchasing goods for resale and hence must keep track of their inventories.

Ramifications: Accrual Accounting and Capitalization Requirements

Once you're required to keep track of inventory, you're faced with additional requirements. The first is that you keep your books using the accrual system of accounting. This system is discussed briefly in the Glossary. To recap, the accrual system of accounting requires you to count as revenues any invoices you send out and count as expenses any bills you receive. When you actually receive payment on your invoice is irrelevant in the accrual system of accounting, as is when you actually pay your bills.

The downside of using the accrual system is that you're paying tax on money you haven't received. Since most businesses are profitable, the fact that you can count billed expenses as paid expenses doesn't offset what amounts to an early payment of tax liability. Over time, those on the accrual system adjust to it. Income (and the taxes associated with it) is always reported a little early, but you learn to live with that.

How much does this system favor the government? The IRS is not shy about its preference for the accrual system. That tells me that staying on the cash system as long as you can is in your long-term best interest.

Can you have an inventory and continue to use cash-basis accounting? Only if your inventory is worth, on average, less than 10 percent of your annual revenues. That 10 percent is a *de minimis* figure, meaning the IRS doesn't consider an inventory worth $8,000 in a business generating $100,000 enough of a factor to influence overall profitability and so doesn't care which system you use. That business owner will, of course, continue to use cash-basis accounting. By the same token, if inventory regularly on hand exceeds 10 percent of annual revenue, the IRS wants that business owner to switch to accrual accounting.

When does such a switch take place? Generally at the end of the first year you meet the requirements. Don't switch your accounting system midyear. You can switch from cash to accrual without obtaining prior IRS approval. Remember, however, that switching the other way around, from an accrual to a cash system, can occur only with prior written IRS approval.

A second complication facing those with an inventory is capitalization. This subject was discussed in detail in Chapter 6. Unless the inventory consists of goods held for resale, capitalization requirements apply. Briefly, capitalization is the process of treating certain expenses as capital assets. This means that, instead of deducting the entire cost of a consumable item in the year it's purchased, the cost of that consumable is capitalized and made part of inventory so that its cost is deducted only as inventory goods are sold.

Capitalization requirements have been part of the tax code for decades, but until recently only businesses with revenues exceeding $10 million annually were subject to their provisions. Capitalization requires significantly more bookkeeping, which used to make sense only at the big-business level. The Tax Reform Act of 1986 changed all that by eliminating the revenue threshold and throwing the mom-and-pop operation in with the Fords and General Motors and IBMs. Now any business with an inventory is required to capitalize expenses. Sole proprietorship, partnership, corporation—business structure doesn't matter. Capitalization requirements apply to all.

Bear in mind that the regulations explaining how to implement the Tax Reform Act of 1986 are still being developed. There is still no publication which deals with the subject. So what do you, the small-business-owner-artist, need to do?

To begin with, avoid having an inventory. That is the simplest approach. If you *do* have an inventory, keep it below *de minimis* levels. Or, if your inventory consists of your own tapes or CD's—goods you manufactured and intend to re-sell—claim an inventory but ignore capitalization requirements.

If, however, you are in the film and video industry, capitalization requirements clearly apply to you. Filmmakers and video artists are such IRS targets that they are named explicitly in the tax code. For more information on capitalization, especially as it affects filmmakers and video artists, see Chapter 6.

Some Information on IRS Enforcement Policies

Periodically, the IRS creates a special task force to evaluate a sampling of tax returns and to determine the degree to which taxpayers are voluntarily complying with the tax code. One task force, at the Ogden service center, found taxpayers noncompliant in sixteen areas. One area was inventory, another capitalization. The 1991 report reads:

Taxpayers are currently expensing amounts which should be inventoried. An example is on Schedule F [the farm schedule] where some taxpayers have the cost of items purchased for resale exceed the gross receipts. This indicates unsold inventory is being expensed.

(Source: Internal Revenue Service, Public Affairs Office, Ogden IRS Center, P.O. Box 9941, Ogden, Utah 84409, pp 11–12).

Expect to see greater attention focused on the inventory issue in the coming years.

What Belongs in Inventory and How to Value It

If you are required to keep track of inventory, include the following, valued at their cost to you: raw materials required to produce the goods you sell; unfinished or partially finished goods; labor costs connected to the manufacture of these items; materials and supplies you need to produce your product or get it to market, such as packing materials or crates; goods based on your work that you intend to resell, such as limited edition prints, cassettes, or CDs; miscellaneous costs such as freight or entry fees to art fairs.

Do not include: overhead expenses (but see discussion on capitalization above); capital assets used to manufacture or display your goods; salaries, unless they're directly attributable to the manufacturing process.

Central to figuring out what expenses should and should not be included in inventory is the title of Part III of Schedule C: "Cost of Goods Sold." If the expense isn't in the product you're selling, it doesn't belong in the inventory section of the tax form. Put it, instead, in the "Expenses" section, Part II of Schedule C.

Inventory is valued at its cost to you. Alternatively, it can be valued at its fair market value, if that figure is less than your cost. Valuing inventory by using either its cost to you or the fair market value, whichever is lower, is why most artists don't need to declare an inventory. A painter, for example, might have sixty finished and thirty unfinished works in her studio, but the cost of each work is insignificant—the paints, the canvas. The value of each work comes from the artist's creativity and ability to translate that creativity into a two-dimensional medium.

What happens when you have an inventory and goods are damaged, perhaps by storm or fire? Their fair market value may now be less than their original cost to you. The same holds true for goods damaged in transit. Perhaps you're a writer who publishes her own line of do-it-yourself guides. You ship thirty books to Cincinnati, and the bookstore owner returns two of them as damaged in transit. The fair market value of those books is now zero.

At the end of the year you count your inventory: so many items at such-and-such a cost (or fair market value), so many items at this other cost, so many now worth nothing. Then you add up all the individual categories to arrive at a final year-end inventory figure.

How do you write off the items you donated to a charity or used for promotional purposes? They're gone from your year-end inventory, aren't they? Therein lies the explanation. If they aren't in your inventory, then when you subtract the cost of your year-end inventory from your purchases, labor, and materials and supplies total, the cost-of-goods-sold figure includes all those items used for business purposes, whether they were sold, destroyed, damaged, or handed out as advertising. An example will shed light on this.

MUSICIAN'S EXAMPLE

Joe Blow is a trumpet player. He and his band, The Blowhards, have been in the music business for three years, playing local and regional gigs and for private parties. Joe operates his business as a sole proprietorship, paying his musicians on a commission basis and giving them 1099-MISC forms at the end of the year. (His accountant wants Joe to make them his employees, but Joe hasn't gotten around to doing that yet.)

During the past year, Joe and his band made one recording of a live concert and a second of solo trumpet chamber music. Joe took the following information to his accountant:

Album #1: Costs: $2,500   sound and recording
technicians

900   editing technician

500   album design

2,200   production costs

Total costs: $6,100

Number produced: 250 records

500 cassettes

100 CDs

Album #2: Costs: $ 800   sound and recording
technicians

800   editing technician

500   album design

625   studio rental

2,300   production costs

Total costs: $5,025

Number produced: 250 records

500 cassettes

100 CDs

The accountant wanted more information from Joe. (Don't they always?) Specifically, the accountant wanted Joe to figure out how many records, cassettes, and CDs of each album were left over (that is, unsold) on December 31 of last year.

So Joe went home and figured out he had sold: Album #1: 62 records, 420 cassettes, and 33 CDs. Album #2: 16 records; 45 cassettes, and 0 CDs. Joe also figured out he'd sent 44 demo cassettes to various stations and stores: 30 for Album #1 and 14 for Album #2.

Oh, yeah. Joe also remembered he'd spent $1,000 to have another 500 cassettes made of Album #1, since he was running kind of low on stock. (Annoying as it must be for a client, it's probably good that accountants ask as many questions as they do. In most cases there's more to learn, and Joe was no exception to that rule.)

Joe actually went to more trouble to answer his accountant than he needed to. All he had to do was provide the number left at the end of the year, not the number he sold. Joe could have saved himself

FIGURE 16
INVENTORY EXAMPLE

Title	Number on Hand		Giveaways to Friends & Relatives	COGS
	12–31–90	12–31–91		
Album #1:				
Records	0	250	188	
Cassettes	0	500	36	3	3992.
CDs	0	100	67		
	@7^{18}			
Album #2:				
Records	0	250	234	
Cassettes	0	500	455	2	349.
CDs	0	100	100		
	@5^{91}			
Album #1A:				
Cassettes	0	500	500		0
	@2^{00}			

Σ COGS = 4341.

some work by simply counting the total number of releases left at the end of the year—records, cassettes, and CDs. But it was good that Joe remembered the extra production.

Now the only other piece of information Joe's accountant needs is the number of albums Joe gave away to his family and friends. Joe gave three cassettes of Album #1 to his nephews and two cassettes of Album #2 to his great aunt in Topeka.

With that information, Joe's accountant develops a chart (Figure 16), from which Joe's cost-of-goods-sold figure is calculated for the current year.

Some hints toward understanding the figures:

1. Divide total production cost by number of units produced to arrive at a cost per unit. Assign that cost per unit to any unit, regardless of medium, unless you have separate production costs for cassettes and CDs and for records. (See special cases, below.)

2. Inventory is always assumed to be sold in this order: oldest

goods first, then newer goods. This is the FIFO (first-in, first-out) system. Joe's year-old inventory is valued at the number of Album #1 records, cassettes, and CDs from the first issue that are unsold at the end of the year, plus the number of Album #2 records, cassettes, and CDs that are unsold at the end of the year, plus the entire cost of producing the reissue of Album #1 (since, by FIFO, none of the reissue units were sold).

3. A reissue is treated as a new release, with its own lower cost per unit.

4. Albums given to relatives are deducted from the manufacturing cost at the cost per unit calculated.

SPECIAL CASES

SEPARATE PRODUCTION COSTS

If you have separate production costs, allocate the costs attributable to overall production proportionately, according to the number produced.

Example: If you produce 500 cassettes and CDs and 250 records, attribute two-thirds of the general production costs (technicians, studio rental, design work) to the cassettes and CDs and one-third to the records. The cost per unit for cassettes and CDs, then, is two-thirds of the production costs plus all the packaging costs (box plus cassettes or CDs), divided by 500, the number of cassettes and CDs produced.

The cost per unit for the records is one-third of the production costs, plus the cost of the album covers and the vinyl, divided by 250, the number of records produced.

REISSUES

Handle these as new releases, and calculate the per-unit cost by dividing production cost by number produced. The per-unit cost of reissues is much lower than the per-unit cost of the first issue, since the general production expenses have already been allocated to the first-issue units.

Don't get the idea that this is an opportunity for creative tax planning. You should plan to produce as many units as you think you'll reasonably sell in an eighteen-month period. Don't over-produce, because the costs involved will be tied up in inventory for years. Don't underproduce with the thought you can write off all the overhead costs on the first 100 units. On self-published albums, make the number produced fit the profile of your business. By the second or third album you will have a track record by which to gauge the size of your production orders.

INVENTORY FOR OTHER ARTISTS

The musician's example is transferable to anyone with an inventory, artists included. It's important to remember:

- You need to have a separate unit cost for items significantly different from one another (purchased at different times, usually).
- To speed year-end counting, mark boxes of bulk purchases (findings, dyes, paints) with the original purchase price so you can eyeball the contents and take the proportion of the container left, times that purchase price, as the value of that item at the end of the year.
- Contemporaneous notes suffice to document "items withdrawn for personal use," the gifts you make to relatives and friends.
- When items are no longer marketable, their fair market value drops to zero. This happens to books written on time-specific topics or items replaced by a newer, significantly different or improved version. Destroy them, or, if they have any use at all (such as clothing sporting "Yankees in '91"), give them to a local charity. You won't have a charitable deduction since the cost of producing the materials is being written off via the year-end inventory figure, but at least the items won't be totally wasted.
- If you take items in trade, develop a cumulative list of them, referenced by trade-in invoice, that shows the allowance you provided. That allowance is listed on the sales invoice. Your reportable revenue on the sale is the cost of the new items

sold, even though the customer paid you less than that because of the trade-in. The cost of the trade-in becomes part of your inventory, and you can write it off when the trade-in item is sold.

For More Information

The IRS does not have a publication focusing on inventories. The issue is discussed here and there in Publication 334, "Tax Guide for Small Business," but no comprehensive examples are offered in any IRS materials.

Inventories are covered in Section 471 of the Internal Revenue Code.

□ 16 □

Sale of Business Equipment

Overview

The sale of any capital asset used in your business is a taxable event that must be reported on your tax return in the year of sale. Capital assets include any item reported by you on Form 4562 (whether it was depreciated or expensed), your personal automobile if you used it for business, and your residence if you claimed a deduction for home-office use. Trade-ins are treated as sales. Use Form 4797 to report the transaction.

Presale Planning

It's advisable to have a general idea of the tax consequences before you sell a piece of business equipment. To calculate your potential tax liability, you must understand the concept of "basis."

Basis is your current investment in a capital asset. Basis changes through the life of an asset as it depreciates and its cost is written off. Take a computer. Its cost to you might have been $2,500. In the year of purchase, you perhaps elected to expense it. In that single year, the basis of the computer drops from $2,500 to zero. (Of course the process is slower if you depreciate the computer, but this gives you an idea of how basis changes.)

Let's assume that you sell the computer the following year for $1,500. (A computer drops dramatically in value as the technology fuels market demand for faster processing units.) A quick glance at the numbers might lead you to the faulty conclusion that you have a deductible loss. True, you took a financial drubbing, but for your taxes you must report a $1,500 profit (the $1,500 sale price, less basis, equals capital gain).

Presale planning is even more important when it comes time to sell your home, if you've claimed a home-office deduction. Most homeowners understand that they can roll any profit from the sale of their home into their next home, provided it costs more than their existing home. What they forget is that claiming a deduction for home-office use divides their property into residential and commercial property according to the percentage of home-office use. The capital gain on the former can be rolled into the replacement residence. (This takes the form of an adjustment to basis, explained below.) But the capital gain on the latter, commercial, property is taxable in the year of sale.

Presale planning in the case of a residence used partly for business is most useful if it's done several years in advance. If you know you're going to move to Washington in two or three years, don't claim home-office use from now until the time you move. Even if you've claimed home-office use in the past and are entitled to claim it now, forget about it. The rules on rolling over the capital gain from your existing house into your replacement residence specify that you must occupy your home three of the five years prior to selling it. If you do not claim a home-office deduction for two full calendar years prior to selling your home, the entire capital gain can be rolled over into your replacement residence.

Of course, if you need to move you'll probably move, with or without understanding the tax consequences. In the case where you can't preplan your move, at least sit down and figure the tax consequences of your action. Pull together the papers establishing the basis of your existing residence and figure the basis. Determine how much depreciation you've claimed on your home for the home-office deduction and calculate overall business use of your home for the years you owned it. Why do this before a move? For the simple reason that the information you need to file the tax forms on the sale of a residence is much easier to get your hands on before you move than after you move.

Sale of a personal automobile generally has no adverse consequences for those deducting expenses using the standard mileage rate deduction. For those using the actual-expense method of deducting expenses for business use of a personal automobile, calculating the potential gain should be done prior to selling or trading, especially if a luxury automobile is involved.

Example 1: SALE OF BUSINESS EQUIPMENT

Effie Stopp is a photographer. Three years ago she bought a Hasselblad camera for $1,500, which she began depreciating. She now has a chance to trade it for two other cameras that together retail for $1,000.

To figure out the tax implications of the trade, Effie digs back through her tax returns to come up with the depreciation taken on the Hasselblad: $300 plus $480 plus $288 = $1,068. Her basis in the Hasselblad is $1,500 − $1,068 = $432. Her tentative capital gain is $1,000 − $432 = $568.

Because Effie owned the Hasselblad more than one year, she uses Part I of Form 4797 to calculate the gain. Figure 17 shows what Effie's Form 4797 looks like.

Any gain from Part I of Form 4797 is transferred to Schedule D as a long-term capital gain. (A loss is reportable on the front of Form 1040.) Both Form 4797 and Schedule D will be part of Effie's tax return this year.

Her basis in the two new cameras is $1,000. She can expense them or begin depreciating them as circumstances dictate.

Example 2: SALE OF RESIDENCE

Case A: With Home Office

JJ Flash is a dancer who's owned his home for four years and who's claimed a deduction for the studio he has on the second floor

FIGURE 17

FORM 4797: CAMERA SALE

| Part I | Sales or Exchanges of Property Used in a Trade or Business and Involuntary Conversions From Other Than Casualty and Theft—Property Held More Than 1 Year |

1 Enter here the gross proceeds from the sale or exchange of real estate reported to you for 1990 on Form(s) 1099-S (or a substitute statement) that you will be including on line 2, 10, or 20 . . . . **1**

(a) Description of property	(b) Date acquired (mo., day, yr.)	(c) Date sold (mo., day, yr.)	(d) Gross sales price	(e) Depreciation allowed or allowable since acquisition	(f) Cost or other basis, plus improvements and expense of sale	(g) LOSS ((f) minus the sum of (d) and (e))	(h) GAIN ((d) plus (e) minus (f))
2 HASSELBLAD	9-4-88	8-16-90	1000.	1068.	1500.		568.

3 Gain, if any, from Form 4684, Section B, line 21 . . . .

4 Section 1231 gain from installment sales from Form 6252, line 22 or 30 . . . .

5 Gain, if any, from line 32, from other than casualty and theft . . . .

6 Add lines 2 through 5 in columns (g) and (h). . . . . (—)   568.

7 Combine columns (g) and (h) of line 6. Enter gain or (loss) here, and on the appropriate line as follows: . . . .   568.

   Partnerships.—Enter the gain or (loss) on Form 1065, Schedule K, line 6. Skip lines 8, 9, 11, and 12 below.

   S corporations.—Report the gain or (loss) following the instructions for Form 1120S, Schedule K, lines 5 and 6. Skip lines 8, 9, 11, and 12 below, unless line 7 is a gain and the S corporation is subject to the capital gains tax.

   All others.—If line 7 is zero or a loss, enter the amount on line 11 below and skip lines 8 and 9. If line 7 is a gain and you did not have any prior year section 1231 losses, or they were recaptured in an earlier year, enter the gain as a long-term capital gain on Schedule D and skip lines 8, 9, and 12 below.

8 Nonrecaptured net section 1231 losses from prior years (see Instructions) . . . .   —

9 Subtract line 8 from line 7. If zero or less, enter -0-. Also enter on the appropriate line as follows (see instructions): . . . . .   568.

   S corporations.—Enter this amount (if greater than zero) on Form 1120S, Schedule D, line 7, and skip lines 11 and 12 below.

   All others.—If line 9 is zero, enter the amount from line 7 on line 12 below. If line 9 is more than zero, enter the amount from line 8 on line 12 below, and enter the amount from line 9 as a long-term capital gain on Schedule D.

in each of those years. Now he has the chance to work in New York, so JJ's in a hurry to hit the big time. His realtor tells him a buyer will pay $90,000 for the home JJ bought for $80,000.

JJ's studio took up 30 percent of the living space in his home. Over the years, his depreciation schedules showed the following deductions:

Year 1: 3,042 percent (he bought the house in January and began using it as a studio immediately) × 30 percent (the business portion of the home) × $70,000 (JJ knows land isn't depreciable) = $639.

Years 2–4: 3.175 percent × 30 percent × $70,000 = $667 + $667 + 667 = $2,001. Total depreciation: $2,640.

JJ made no capital improvements to his home during those four years, so his basis in the house is $80,000 plus some of the closing costs he paid when he bought the house but that he couldn't deduct on that year's tax return. For JJ, those costs totaled $1,850. JJ's basis in the house, then, is $81,850.

To report the sale of his house, JJ needs to use Form 2119 to calculate the gain (or loss) on the residential portion of his home and Form 4797 to calculate the gain (or loss) on the business portion.

FIGURE 18
FORM 4797: HOUSE SALE

Form 4797 (199)   Page **2**

Part III Gain From Disposition of Property Under Sections 1245, 1250, 1252, 1254, and 1255

19 Description of section 1245, 1250, 1252, 1254, and 1255 property:	Date acquired (mo., day, yr.)	Date sold (mo., day, yr.)
A RESIDENCE WITH 30% HOME OFFICE	6-4-87	11-12-91
B		
C		
D		

Relate lines 19A through 19D to these columns ▶	Property A	Property B	Property C	Property D
20 Gross sales price (Note: See line 1 before completing.) 30% X 90,000	27000			
21 Cost or other basis plus expense of sale 24555 + 2190	26745			
22 Depreciation (or depletion) allowed or allowable	2640			
23 Adjusted basis. Subtract line 22 from line 21	24105			
24 Total gain. Subtract line 23 from line 20.	2895			

25 If section 1245 property:
a Depreciation allowed or allowable from line 22
b Enter the **smaller** of line 24 or 25a

26 If section 1250 property: If straight line depreciation was used, enter zero on line 26g unless you are a corporation subject to section 291.
a Additional depreciation after 12/31/75 (see instructions)
b Applicable percentage multiplied by the **smaller** of line 24 or line 26a (see instructions)
c Subtract line 26a from line 24. If line 24 is not more than line 26a, skip lines 26d and 26e.
d Additional depreciation after 12/31/69 and before 1/1/76
e Applicable percentage multiplied by the **smaller** of line 26c or 26d (see instructions)
f Section 291 amount (corporations only)
g Add lines 26b, 26e, and 26f

27 If section 1252 property: Skip this section if you did not dispose of farmland or if you are a partnership.
a Soil, water, and land clearing expenses
b Line 27a multiplied by applicable percentage (see instructions)
c Enter the **smaller** of line 24 or 27b

28 If section 1254 property:
a Intangible drilling and development costs, expenditures for development of mines and other natural deposits, and mining exploration costs (see instructions)
b Enter the **smaller** of line 24 or 28a

29 If section 1255 property:
a Applicable percentage of payments excluded from income under section 126 (see instructions)
b Enter the **smaller** of line 24 or 29a

Summary of Part III Gains (Complete property columns A through D, through line 29b before going to line 30.)

30 Total gains for all properties. Add columns A through D, line 24	2895.
31 Add columns A through D, lines 25b, 26g, 27c, 28b, and 29b. Enter here and on line 13. (See the Instructions for Part IV if this is an installment sale.)	—
32 Subtract line 31 from line 30. Enter the portion from casualty and theft on Form 4684, Section B, line 15. Enter the portion from other than casualty and theft on Form 4797, line 5	2895.

Part IV Election Not to Use the Installment Method (Complete this part only if you elect out of the installment method and report a note or other obligation at less than full face value.)

33 Check here if you elect out of the installment method	▶ ☐
34 Enter the face amount of the note or other obligation	▶ $
35 Enter the percentage of valuation of the note or other obligation	▶ %

Part V Recapture Amounts Under Sections 179 and 280F When Business Use Drops to 50% or Less (See Instructions for Part V.)

	(a) Section 179	(b) Section 280F
36 Section 179 expense deduction or section 280F recovery deductions		
37 Depreciation or recovery deductions (see Instructions)		
38 Recapture amount. Subtract line 37 from line 36. (See Instructions for where to report.)		

He begins by allocating basis between the residential and business portions of his home:

70% × $81,850 = $57,295, his basis in his residence,

30% × $81,850 = $24,555, his basis in the business portion of his residence.

Next he takes the settlement statement from the sale and distributes the sale price ($90,000) and cost of sale (amounting to $7,300, including realtor's fee) as follows:

70% residence: Proceeds = 70 percent × $90,000 = $63,000.
Cost of sale = 70% × $7,300 = $5,110;
30% office: Proceeds = 30% × $90,000 = $27,000.
Cost of sale = 30% × $7,300 = $2,190.

After JJ double-checks his figures to make sure the proceeds from the residential and business portion add up to the total reported to him on Form 1099-S, and after checking his arithmetic on divvying up the cost of sale and basis, JJ's ready to tackle his tax forms.

He begins with Form 4797. He has to use Part III and then Part I to report the sale of a business office. Figure 18 shows JJ's entries in Part III.

The depreciation is what does JJ in, handing him a gain of $2,895. Without it, he'd show a minimal gain, commensurate with his slim profit after closing costs. This illustrates a common problem. You may sell a property at a slight gain or even at a loss (in dollar terms, meaning money out of your pocket) and still show a taxable gain because of the depreciation you've taken.

JJ's $2,895 gain is transferred to Part I of Form 4797, and from there to the line on Schedule D reserved for Form 4797 gains, and from Schedule D to Form 1040 as taxable income.

When JJ turns to work on Form 2119, he's going to face a dilemma. His basis in the residential portion of his home is $57,295. The residential portion of the sale price is $63,000 and the cost of sale attributable to the residential portion is $5,110. Quick arithmetic shows a gain of $595. Figure 19 shows JJ's Form 2119.

JJ can roll this gain over into a new residence, provided it costs more than $90,000. But JJ knows he won't be able to afford to buy in the New York area, so he's well-advised to check "no" when asked if he plans to replace his residence within two years. Checking that "no" box means JJ reports the $595 gain on Schedule D, on the line reserved for Form 2119 gains.

FIGURE 19
FORM 2119: HOUSE SALE

Tax Return

Part I General Information

1a	Date your former main home was sold (month, day, year) . . . . ▶			4 / 21 / 91
b	Enter the face amount of any mortgage, note (e.g., second trust), or other financial instrument on which you will receive periodic payments of principal or interest from this sale (see Instructions) . .	1b		—
2	Have you bought or built a new main home?			☐ Yes ☒ No
3	Is or was any part of either main home rented out or used for business? (If "Yes," see Instructions). .	30.7% .		☒ Yes ☐ No

Part II Gain on Sale *(Do not include amounts you deduct as moving expenses.)*

70% x ?o

4	Selling price of home. (Do not include personal property items that you sold with your home.) . . .	4	63 000	00
5	Expense of sale. (Include sales commissions, advertising, legal, etc.)	5	5 110	00
6	Amount realized. Subtract line 5 from line 4	6	57 890	00
7	Basis of home sold. (See Instructions.)	7	57 295	00
8a	Gain on sale. Subtract line 7 from line 6	8a	595	00

    • If line 8a is zero or less, stop here and attach this form to your return.

    • If you answered "Yes" on line 2, go to Part III or Part IV, whichever applies. Otherwise, go to line 8b.

b	If you haven't replaced your home, do you plan to do so within the replacement period (see Instructions)?	☐ Yes	☒ No

    • If "Yes," stop here, attach this form to your return, and see Instructions under **Additional Filing Requirements.**

    • If "No," go to Part III or Part IV, whichever applies.

Part III One-Time Exclusion of Gain for People Age 55 or Older *(If you are not taking the exclusion, go to Part IV now.)*

☐ Yes ☐ No

Case B: Without Home Office

Assume the same facts, except JJ's moving home to Kansas City. In 1986, he decided to give himself four years in another place and then return home. JJ knew from the start that he would claim a deduction for business use of his home those first two years of ownership. He wouldn't claim the deduction the last two years because of the impending move.

This JJ has different calculations to make. His basis is $81,850, less the depreciation he claimed for home-office use the first two years only, or: $81,850 − $639 the first year - $ 667 the second year = $80,544.

His sale price is still $90,000 and his cost of sale is still $7,300.

Quick calculating on Form 2119 shows his gain is $2,156. Moving to Kansas City, JJ can afford to buy a house. In fact, he already has one picked out. It'll cost him $100,000, but it's a beauty. Figure 20 shows how JJ's Form 2119 will look and how rolling over the gain from his old house lowers the basis of his new residence.

These two scenarios would have almost the same net effect if JJ weren't replacing his residence. In fact, had JJ known his home would sell for little more than he paid for it, he'd have been better off claiming a home-office deduction for every year he owned the

FIGURE 20

FORM 2119: HOUSE SALE

Form **2119** Department of the Treasury Internal Revenue Service	**Sale of Your Home** ▶ Attach to Form 1040 for year of sale. ▶ **See Separate Instructions.** ▶ **Please print or type.**		

Your first name and initial (If joint, also give spouse's name and initial.)	Last name	Your social security number

Fill In Your Address Only If You Are Filing This Form by Itself and Not With Your Tax Return	Present address (no., street, and apt. no., rural route, or P.O. box no. if mail is not delivered to street address)	Spouse's social security number
	City, town or post office, state, and ZIP code	

Part I General Information

1a	Date your former main home was sold (month, day, year) . . . . ▶		11 / 12 / 91
b	Enter the face amount of any mortgage, note (e.g., second trust), or other financial instrument on which you will receive periodic payments of principal or interest from this sale (see Instructions) . .	**1b**	—
2	Have you bought or built a new main home?		☒ Yes ☐ No
3	Is or was any part of either main home rented out or used for business? (If "Yes," see Instructions.)		☒ Yes ☐ No

Part II Gain on Sale *(Do not include amounts you deduct as moving expenses.)*

4	Selling price of home. (Do not include personal property items that you sold with your home.) . . .	**4**	90 000 00
5	Expense of sale. (Include sales commissions, advertising, legal, etc.)	**5**	7 300 00
6	Amount realized. Subtract line 5 from line 4	**6**	82 700 00
7	Basis of home sold. (See Instructions.) . 81,850 – 639 – 667 =	**7**	80 544 00
8a	**Gain on sale.** Subtract line 7 from line 6	**8a**	2156 00
	• If line 8a is zero or less, stop here and attach this form to your return.		
	• If you answered "Yes" on line 2, go to Part III or Part IV, whichever applies. Otherwise, go to line 8b.		
b	If you haven't replaced your home, do you plan to do so within the replacement period (see Instructions)?		☐ Yes ☐ No
	• If "Yes," stop here, attach this form to your return, and see Instructions under **Additional Filing Requirements.**		
	• If "No," go to Part III or Part IV, whichever applies.		

Part III One-Time Exclusion of Gain for People Age 55 or Older *(If you are not taking the exclusion, go to Part IV now.)*

9a	Were you 55 or older on date of sale?		☐ Yes ☒ No
b	Was your spouse 55 or older on date of sale?		☐ Yes ☐ No
	If you did not answer "Yes" on either line 9a or 9b, go to Part IV now.		
c	Did the person who answered "Yes" on line 9a or 9b own and use the property as his or her main home for a total of at least 3 years (except for short absences) of the 5-year period before the sale? (If "No," go to Part IV now.) . .		☐ Yes ☐ No
d	**If you answered "Yes" on line 9c, do you elect to take the one-time exclusion?** (If "No," go to Part IV now.) .		☐ Yes ☐ No
e	At time of sale, who owned the home?	☐ You	☐ Your spouse ☐ Both of you
f	Social security number of spouse at time of sale if you had a different spouse from the one above at time of sale. (Enter "None" if you were not married at time of sale.) . . . . ▶		
g	Exclusion. Enter the **smaller** of line 8a or $125,000 ($62,500, if married filing separate return) . .	**9g**	

Part IV Adjusted Sales Price, Taxable Gain, and Adjusted Basis of New Home

10	Subtract the amount on line 9g, if any, from the amount on line 8a	**10**	2156 00
	• If line 10 is zero, stop here and attach this form to your return.		
	• If you answered "Yes" on line 2, go to line 11 now.		
	• If you are reporting this sale on the installment method, stop here and see line 1b Instructions.		
	• All others, stop here and enter the amount from line 10 on Schedule D, line 3 or line 10.		
11	Fixing-up expenses (See Instructions for time limits.)	**11**	—
12	**Adjusted sales price.** Subtract line 11 from line 6	**12**	82700 00
13a	Date you moved into new home (month, day, year) ▶ 12/ 1 /91 **b** Cost of new home .	**13b**	100 000 00
14a	Add the amount on line 9g, if any, and the amount on line 13b and enter the total	**14a**	100 000 00
b	Subtract line 14a from line 12. If the result is zero or less, enter -0-	**14b**	0
c	**Taxable gain.** Enter the **smaller** of line 10 or line 14b	**14c**	0
	• If line 14c is zero, go to line 15 and attach this form to your return.		
	• If you are reporting this sale on the installment method, see line 1b Instructions and go to line 15.		
	• All others, enter the amount from line 14c on Schedule D, line 3 or line 10, and go to line 15.		
15	Postponed gain. Subtract line 14c from line 10	**15**	2156 00
16	**Adjusted basis of new home.** Subtract line 15 from line 13b	**16**	97844 00

Sign Here Only If You Are Filing This Form by Itself and Not With Your Tax Return	Under penalties of perjury, I declare that I have examined this form, including attachments, and to the best of my knowledge and belief, it is true, correct, and complete
	Your signature _____ Date _____ Spouse's signature _____ Date _____
	(If a joint return, both must sign.) ▶

For Paperwork Reduction Act Notice, see separate Instructions.   Form **2119** (1990) house, even though he planned to move. Remember that a portion of utilities and homeowner's insurance are deductible to those who use part of their homes for business. These items aren't deductible to homeowners who don't claim business use of part of their homes. True, both the home-office and non-home-office taxpayer can deduct mortgage interest and property taxes, but for the home-office taxpayer the portion taken on Schedule C offsets Social Security tax as well as income tax.

Most of JJ's tax liability in the first scenario came from depreciation, which was probably more than offset by the 30 percent of utilities and homeowner's insurance he deducted. Add to that the Social Security tax savings from deducting 30 percent of mortgage interest and property taxes, and you begin to see why claiming home-office space is so desirable to taxpayers and so closely monitored by the IRS.

In general, if you know property in your area hasn't appreciated much in value since you bought it, claim a home-office deduction as long as you're entitled to do so. (Watch the restrictions on the new Form 8829.) If you're moving from an area of relatively low property values, like the Midwest, to one of relatively high property values, like Los Angeles or New York, assume you will not be able to afford a replacement residence and plan accordingly. If you're moving from a high-property-value area to a lower one, and you've owned a home for many years so you'll realize a significant gain when you sell, don't claim a home-office deduction for two full calendar years prior to sale. The capital gain on houses that have appreciated significantly can be staggering.

A capital gain on the sale of that part of your home used for business becomes taxable income in the year of sale; a capital loss on the sale of that part of your home used for business becomes a deductible loss. Any gain on the sale of the personal-use portion of your residence becomes taxable income in the year of sale, unless it's rolled over into a residence costing more. Any loss on the sale of a residence is not deductible.

Example 3. SALE OF AN AUTOMOBILE
Case A: Used Standard Mileage Deduction for Business Use

Lil O'Lady, a watercolor painter, traded in her 1987 Corvette on a brand new 1991 model, getting $14,000 in trade after she swore to the dealer that she'd only driven it to church. (She didn't use one of the Pasadena dealers.) Lil had paid $28,000 for the car in 1987 and had used the standard mileage deduction because she didn't want to be slowed down with all those gas and oil receipts.

To calculate her gain or loss on the trade-in, Lil first needed to calculate overall business use during her ownership. She went back through her tax records to come up with total miles driven and business miles driven, and then made up this chart (Figure 21):

FIGURE 21
MILEAGE USE

Year	Total miles	Business miles	Depreciation rate (in cents)	Depreciation allowed
1987	14,236	8,962	@ 10¢	896
1988	16,918	12,414	@ 10.5¢	1303
1989	17,224	11,627	@ 11¢	1279
1990	15,962	14,710	@ 11¢	1618
1991	9,651	8,291	@ 11¢	912
Totals	73,991	56,004	—	6008

Business % use = 75.69%

Lil's overall business percentage use is 75.69 percent (56,004 business miles divided by 73,991 total miles). Lil has mileage logs to back up what might seem to an IRS auditor like a suspiciously high number of overall miles, given Lil's age, and an even more suspicious number of business miles. An auditor finds that Lil has not only the logs to back up her claims, but also galleries up and down the coast selling her works that she visits on a regular basis, thereby supporting her claim that these are business miles and not just stopovers at the next surfing spot.

Lil begins by calculating the business cost of her vehicle and the business sale price of her vehicle. The entire vehicle cost $28,000 in 1987. Business use at 75.69 percent means the business part of that vehicle cost her $21,193. Her trade-in sale price was $14,000 for the entire car, or $10,597 for the business portion of the car.

Next, Lil looks at the Form 4797 instructions to find the depreciation part of the standard mileage rate she used each of those years and enters those numbers in the chart. Multiplying the depreciation

FIGURE 22

FORM 4797: CAR SALE

Part I	Sales or Exchanges of Property Used in a Trade or Business and Involuntary Conversions From Other Than Casualty and Theft—Property Held More Than 1 Year						

1 Enter here the gross proceeds from the sale or exchange of real estate reported to you for 1990 on Form(s) 1099-S (or a substitute statement) that you will be including on line 2, 10, or 20 . . . . **1**

(a) Description of property	(b) Date acquired (mo., day, yr.)	(c) Date sold (mo., day, yr.)	(d) Gross sales price	(e) Depreciation allowed or allowable since acquisition	(f) Cost or other basis, plus improvements and expense of sale	(g) LOSS ((f) minus the sum of (d) and (e))	(h) GAIN ((d) plus (e) minus (f))
2 AUTO	4-10-87	6-5-91	10597	6008	21193		4584

3 Gain, if any, from Form 4684, Section B, line 21 . . . .

4 Section 1231 gain from installment sales from Form 6252, line 22 or 30 . . . .

5 Gain, if any, from line 32, from other than casualty and theft . . . .

6 Add lines 2 through 5 in columns (g) and (h) . . . . (4584) —

7 Combine columns (g) and (h) of line 6. Enter gain or (loss) here, and on the appropriate line as follows: . . . . (4584)

    Partnerships.—Enter the gain or (loss) on Form 1065, Schedule K, line 6. Skip lines 8, 9, 11, and 12 below.

    S corporations.—Report the gain or (loss) following the instructions for Form 1120S, Schedule K, lines 5 and 6. Skip lines 8, 9, 11, and 12 below, unless line 7 is a gain and the S corporation is subject to the capital gains tax.

    All others.—If line 7 is zero or a loss, enter the amount on line 11 below and skip lines 8 and 9. If line 7 is a gain and you did not have any prior year section 1231 losses, or they were recaptured in an earlier year, enter the gain as a long-term capital gain on Schedule D and skip lines 8, 9, and 12 below.

8 Nonrecaptured net section 1231 losses from prior years (see Instructions) . . . .

9 Subtract line 8 from line 7. If zero or less, enter -0-. Also enter on the appropriate line as follows (see instructions). . . . . . .

    S corporations.—Enter this amount (if greater than zero) on Form 1120S, Schedule D, line 7, and skip lines 11 and 12 below.

    All others.—If line 9 is zero, enter the amount from line 7 on line 12 below. If line 9 is more than zero, enter the amount from line 8 on line 12 below, and enter the amount from line 9 as a long-term capital gain on Schedule D.

rate for each year times the number of business miles gives Lil the amount of depreciation she put on the vehicle during the time she owned it.

Lil now has all the information she needs to complete her Form 4797. She uses Part I, since she owned the vehicle for more than a year. Figure 22 shows how she arrived at a loss of $4,584. This loss is deductible directly on the front of Lil's Form 1040.

Any accountant would be thrilled at producing this kind of tax loss for a client, but Lil is less than impressed. She's still feeling ripped off at the low trade-in allowance she was given. After all, the car was almost new . . .

Case B: Used Actual-Expense Method to Deduct for Business Use

Assume the same facts as in the case above, but this time Lil used the actual-expense method of deducting expenses.

Lil begins the same way, determining business-use percentage. It's still 75.69 percent. From her annual tax records, she jots down the amount of depreciation she took each year: $1,611 in 1987, $3,008 in 1988, $1,653 in 1989, $1,359 in 1990. Lil doesn't claim deprecia-

FIGURE 23

FORM 4797: CAR SALE

Part I	Sales or Exchanges of Property Used in a Trade or Business and Involuntary Conversions From Other Than Casualty and Theft—Property Held More Than 1 Year						

1 Enter here the gross proceeds from the sale or exchange of real estate reported to you for 1990 on Form(s) 1099-S (or a substitute statement) that you will be including on line 2, 10, or 20 . . . . **1**

(a) Description of property	(b) Date acquired (mo., day, yr.)	(c) Date sold (mo., day, yr.)	(d) Gross sales price	(e) Depreciation allowed or allowable since acquisition	(f) Cost or other basis, plus improvements and expense of sale	(g) LOSS ((f) minus the sum of (d) and (e))	(h) GAIN ((d) plus (e) minus (f))
2 AUTO	4-10-87	6-5-91	10597	7631	21193	2965	

3 Gain, if any, from Form 4684, Section B, line 21 . . . .

4 Section 1231 gain from installment sales from Form 6252, line 22 or 30 . . . .

5 Gain, if any, from line 32, from other than casualty and theft . . . .

6 Add lines 2 through 5 in columns (g) and (h) . . . . (2965) —

7 Combine columns (g) and (h) of line 6. Enter gain or (loss) here, and on the appropriate line as follows . . . . (2965)

Partnerships.—Enter the gain or (loss) on Form 1065, Schedule K, line 6. Skip lines 8, 9, 11, and 12 below.

S corporations.—Report the gain or (loss) following the instructions for Form 1120S, Schedule K, lines 5 and 6. Skip lines 8, 9, 11, and 12 below, unless line 7 is a gain and the S corporation is subject to the capital gains tax.

All others.—If line 7 is zero or a loss, enter the amount on line 11 below and skip lines 8 and 9. If line 7 is a gain and you did not have any prior year section 1231 losses, or they were recaptured in an earlier year, enter the gain as a long-term capital gain on Schedule D and skip lines 8, 9, and 12 below.

8 Nonrecaptured net section 1231 losses from prior years (see instructions) . . . .

9 Subtract line 8 from line 7. If zero or less, enter -0-. Also enter on the appropriate line as follows (see instructions): . . . . .

S corporations.—Enter this amount (if greater than zero) on Form 1120S, Schedule D, line 7, and skip lines 11 and 12 below

All others.—If line 9 is zero, enter the amount from line 7 on line 12 below. If line 9 is more than zero, enter the amount from line 8 on line 12 below, and enter the amount from line 9 as a long-term capital gain on Schedule D.

tion in the year of sale because IRS regulations don't allow it. Total depreciation taken equals $7,631.

Remember the limitations placed on depreciation allowed for luxury automobiles? Annual depreciation allowed is the annual allowance times the business percentage use for that year. See Form 4562 instructions for the annual caps. They're indexed to inflation, so don't assume that what works for one year will still be in effect the next.

Lil's cost for the business part of the car is still $21,193, and her trade-in allowance on the business part of the car is still $10,597. Figure 23 shows Lil's loss.

By using the actual-expense method of claiming a deduction for business use of her automobile, Lil was able to deduct expenses earlier. Otherwise, her overall loss on the Corvette was the same, whether she used the standard mileage rate or the actual-expense method.

Generally, using the standard mileage deduction gives you a larger deduction if you put a lot of business miles on your car each year (more than 10,000) or if your pattern is to buy a new car, drive

FIGURE 24
FORM 4797: CAR WITH OVERDEPRECIATION

Part I Sales or Exchanges of Property Used in a Trade or Business and Involuntary Conversions From Other Than Casualty and Theft–Property Held More Than 1 Year

1. Enter here the gross proceeds from the sale or exchange of real estate reported to you for 1990 on Form(s) 1099-S (or a substitute statement) that you will be including on line 2, 10, or 20. . . . . | 1 |

2 (a)Description of property	(b) Date acquired (mo., day, yr.)	(c) Date sold (mo., day, yr.)	(d) Gross sales price	(e) Depreciation allowed or allowable since acquisition	(f) Cost or other basis, plus improvements and expense of sale	(g) LOSS (f) minus the sum of (d) and (e))	(h) GAIN ((d) plus (e)) minus (f))
1981 honda	01/01/81	06/01/90	51.	1,313.	796.		568. 0

3. Gain, if any, from Form 4684, Section B, line 21 . . . .
4. Section 1231 gain from installment sales from Form 6252, line 22 or 30 . . . . .
5. Gain, if any, from line 32, from other than casualty and theft . . . .
6. Add lines 2 through 5 in columns (g) and (h) 568. 0
7. Combine columns (g) and (h) of line 6. Enter gain or (loss) here, and on the appropriate line as follows: 568. 0
   Partnerships. –Enter the gain or (loss) on Form 1065, Schedule K, line 6. Skip lines 8, 9, 11, and 12 below.
   S corporations. –Report the gain or (loss) following the instructions for Form 1120S, Schedule K, lines 5 and 6. Skip lines 8, 9, 11, and 12 below, unless line 7 is a gain and the S corporation is subject to the capital gains tax.
   All others. – If line 7 is zero or a loss, enter the amount on line 11 and skip lines 8 and 9. If line 7 is a gain and you did not have any prior year section 1231 losses, or they were recaptured in an earlier year, enter the gain as a long-term capital gain on Schedule D and skip line 8, 9, and 12 below.
8. Nonrecaptured net section 1231 losses from prior years (see Instructions) . . . .
9. Subtract line 8 from line 7. If zero or less, enter zero. Also enter on the appropriate line as follows (see instructions): . . . .
   S corporations. –Enter this amount (if greater than zero) on line 11 Form 1120S, Schedule D, line 7, and skip lines 11 and 12 below.
   All others. – If line 9 is zero, enter the amount from line 7 on line 12 below. If line 9 is more than zero, enter the amount from line 8 on line 12 below, and enter the amount from line 9 as a long-term capital gain on Schedule D.

Part II Ordinary Gains and Losses

10. Ordinary gains and losses not included on lines 11 through 16 (include property held 1 year or less)

11. Loss, if any, from line 7 . . . .
12. Gain, if any, from line 7, or amount from line 8 if applicable . . . . . .
13. Gain, if any, from line 31 . . . .
14. Net gain or (loss) from Form 4684, Section B, lines 13 and 20a . . . . .
15. Ordinary gain from installment sales from Form 6252, line 21 or 29 . . . .
16. Recapture of section 179 deduction for partners and S corporation shareholders from property dispositions by partnerships and S corporations (see Instructions) . . . . . .
17. Add lines 10 through 16 in columns (g) and (h) . . . .
18. Combine columns (g) and (h) of line 17. Enter gain or (loss) here, and on the appropriate line as follows: . . . . 0.
    a. For all except individual returns: Enter the gain or (loss) from line 18 on the return being filed.
    b. For individual returns:
    (1) If the loss on line 11 includes a loss from Form 4684, Sec. B, Part II, column(b)(ii), enter that part of the loss here and on line 21 of Schedule A (Form 1040). Identify as from "Form 4797, line 18b(1)". See Instructions . . . . . . 0.
    (2) Redetermine the gain (loss) on line 18, excluding the loss, if any on line 18b(1). Enter here and on Form 1040, line 15. . . . . . . 0.

For Paperwork Reduction Act Notice, See Instructions   Tax Resources, Inc. (1990) 96-0169940   Form 4797 (1990)

NO GAIN RECOGNIZED DUE TO OVERDEPRECIATION OF VEHICLE WHERE STANDARD MILEAGE DEDUCTION WAS USED

it for ten years, and then buy another new one. If you buy a luxury car, the actual-expense method of deducting expenses works well only if you have a high percentage of business use. Lil sure did, so she came out with approximately the same net effect.

A danger with using the actual-expense method is recapture, triggered when your business use falls below 50 percent. This subject is discussed in greater detail below. Had Lil trusted a phone and a fax more than her eyes, she could have cut down on her driving time. Her accountant was always after her to do just that, since time spent in a car is time wasted for producing art. But then, what do accountants know about Route 1?

Sometimes, when you've owned a car a long time and have run up significant business miles on it, the depreciation included in the standard mileage rate ends up causing you to show a gain on the sale of the car. Relax. That gain is a paper gain only. It's not recognized as income. You can never have a gain on the sale or disposition of a vehicle when you used the standard mileage rate to deduct expenses for business use of your car, due to "overdepreciating" the vehicle.

Figure 24 shows how this works. This car, which was junked in 1990, was driven a lot for business. The depreciation included in the standard mileage rate for all the business miles this car was driven created a paper gain. Figure 24 shows the notations you should use to zero out the gain.

Other Dispositions

What happens if you stop being self-employed? What happens if you give away your equipment to a nonprofit organization? What if you give it to your nephew to start his own business? These three seemingly different scenarios have one thing in common: You've retired the asset prior to the end of its tax life. You've removed it from service before its life, as the IRS figures it, is done. When that happens, you're subject to recapture of part of the depreciation taken on that capital asset.

Let's say you buy a computer in June for $2,000. In your tax return filed for the year you bought it, you elect to expense it (Internal Revenue Code Section 179), deducting the full cost in the year of purchase. The following year, you get an offer for a W-2 job you find you can't refuse. Since you're no longer self-employed, you must pay tax on the difference between your basis (zero) and the basis you should have if you'd used straight-line depreciation for one year ($2,000 − [$400 × ½ year] = $1,800).

Sound unfair? Maybe it is, but it's one of those strictures that made expensing possible in the first place. The IRS doesn't want taxpayers dropping in and out of self-employment for the sake of buying some equipment they write off at the expense of other tax-payers and then get to use, scot-free, for the duration of its use-fulness.

Recapture also occurs when you give away a piece of equipment. If you give it away to a nonprofit organization, you can deduct your basis in the equipment as a charitable contribution of materials on your Schedule A. (Contributions of business property to nonprofit organizations are never deductible on Schedule C.) But if you ex-pense it, you have no additional charitable contribution because your basis in it is zero. In either case, you gave it away before its five-year life was over. You may have a charitable contribution deductible on Schedule A; for sure, you're subject to recapture. If you give away a capital asset to a relative or retire it from business use to personal use, you're subject to recapture.

Recapture is figured on Form 4797. It equals the difference be-tween your actual basis and your allowable basis. Your actual basis is your purchase price less depreciation taken including expensing. Your allowable basis is your purchase price less depreciation allowed, using the straight-line method over the IRS-defined life of the asset.

Recapture results in taxable income to you if you've used any of the accelerated methods of depreciating capital assets (ACRS or MACRS), because allowable depreciation is figured using straight-line percentages for the life of the asset.

LESS THAN 50 PERCENT BUSINESS USE

Recapture also occurs when business use of an asset drops to less than 50 percent in any given year.

Let's say your spouse goes into business and starts using the com-puter you bought in 1989. First of all, you need to begin keeping a his-and-her log on computer use. By the end of the year, that log shows that he's been on the machine 60 percent of the time. At that point, you call a divorce attorney. (Little joke, but not by much.)

Better to buy a second computer than to share it. Files can be erased, work patterns disrupted, and aggravation injected into your personal relationship. And on top of all that you have to keep a log for the IRS showing who's using the computer when. Adding insult to inconvenience, you're faced with recapture when you file your tax return: more tax forms to include in your return and, probably, some additional taxable income.

Recapture due to business use falling below 50 percent most often occurs with cars. Say you've been claiming a deduction using the actual-expense method at something like 63 percent business use, when all of a sudden you find you're using your car less for business, less than 50 percent to be exact. Your recapture amount equals the difference between your purchase price and the depreciation actually taken less your purchase price and the depreciation allowed using the straight-line method.

THE DOWNSIDE OF RECAPTURE

Sale of a business asset results in a gain or loss figured on Form 4797. The gain almost always results in taxable income; sometimes, depending on the nature of the asset, a loss results in a taxable loss that can offset other income. Recapture is different. It's a double whammy. Gain is still figured on Form 4797 but then is transferred to the "other income" line of Schedule C. There it becomes part of your total income and is subject to self-employment tax.

This distinction is significant enough to merit repeating: Sale of an asset results in ordinary gain or loss; recapture results in additional self-employment income.

Does this mean you should turn cheapskate and keep your assets forever? No. But it does mean you continue to use your business assets in your business until their tax life has expired. Then it's safe to give them away (but no tax-deductible contribution to a nonprofit organization, since your basis is zero) or to give them to your relatives. (Just make sure they know how to use the equipment.)

Update on Enforcement

Business equipment provides a great opportunity for self-employed people to cheat on their taxes. Bear in mind the relevant term: *cheat* on their taxes.

Cheaters are caught only half the time, maybe less. If you don't want to gamble with your life, your fortune, and your professional reputation, don't even entertain the thought of cheating on your taxes. You'll rest easier. When that dreaded letter comes from the IRS announcing an audit, all you'll face is the certainty of hours spent reorganizing your materials to meet an auditor for an hour or so. The worst that can happen is a disagreement over some minor interpretation of tax law, such as writing off small tools instead of including them in a "small equipment" category and depreciating or expensing them.

Cheaters, on the other hand, don't know which way to turn when that audit letter comes. They can't remember which figures are right, which set of books is accurate, or what they included or excluded. To keep yourself safe and sane, file Form 4797 with your tax return when you retire an asset from business use before its tax life is over or when you start using a piece of equipment less than 50 percent. In the context of an entire life of taxpaying, recapture doesn't represent much of a financial burden.

By all means, when you sell business equipment, report the sale of business equipment. If you've been expensing television monitors for each of the past six years, it doesn't take a nuclear scientist to figure out something might be fishy if they are not expensed in the current year. The main purpose of field audits now is to check on the kinds of equipment the business owner says he's using in his business and to do a nose count on the premises.

For Further Information

Consult IRS Publication 544, "Sales and Other Dispositions of Assets."

□ 17 □

Pricing and Profits

Setting Objectives

As your business matures, it's no longer enough that it pays for itself. You, the owner, want certain things from it. Maybe you want your own home; maybe you want to pay for your kids' college education; maybe you want a decent retirement plan. As your financial wants increase, so do the pressures on your business to meet your expectations.

Building a Model

To get a grip on what your business must produce to meet your needs, begin with a monthly budget. Figure 25 is a budget worksheet. Enter personal monthly or annual expenses for each item.

FIGURE 25
BUDGET SHEET

BUDGET	MONTHLY	ANNUAL
Mortgage		
Utilities		
Food		
Entertainment (shows, eating out)		
Travel (escrow)		
Auto		
Insurance (escrow)		
Auto or Credit Card Payments		
Health Expenses, incl. insurance		
Wardrobe (escrow)		
Cleaning		
Contributions		
Gifts		
"Allowances"/Pocket Money		
Other: identify:		

Use the monthly total plus a 10 percent slush factor as the amount you need to make in your business to meet your monthly living expenses. That's step one in developing your pricing model.

Step two is working out a budget for your business. Begin by identifying your predictable overhead costs: rent, utilities, studio telephone, office supplies, postage and fax, overnight mail and delivery service charges, dues and publications, conferences and continuing education, advertising, tools and small equipment. Look at last year's tax return as a guide and adjust upward or downward in any category that doesn't seem typical. Take this total and divide by twelve for a monthly average. Add 10 to 15 percent to cover business expansion and inflation.

Next, identify the costs of making your product: supplies that go into it, payments to outside vendors (including independent contractors), freight. Figure how many units you produce for the dollars you've estimated, and divide the dollar figure by the unit figure to arrive at a cost per unit.

At this stage, you need to think about some of the variable costs you inevitably incur. If you have a new product line, you will spend more on advertising to introduce it than you will later to keep it moving. New products also generally require some extraordinary start-up expense: casting a prototype, building a mold, or generating sketches for a presentation. Determine how many new products you'll introduce next year, add up the special costs, and divide the total by 12 to arrive at a monthly set-aside for new-product development and marketing.

A final entry is a set-aside for new equipment purchases. As your business matures you need to buy less equipment. You may want the latest gizmo, but your wants can be modulated and scheduled. Usually you'll settle on a figure you're willing to invest each year for capital assets. Take this figure and divide it by 12 for a monthly set-aside for equipment purchases.

Thus far you have:

- monthly personal budget
- monthly business overhead
- cost per unit
- new product special costs

- set-aside for new product development and marketing
- set-aside for capital assets

TESTING THE MODEL

Let's begin to put some hypothetical numbers to this model. Let's assume your monthly personal budget is $2,000. And let's put your monthly business overhead at $800. The cost per unit produced is $60. New-product special costs maybe average $100 per month. You plan to introduce one new product next year, at a cost of $6,000, or $500 per month. You plan to spend $3,000 on equipment, or $250 monthly. Totals thus far:

Monthly personal budget	$2,000.
Monthly business overhead	800.
New-product special costs	100.
New-product development and marketing	500.
Equipment set-aside	250.
Working figure	$3,650.

So far, you know you need to generate at least $3,650 each month, or around $44,000 per year. This is before taxes and your personal draw. Taxes on this kind of income run on the average 20 percent (a blending of the 15 and 28 percent rates). For this exercise, use 15 percent, because tax will be paid on net profit, and you're using gross revenue in this planning model. Self-employment tax eats up another 15 percent, but figure this at 10 percent because FICA rates apply only to net profit. State taxes account for another 5 percent. Total tax factor is about 30 percent (15 percent federal, 10 percent FICA, 5 percent state). This means that 30 percent of whatever gross figure you calculate should be allocated for taxes. How much should you pay yourself? How about $1,000 per month? And what about your future? Let's put some money aside for a retirement plan contribution.

Your budget begins to look like this:

Monthly personal budget	$2,000.
Monthly business overhead	800.

New-product special costs	100.
New-product development and marketing	500.
Equipment set-aside	250.
Taxes: 30 percent of gross	(unknown)
Your pay	1,000.
Retirement plan contribution: 20 percent of net profit	(unknown)
Working figure	$4,650, plus two unknowns

Setting Sales Objectives

Put the model aside for now and focus on sales needed to generate what now amounts to approximately $55,000 per year. You know that the unit cost of your product is $60. Then: $x - \$60 = y$, where x is the price you get for the product and y is your net profit on each item. It's y that should equal $55,000 per year. The higher x is, the higher y is (to a point—more on that later).

Your estimates of how many products to sell needs to be realistic. Base your estimates on past performance or on a marketing pyramid:

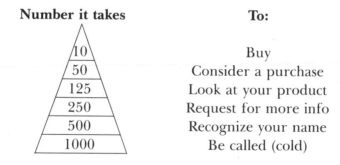

Number it takes	**To:**
10	Buy
50	Consider a purchase
125	Look at your product
250	Request for more info
500	Recognize your name
1000	Be called (cold)

The marketing pyramid tells you your "hit ratio"—your ratio of sales to contacts made. Read up from the base: If you send your card to a thousand people you don't know, you're likely to end up selling only ten products. The clue to effective marketing is to enter the pyramid at a higher level. In business this is called "qualifying" the customer.

Qualifying, in the art world, most likely involves identifying studios or galleries compatible with your style, as well as finding a market for specialty products. Send information to the 125 people (fourth level) who, you already know, will look at your product. You can still sell ten products, but with a smaller investment of time and money. If you can jump to level five (the fifty who, you already know, will seriously consider purchase), your hit ratio becomes ten of fifty, or a 20 percent ratio of sales to contacts.

The realistic estimate of the number of pieces you can sell multiplied by y (your net profit per piece) gives you the likely revenue total. Consider the big picture for a moment; price is discretionary and you've included a number of variables in your equation. But let's assume the number of pieces sold times y is reasonably close to the income you need to generate, and let's test the model.

REFINING THE MODEL

Assume net profit per unit is $2,000 and you realistically can sell thirty units per year, for total net profit of $60,000. You now have a working figure to use to estimate the two unknowns in your equation. Taxes eat up 30 percent ($18,000), and the retirement plans require about $12,000 (20 percent of likely net profit).

Your worksheet looks like this:

Monthly personal budget	$2,000.
Monthly business overhead	800.
New-product special costs	100.
New-product development and marketing	500.
Equipment set-aside	250.
Taxes ($18,000 ÷ 12)	1,500.
Your pay	1,000.
Retirement ($12,000 ÷ 12)	1,000.
Working monthly budget =	$7,150
Working annual budget =	$85,000
	(approximately)

Can you make that much? Do you (can you) raise prices? Do you try to sell more? Do you scrap plans to buy equipment? Do you stop paying yourself?

Before you go too crazy contemplating these options, test out your assumptions. Begin with the tax figure. To gross $85,000 you'll spend the following:

Studio overhead: 800 × 12	$ 9,600
New-product costs: 600 × 12	7,200
Equipment purchases: 250 × 12	3,000
Cost of goods sold: 60 × 30	1,800
Total expenses	$21,600

Your net profit is around $60,000. That means FICA will be about $9,000, and you can put $12,000 away for retirement. Your federal income tax is about ten thousand dollars, with your state tax adding maybe another $2,500. Thus far it looks as though you still need to gross $85,000. Cut overhead? Improbable. Cut your monthly budget? Maybe. But maybe the $1,000 draw can go. After all, the business is already supporting you totally (including paying your taxes), on top of adding $1,000 per month to your retirement nest egg.

Interrupt yourself at this point. The option of increasing prices or increasing sales should be investigated before deciding to cut your pay. This is the stage where you need to look seriously at your prices. If you're not making enough to support yourself in a reasonable style (reasonable to you, of course), you're probably not going to stay in business very long.

It's hard to ask for more money. But do it anyway. Make your prices (and your sales volume) cover your living expenses, the cost of operating your studio, the cost of making your art, and your pay.

A Critique

The model developed in this exercise oversimplifies some issues. It uses only one product where, in reality, you probably have several product lines, differentiated by size and market. Multiple product lines require more sophisticated number crunching. In that real-world situation, figure the profit per unit in each product line and multiply that figure by the number of each you're likely to sell during the year.

Within this context, consider developing at least one "cash cow": a product you don't necessarily like to make but that provides a wide profit margin and can be sold almost at will. The presence of a cash cow in your repertoire makes achieving your budgetary goals considerably easier.

Another point of oversimplification in the model is the linear treatment of profit per unit and number of units produced. You cannot, for example, continue to turn out more and more works in the same space and with the same profit margin. At some production level you'll reach what's called the point of diminishing returns, where productivity, efficiency, and unit profit begin to decrease. You also remain limited by your own time and energy.

You may also think it oversimplification to assume you can actually move art products through the door. This is not as great a stretch of imagination as it appears at first blush. Even in the art world, sales build steadily. Sometimes they leap sharply—when you're "discovered" or come into vogue—but more likely they grow steadily as gallery owners or reps become more comfortable with your work and with the customers who like it. Knowing exactly when you'll get that check in the mail will probably remain a mystery, but predicting annual gross sales is not as hard as it seems.

Performing artists: Feeling left out? Hard as it may seem to believe, you, too, create a product. "New-product development" means the budget you put together for the next recital or opening. "Cost per unit" will probably include some hefty fees to independent contractors. Modify the model to fit your business.

Concluding Comment

The prices of your product must be related to how much you need to earn. How much you need to earn is, in turn, dependent on your personal circumstances. Customize this model to fit your business and your personal profile. Use it, over time, with your books, to manage your art business, with a goal of refining your objectives in the areas of pricing, productivity, and profits.

□ 18 □

Audits

Overview

In 1985 the IRS undertook a massive computerization of its recordkeeping and issued new requirements for third-party payments,
among them interest paid to you by banks and payments made to
you by agencies or individuals who hire you as an independent
contractor. Taxpayers in general saw more 1099-MISC forms issued
to them; even the art world noticed the difference. As the IRS levied
penalties for failure to file 1099s, compliance jumped and the day of
under-the-table payments appeared to be over.

The increase in reports from third-party payers has allowed the
IRS to monitor the typical taxpayer with great accuracy. The "typical
taxpayer" has a W-2 job, several bank accounts, a mortgage, maybe a
mutual fund, and possibly a child or two. This person presents no
difficulties for the IRS, since it has already received a copy of almost
every tax document he or she needs to file a tax return even before
the return itself has been filed. What computer reports on what the

"typical taxpayer" has earned and what the "typical taxpayer" owes means is that the IRS has been able to focus its audit attention on people in business for themselves—a group that includes artists. The function of an audit is to ascertain that you have reported all your taxable income and have taken only legitimate deductions.

The threat of audit is the greatest, most effective compliance tool in the IRS arsenal. This threat is diminished, some think, by the overall decrease in the percentage of returns audited each year. It stands to reason that the IRS can't audit all small-business owners. But if you are audited, the auditor will confront you on the legitimacy of your deductions. Even if you come out of the audit clean, the auditor can check a box on the internal audit form to recommend a subsequent-year audit.

Auditors are also more up to date on tax law and regulations than in the past. Increased training has led to more successful compliance efforts, which means more money for the IRS. More than ever before, an artist or small-business owner needs to become somewhat familiar with tax law to achieve some level of sophistication in completing a tax return or in working effectively with a tax accountant.

The Chances of Being Audited

Only about 1 percent of all federal tax returns are audited. States seldom audit individual tax returns, relying instead on the IRS to uncover unreported income. Most audits of employers, however, are initiated at the state level.

Self-employed people are twice as likely to be audited. The volume of paperwork a self-employed person has to process makes it more likely some information is lost or ignored. Also, there are few reporting documents, such as 1099 forms, to verify the income a self-employed individual earns. Finally, expenses can be padded more easily by the self-employed person than by someone's employee.

A recent IRS study concluded that more than half of all self-employed people underreport income on their tax returns. This shockingly high level of noncompliance has led to increased audits to catch the cheaters, making life miserable for law-abiding sole proprietors.

Taxpayers who earn more than $100,000 are five times as likely to be audited. Other activities that increase the chances of being audited include ownership of rental property, participation in limited partnerships and other tax shelters, and ownership of a closely held corporation.

WHAT TRIGGERS AN AUDIT

Audits occur primarily because of unreported income. They also happen when the tax return is internally inconsistent or when expenses are excessive compared to other taxpayers reporting the same income, especially if the figures in some red-flag areas, such as travel or business entertainment or home-office expense, appear inflated.

Taxpayers who file their returns late stand a higher chance of being audited than those who file tax returns on time. If you haven't filed tax returns for several years, know that the IRS is trying to contact you. It's now almost impossible for an individual to escape the computer reporting that invades every segment of our economy. If the IRS can find you, it will offer you the opportunity to file past-due tax returns; if it can't find you, it will file them on your behalf and send a bill to your last known address. Penalties for late filing and late payment are added to interest penalties, virtually doubling the amount you originally owed. If you had a refund coming from the IRS, after three years it's lost. And, after all that's befallen you, you may still be audited!

Types of Audits

The *mail audit* is the most common. It's used only for cases of unreported income. You open that dreaded brown envelope and find a letter announcing in the most respectful terms imaginable that the IRS has discovered a discrepancy between what you reported on your tax return and what outside payers reported to the IRS about you. The next page identifies the amount of the discrepancy and computes the amount of tax the IRS thinks you need to pay. A third page lists the reports received by the IRS, grouping similar kinds of income in the category where the discrepancy exists.

Presumably you already reported most, if not all, of these items on your tax return. What you need to do is figure out which item the IRS thinks you didn't include, and then tell the IRS where it is on the return you filed.

The last page gives you the option of: 1. agreeing and paying in full; 2. agreeing partially, which requires you to write a letter identifying where you agree with the IRS and where you disagree and why; or 3. disagreeing totally, which also requires you to write a letter. Generally you disagree only when the income is already on your tax return, although not where the IRS expected to find it.

After reviewing your return, you may find that where you put something has resulted in avoiding a tax the IRS thinks you should pay. For example, you may have reported a commission on the "other income" line of Form 1040. Write a letter agreeing to pay the Social Security tax on that commission, but disagreeing on the income tax assessment. In fact you already paid the income tax when you included the commission as income on the "other income" line, but since the IRS thinks you didn't report it at all, it's billed you for income tax as well as Social Security tax.

When writing the IRS in response to a mail audit, organize your letter well so your case can be settled quickly. Be sure to use the fourth page—which lists your options—as a cover sheet for your letter and any accompanying documentation. Fold that page so the correct IRS office will show through the window envelope provided by the IRS.

Mail it within the time indicated on the first page and wait for a response. This usually takes six to eight weeks and is a process that cannot be hurried. If you partially agreed with the IRS findings, the response will take the form of a final bill you should pay in full. If you totally disagreed and the IRS is convinced, you will receive a brief acknowledgement. If you disagreed but were unable to convince the IRS of your position, you will receive a bill accompanied by a letter reaffirming the IRS position.

Do not call the IRS. Discussing your tax account with an IRS representative does not usually lead to a settlement. Put your energy into the letter you write in response to the mail audit, and make it prove your case.

Remember to amend your state income tax return if the IRS adjusts your federal tax return.

The second kind of audit is the *office audit*. The IRS letter informs you that your return has been selected for examination, and gives you a local telephone number to call to schedule a meeting with an IRS auditor in an IRS office. You're expected to call within ten days to schedule an appointment within thirty days of the letter date.

The letter goes on to identify the items that will be examined at the audit. Sometimes unreported income is an issue and the office audit always includes the examination of some of the deductions you claimed on your tax return. The letter also asks you to bring along copies of tax returns for the year before and the year after the return being examined. These are requested mainly to ensure you've filed them. Sometimes items are cross-checked for duplicate deductions (especially in the depreciation schedules) or for continuity from year to year. (The office audit is described in more detail on page 186.)

The third kind of audit is the *field audit*. In the past few years these have become comparatively rare as IRS agents' time has become more limited. If your return is selected for a field audit, you receive a letter similar to that sent for an office audit, but when you call to schedule an appointment, you're scheduling a time for an auditor to come to your office and examine your books, receipts, equipment, and physical space.

If you're selected for a field audit, chances are good the IRS thinks there's something phony about your claimed deductions or the equipment you say you have. Prepare for these audits with the utmost care; the IRS comes to the audit suspecting more than honest mistakes in addition.

The last kind of audit is the *taxpayer compliance monitoring program,* or TCMP. It's conducted every three years (most recently in 1990) on a tiny cross-section of taxpayers. Unlike every other kind of audit, the TCMP is not based on any assumption of error. It's more like an IRS-initiated research program to determine what's really going on in the world.

Every entry on your tax return—from your name and address through the birth of any and all dependents through each item of income on to and through each deduction—*every* entry on a tax return must be verified. A TCMP audit takes days to complete. Findings are collected nationally and used to establish typical deductions for various categories of taxpayers at various income levels. As with any audit, adjustments can and will be made for discrepancies uncovered in the process, but that is not the primary purpose of a TCMP audit.

Note: Never use these "typical" deduction figures in determining your own deductions. The only deductions you should be taking on your tax return should be supported by receipts and cancelled checks. If you don't have 'em, don't claim 'em.

What Happens at an Audit

An audit begins with the agent asking you background questions. One of these will be whether or not you belong to a barter or trade organization. You may also be asked about educational background, address and telephone numbers, or employment history. You are asked, by category, whether or not you have reported all your income. The auditor then examines the items listed in the letter inviting you to the audit. Respond to the auditor's specific questions. Do not volunteer information. The auditor is in charge: Don't get into power plays over who is controlling the conversation.

The better prepared you are, the neater your records will be and the easier it will be for the auditor to examine the deductions you claimed. It's not to your advantage to toss the auditor your check register and tell her to figure out telephone expense. If you made an entry on your tax return, you must be able to substantiate that entry.

Have canceled checks bundled together with receipts for each item being investigated. Your objective is to get out of that office with as little damage as possible. If the auditor adds up a bundle of checks and finds a discrepancy between the figure you have on your return and the total, be prepared to explain how and why that mistake happened. Be candid, but don't go into too much detail. Blabbing or running on may result in more items added to the audit list if the auditor suspects other problems.

If the auditor finds several discrepancies, you can bet she will run totals on all the packets you have and may request documentation on items not originally included in the audit list. An auditor can request the information, but if it was not included in the letter sent you, you have the right to request time to gather those records and bring them in. Be firm in stating your case, reiterating if necessary that you prepared only those items identified in the IRS audit letter.

Be aware that the IRS has access to your bank records. At an office audit, you're likely to hear the auditor say: "I find $x in deposits reported for you in 199X. Please show me where you've reported that income on your tax return." That $x figure is likely larger than the amount you listed on your tax returns, because most people shift money from one bank account to another or they take out loans or were given an inheritance or sold an asset or received a gift.

How do you prove to the auditor that $x isn't really all taxable income? You need documentation: loan agreements, deposit slips showing transfers from one account to another, terms of a will, a sales contract. Ideally, you've listed the source of each item on your deposit slips. If you haven't, you're in for some time-consuming, tedious work prior to the audit: finding and identifying checks written on one account and deposited into another, obtaining certified statements of transactions, or requesting copies of documents you did not keep or can't find.

If you're self-employed, it's particularly important that you're able to identify where each income item is reported on your tax return. If you can't, the auditor will consider it all self-employment income, subject to income tax *and* self-employment tax.

Once you're asked that question—"Where did you report $x on your tax return?"—your work is cut out for you. Since the IRS figures there's a fifty-fifty chance you underreported your income, it's become virtually essential that you detail on the deposit slip the source of each item you deposit in a bank account. It follows, then, that you don't want to use a bank where your deposit slips aren't returned to you with your monthly statements.

Most audits last one to one and one-half hours. At the end of the audit, you usually know about any discrepancies the auditor has uncovered. If additional tax is owed, you are asked if you agree with the findings. Sometimes you are allowed to pay an undisputed amount on the spot; other times the auditor may need to check with a supervisor to see if the audit results are acceptable.

If you do not agree with the findings, you have the option of requesting a second interview with the same auditor to bring in the records that will substantiate your case. If you disagree with the auditor's findings because of a different interpretation of the law, then you have the right to appeal to the office supervisor. Going to tax court to argue a point is a third course open to you, but since the minimum fee to file your dispute is $5,000, this is not generally viable for individuals.

How to Protect Yourself

Since 1986, computerization has made tax filing a rigorous exercise, a little like playing Russian roulette with all loaded chambers; the IRS computers won't miss a 1099 form, so you can't either. Take your legitimate deductions, but:

1. Don't press your luck and deduct something you can't document in the hope of slipping one past the IRS. Penalties for claiming a deduction you could or should reasonably have known wasn't allowed results in penalties large enough to dwarf the tax savings.

2. Don't estimate your expenses. Know that you can, if called on in a year or two, pull together receipts and canceled checks to support each expense you claim.

3. Don't try to deduct travel expenses for study unless you're enrolled in a structured program with a curriculum directly and integrally related to your business.

4. Don't try to deduct entertainment where personal pleasure is a material factor.

5. Make sure your equipment is in service (up and running and in use) if you claim a deduction for it in a specific tax year.

6. Keep adequate documentation, including a mileage log for business miles driven, a contemporaneous log for cash expenditures, and receipts or canceled checks for any other expenses.

7. Keep track of your income as you receive it, taking care to separate the W-2 income from independent contractor income. There's withholding on the former, not on the latter.

An Editorial Comment

The process of selecting returns for audit and the audit itself have become so sophisticated over the past few years that the IRS comes out of very few office audits empty-handed. Field audits almost always show a change in favor of the IRS. Mail audits result in increased tax revenues approximately sixty percent of the time.

In other words, if you're selected for an audit, count on the probability that the audit will cost you money. Either you forgot to report some income the IRS has found or you claimed deductions you cannot substantiate or you took a deduction where none is allowed.

Occasionally an audit reveals no errors on a taxpayer's return; on some rare occasions a taxpayer may even receive a refund. But these outcomes are becoming more and more rare as selection techniques, interview skills, and computerized reporting systems improve.

□ 19 □

Retirement Plans

Baby Boomers

If you're old enough to be reading this book, count on the fact that the federal government will not be able to support you in your old age. I'm an early baby boomer, and things don't get easier for people born after I was. The reason is demographics. Baby boomers find themselves smack-dab in the middle of a population glut.

The boomers' overwhelming voting power to raise taxes to support themselves will be offset by the fiscal reality of the deficit they are handing down to younger generations. That leaves many of us with the need to fend for ourselves. We can do that by establishing and then contributing to retirement plans.

Introduction

Retirement planning depends on where you are in your life cycle. If you're forty or older, you need to be making contributions to a retirement plan whether you think you can afford to or not. You need to make your retirement contributions a priority, taking precedence even over your children's college educations. There's no valid excuse for not setting up a retirement plan for yourself if you're older than forty.

If you're under forty, contribute to a retirement plan only if you already own a home and have established a college-education fund for each of your children. There are, of course, exceptions.

Say you're twenty-six, don't own a home because you don't want to, and earn enough money to push some of it into the 28 percent tax bracket. You may want to consider contributing to a retirement plan simply to save on taxes. Ideally, you've already put together a monthly budget using the budget sheet offered in Chapter 17. You've saved up one month's operating expenses and put it in an interest-bearing checking account. You've saved up six months' operating expenses and invested that in short-term certificates of deposit. Once you have this cushion, the next logical step for you is to put money into tax-sheltered retirement funds.

Overview

Retirement plans are divided into pre-tax and post-tax plans. Pre-tax plans are offered by W-2 employers. They're known as 401(K) plans if the employer is a for-profit corporation, and as 403(B) plans if the employer is a nonprofit corporation. Colloquially, they're known as TDAs (tax-deferred annuities) because virtually all of them offer insurance annuities as an investment option. Post-tax plans include Individual Retirement Accounts (IRAs), Simplified Employee Pension (SEP) plans, and Keogh plans. Any taxpayer can open an IRA for as much as that individual's earned income. Whether a contribution to it is deductible depends on the taxpayer's income and status as a "covered" employee at his or his spouse's W-2 job.

SEPs are available in small companies and to self-employed individuals. Contributions are limited by the way your employer structured the plan and by how much you earn. If you're self-employed, contributions are limited to a percentage of your net profit for the year.

Keoghs are available only to self-employed people. Contributions are limited to the net profit shown in self-employment activities (Schedule C sole proprietorships and Schedule E general partnerships).

Of the two types of plans, pre-tax plans are more valuable. Keeping money out of the tax system in the first place is always worth more than deducting it from taxable income. Better still is to double up. Contribute the maximum you can to your pre-tax plan at your W-2 job and then also contribute to an IRA, or to an SEP or Keogh if you're self-employed.

Any retirement plan carries penalties if you withdraw funds from it prematurely, that is, before you reach the age of fifty-nine and one-half. The federal penalty for early withdrawal is 10 percent. Several states already add their own penalties; more are sure to follow.

Money put aside for retirement must be left there for retirement. Don't expect to get a tax break and then use the money as you would money in a savings account.

Individual Retirement Accounts (IRAs)

A single person can contribute up to $2,000 per year to an IRA account, provided that person has at least $2,000 in earned income. If that person has an adjusted gross income (AGI) less than $25,000, the IRA is fully deductible from taxable income.

If the AGI is between $25,000 and $35,000 and the person is covered by a pension plan at work, the IRA contribution is only partly deductible. With an AGI above $35,000 and inclusion in a pension plan, no part of the IRA contribution is deductible, but earnings within the IRA account are tax-deferred until withdrawal.

A married couple can contribute up to $4,000 per year to their IRA accounts ($2,000 each), provided each has earned income of at least $2,000. If one is gainfully employed and the other isn't, the limit on the IRA contribution is $2,250 ($2,000 and $250, respectively, split any way the couple wants, up to $2,000 to either spouse).

Deductibility of the IRA contribution again hinges on AGI and pension plan coverage. For a married couple with an AGI less than $40,000, the IRA contribution is fully deductible; between $40,000 and $50,000, partly deductible if one or both are covered by a pension plan; over $50,000, not deductible at all unless neither spouse is covered by a pension plan.

If you're self-employed and have an SEP or Keogh plan, you are considered covered by a pension plan and, hence, subject to these income limits in figuring deductibility of IRA contributions.

An IRA account is held in trust for you by a fiduciary institution such as a bank or brokerage house. You cannot set aside money in a regular savings account, for example, and call it an IRA. Money invested in an IRA cannot be withdrawn until you have reached the age of fifty-nine and one-half. Withdrawals prior to that time are considered premature and incur a penalty of 10 percent of the amount withdrawn *in addition to* income tax levied on the amount withdrawn. That means that taxpayers who withdraw money prematurely from a retirement account, pension, or annuity will lose at least 25 percent of the amount withdrawn (10 percent penalty and 15 percent income tax rate), plus a percentage to the state where they live (tax and/or penalty). In the case of upper-bracket taxpayers, over half of a premature withdrawal can be lost to taxes.

Even if your IRA contribution isn't deductible, make it anyway if you already own a house, contribute the maximum to the pre-tax retirement plan at work, have at least six months' operating expenses in short-term investments, and have accounts established for your children's education. The principal you contribute won't be a deduction, but whatever it earns is tax-sheltered until you withdraw it.

Let's say that your combined federal and state tax rate is 35 percent. If you put $2,000 into a passbook savings account and earn 5 percent interest on it, you'll have $100 in interest in a year. After taxes, you get to keep $65. Put that same $2,000 into a retirement account and you're likely to earn at least 8 percent. That $160 earned in one year is yours to keep, at least until you start withdrawing it after you're fifty-nine and a half.

If you make nondeductible contributions to your IRA retirement plan, be sure to file Form 8606 with your tax return. It establishes your basis in the plan. This keeps you from being taxed on the nondeductible part of your retirement fund when you withdraw it.

A word of caution: If your retirement account consists of contributions that were deductible and contributions that weren't, you can't withdraw funds just from the nondeductible part of the account. A withdrawal of $6,000 comes proportionately from the deductible contributions and the nondeductible contributions.

Simplified Employee Pension (SEP) Plan

SEPs were devised to help small employers offer pre-tax retirement plans to their employees. The high administrative cost associated with the more elaborate 401(K) or 403(B) plans left out small employers, to the detriment of wage earners. SEPs were structured for the small employer and are available to companies with fewer than thirty-five employees. Obviously, single-person companies, also known as sole proprietorships, qualify.

As the owner of your company, you can open an SEP for yourself and any employees you have in your business. There's very little paperwork to complete to open an SEP. You can initiate the application process, open an account, and make a contribution to it, all within ten days. Cutting things razor-close to the April 15 deadline is not advisable. Give yourself some time to determine the kind of investment you want to make, since SEPs usually involve larger contributions and you don't move money from one SEP plan to another as often as you might move IRA funds.

Annual contributions are flexible and can be made up to the April 15 filing deadline or the date you file your taxes, whichever is earlier. The size of your annual contribution depends on your net profit from self-employment (Schedule C sole proprietorship or Schedule E partnership). The maximum contribution is 13.043 percent of your net profit less half of the self-employment tax you deduct on the front of the current year's Form 1040, up to $30,000.

If you finish your taxes in March and find you have a little cash to spare, consider opening an SEP plan and making a deductible contribution. To figure out your maximum deduction, deduct half your self-employment tax (the same figure you entered in the adjustments-to-income section on the front of Form 1040) from your net profit. Then multiply that figure by 13.043 percent. Be sure to make the contribution a week before you plan to mail your tax return to allow the paperwork to clear at the trustee's office.

In the instructions for SEP plans, 15 percent is the figure identified as the percentage you should use to figure your maximum contribution. This 15 percent means 15 percent of your net profit less the SEP contribution, or 13.043 percent of your net profit. As a client asked rhetorically, "Why can't the IRS just speak English?" Check out the 13.043 figure if you don't believe me, but make sure that's the one you use to figure your maximum allowable contribution.

SEP plan contributions are subject to the same early-withdrawal penalties described earlier for IRA contributions. An SEP plan's main advantage over an IRA is the larger amount you can contribute annually. If you have an unemployed spouse, however, remember that your being covered by an SEP plan means both of you are "covered employees" for the purpose of determining eligibility for deductible IRA contributions. Figure your options both ways (IRAs for one or both versus SEP for one) to maximize your contributions and fit your personal financial objectives. Your SEP plan contributions go only to your retirement account, never to your spouse's.

Keogh Plans

Keogh plans (Keoghs) are the granddaddies of retirement funds, allowing you to sock away 20 percent of your net profit, up to $30,000 annually, whichever is less. Keoghs are also referred to as H.R. 10 plans, for the House of Representatives bill that established them. Keogh was the congressman who wrote the bill that eventually became the law that now bears his name.

Keogh plans require more planning and more paperwork. First, they must be opened by December 31 of the year in which you intend to make your first contribution. Second, they require an annual report (due by July 31) for any plan with more than one participant or more than $100,000 in assets. Third, you must decide among several options available to you within the Keogh plan framework, as follows:

1. *Defined contribution*. One of two kinds: a. *Profit sharing*. This Keogh version operates just like an SEP. You can contribute up to 13.043 percent of your net profit less the self-employment tax deduction on the front of Form 1040, up to $30,000, whichever is less. No minimum contribution is required. This kind of Keogh plan is appropriate for individuals in the early stages of self-employment who cannot count on making enough profit to contribute regularly to a retirement account. b. *Money purchase*. This Keogh version requires you to contribute a minimum percentage of net income per year. Maximum contribution with profit sharing and defined-contribution Keogh plans is 20 percent of net income less the self-employment tax deduction on the front of Form 1040, or $30,000, whichever is less. Open a defined-contribution Keogh account if your business is firmly established and you're older than forty.

2. *Defined benefit*. This plan requires you to accumulate a certain amount of money by a certain date in the retirement plan, so that the plan will generate defined benefits of a certain dollar figure over your actuarially determined life as a retiree. This type of Keogh plan might be appropriate for the older sole proprietor who is at the peak of her earning potential and knows what she needs in monthly retirement income from this investment. But administrative costs are unreasonably high for this kind of plan, making it sensible only if you have many employees.

The advantage of Keogh plans is that they offer more flexibility than other retirement plans do. You can make a contribution to a Keogh plan up to the date you file your taxes, including extensions. Your percentage contribution is higher than SEP plans allow. As with IRAs and SEP plans, Keogh accounts are held in trust for the sole proprietor by a bank or brokerage house. Early-withdrawal penalties apply.

If You Have Employees

Setting up a retirement plan for yourself generally involves extending proportionate benefits to your employees. If you open an SEP or Keogh plan pior to having employees, you can establish minimum service requirements which subsequent "hires" must meet to qualify, but which can be waived for any employee (read: you) as of the date the plan is adopted. If you already have employees and wish to set up an SEP or Keogh plan for yourself, understand that you'll be contributing the same percentage of salary to an employee's retirement plan that you're contributing for yourself.

Major reforms of the nation's pension plans have made them more equitable. If an employee has met the service requirements you stipulated when establishing the plan, you must contribute the same proportion of profits to his retirement account as you do to your own—and continue to do so in any year he meets minimum requirements. Annual eligibility requirements for an SEP are $400 in W-2 wages in the calendar year (note that this 1991 figure is indexed for inflation), and for a Keogh, one thousand hours of service in the calendar year.

Employee contributions are made to employee IRAs in the case of an SEP plan established by an employer. Contributions made by the employer are deductible to the employer on her business schedule (Schedule C, Form 1065, Form 1120, or 1120-S) and are not deductible to the employee.

For a Keogh, the plan is established in the name of the business and contributions are made to the employer's plan for each qualified employee. This requires a separate accounting of annual contributions so that when an employee resigns or is terminated, the benefits allocable to that employee can be distributed to him. Deductions for employees are taken by the business on the business schedule (Schedule C for sole proprietors or Form 1065 for partnerships). Contributions for owners—sole proprietors or general partners—are not deductible on the business schedules but can be deducted on the individual owner's tax return on the front of Form 1040.

Owners cannot borrow from retirement accounts. With an SEP, an owner can withdraw funds and use them for sixty days, before rolling them over into another IRA plan, without incurring penalty. No such option is available with a Keogh plan.

Investment Options

The same investment vehicles are available regardless of the kind of retirement plan you choose. You can select from: certificates of deposit, mutual funds, stocks, bonds, limited partnerships, and insurance annuities.

Recommendations

What do you choose? I'm going to make some suggestions to you on the assumption you are looking for some guidance.

Under no circumstances choose a limited partnership. A limited partnership is about as good an investment as betting fifty dollars on Aragorn in the seventh race at Finger Lakes. Or playing the lottery. Limited partnerships are *not* investments. They're gambles.

Under no circumstances choose a tax-free investment vehicle. You don't want tax-free municipal bonds in a retirement account that's already tax-free. This seems obvious, once you read it, but I'm constantly shocked by the number of tax-free investment vehicles I see in tax-deferred accounts.

I'm negative about insurance company annuities. They seem so attractive on their faces, advertising an 8 or 9 percent guaranteed rate of return. It seems you can't lose. My skepticism about insurance company annuities is rooted in the health-care crisis I see building, and that skepticism predates the current real estate crisis shaking the insurance industry to its roots.

To make those above-market rate guarantees, insurance companies bought highly leveraged real estate developments or junk bonds that offered high rates of return at what turned out to be an unacceptably high level of risk. As insurance companies fail, and Executive Life and Mutual Benefit are just the tip of the iceberg, insurance companies will eventually be unable to pay any claims other than death benefits and some retirement payouts. Most annuitants will be out of luck.

Aha! Think the states will step in with state guarantees and make good on the contracts? Guess again. I live in a high-tax state. That means, I presume, there are vast coffers of cash somewhere under the capital dome. But Minnesota doesn't have the reserves to pay for all the defaults that might occur as insurance companies collapse. As a taxpayer, I sure don't want to see a tax increase so some retiree can get what he thinks was promised to him when he signed up for that premium rate of return. I am not the guarantor on his gamble. Heartbreaking stories will abound, no doubt, and the press will tell them in its own inimitable way, but the overall capacity of the average taxpayer to absorb more tax levies will come to bear. We simply can't pay any more.

Of course my negativity toward insurance companies is open to discussion. I just know I don't want to see any of my clients buying insurance annuities, and I do my best to steer them in other directions.

A point of information is appropriate here. I don't sell securities and I won't sell securities because this would compromise my position as a financial advisor. So the information here is based on my knowledge of economics and the marketplace, on my experience in following various types of investments over the past fifteen years or so, and on my need to sleep at night, untroubled by speculation about the latest scheme (or scam). My advice may seem pedestrian to some, but we midwesterners put a heckuva premium on a good night's sleep.

What do I like? In general, for most small investors (those with less than $300,000 to invest) I like mutual funds because they spread the risk among a range of investment vehicles. Also, they're professionally managed, so your hysteria at the market's ups and downs is buffered. Most mutual funds are comprised of stocks, but also contain some bonds and debentures. The mix determines their degree of volatility and risk, and leads to their being given names like "growth-and-income" or "speculative" or "income."

Beyond the generic recommendation to invest in mutual funds, the kind of fund you select depends on your age. Generally, the older you are, the more conservative your investment should be. What's older? By the time you hit your fifties, you need to begin shifting investments from growth-and-income investments to income investments. As you progress into your late sixties, you need to move from income toward fixed-income investments that preserve your principal.

From your midthirties through your forties, invest in growth-and-income investments, those blends of small capitalization companies, that might be the Xeroxes of the future (the growth part of the fund), and of blue-chip Fortune 500 companies (the income part of the fund).

If you're under thirty-five, you should be investing in growth companies. Especially if you're opening an educational account for a child, put the money into growth kinds of investments.

Is the stock market safer than insurance companies? Yes. By the time the stock market collapses, the entire economy has collapsed, we're in chaos, and you're better off playing out your own version of Armageddon.

What you don't want to do is put yourself in a position where you can't ride out the fluctuations the market continually shows. Don't turn sixty and decide you need the bigger returns a growth-and-income fund will give you. You may need your funds when you're sixty-five. If the market is in a downturn, you won't get back what you put in. Stock markets run in ten- to fifteen-year cycles, so the sooner you may need the money, the less risk you want to run.

Why not just invest in certificates of deposit? Because by the time you factor in inflation, you've barely kept ahead of the game. You want to choose an investment where your money will grow on its own. In general, you should aim at investments that give you a 10 percent return over the years. Note I did not say over the year. Don't dump an investment because it yielded only 6 percent last year.

I don't like individual stocks for small investors because of the level of risk involved. A mutual fund smoothes out risks for the small investors. Bonds fall into the same category. Always invest only in investment-grade bonds. If you're looking at tax-free municipal bonds for non-retirement-fund contributions, make sure they're general obligation bonds, not just something your city lent its name (and reputation) to.

My investment advice boils down to this. Pick a solid investment vehicle and then stick with it. I prefer to spend more time figuring out where I want to put money than worrying about how it performs from year to year. I am skeptical to the point of hysterical laughter when someone boasts about the twenty-plus percent killing he made on his latest investment. Sure, 20 percent gains occur. So do 20 percent losses. I'm a bit more middle-of-the-road, looking for that solid investment that will, year on year, give me an average 10 percent return on my investment.

With a 10 percent annual return, my money will double every seven years. I can figure this according to the "Rule of 72s," which works this way: Divide 72 by your annual rate of return to give you the number of years it takes for money to double. An investment giving you 6 percent annually will double in twelve years. Remember those wild early-1980 interest rates of 12 percent? Money doubled every six years then.

Don't get greedy. It doesn't pay. Settle for a solid investment and then stick with it. One of the richest people in the country was recently quoted as boasting he never sold an asset he bought. You don't need to wheel and deal to make some money. What you need is confidence in your choice of investment and then the nerve to hang onto it in tough times. This is not to say you don't dump a bad investment. Let's say you bought a limited partnership, either in the eighties when they seemed to be a great way to make easy money or in the early nineties when they were dirt cheap and still seemed to be a great way to make easy money. Either time I think you knew deep down it was a lousy investment. Trust that feeling and get rid of the limited partnership.

A good investment won't seem like "easy money" and won't give you a feeling in the pit of your stomach that you're pulling a fast one. You know the feeling. Now that you're an adult, avoid it.

An Investment Primer

I'll take you one step further and recommend no-load mutual funds for your IRA, SEP-plan, or Keogh-plan contribution. From Sylvia Porter to *Wall Street Journal* analyses, from William Doyle to Jane Bryant Quinn, there's universal agreement that no-load funds perform as well as, or better than, load funds.

What's "load"? It's the percentage charged up front on the purchase of an investment vehicle. Loads can be full-, equal to 8.5 percent of your investment (though these are increasingly rare, due to market pressures); mid, equal to 4.5 percent (charged on the mutual funds you buy through a broker); low, equal to 2 or 3 percent (Fidelity funds spring to mind); and no-load. Although I own some midload fund shares, I prefer no-load funds for beginning investors.

No-load funds can be "true" or "phony." The true no-load funds charge only a set fee to manage your money each year. That charge is spelled out in the fund's prospectus. The phony no-load fund charges no sales commission up front but takes advantage of the 12(b)(1) provision of the Securities and Exchange laws regulating the industry to charge monthly fees on the basis of your investment.

Mutual funds are listed in the financial pages of the newspaper, under the "Mutual Fund Quotations." Phony no-load funds have a "p" designation. Avoid them.

How do you read the information on mutual funds? "NAV" means net asset value, the value of the assets the fund holds divided by the number of shares outstanding. "Offer price" is the price you'll pay to buy shares; "sell price" is the price you'll receive when you sell. Expect the offer price to be higher than the sell price.

You'll also notice that there are various funds in each family of funds. The Fidelity listing, for example, includes maybe sixty individual funds. The advantage of buying into a fund that offers a wide range of individual funds is that you can generally sell shares in one fund and transfer the proceeds to another fund without incurring an additional sales charge.

Remember, because this is a tax-sheltered investment you don't need to report any sale transaction on your tax return. Capital gain will be handled when you withdraw funds in a very simple way: Any withdrawal is treated as ordinary income. But the savings in service charges can significantly affect how much you end up with in your retirement pot.

CALCULATING RETURN ON INVESTMENT (ROI)

Periodically, you may check in on how your investment is doing. I don't think it's a required exercise. Since we're all such small potatoes, the pick-'em-right-the-first-time strategy protects your long-range interests.

I have a peculiar way of figuring how much my investment has earned since I bought it. The traditional way is to multiply the number of shares you own by the current market price. I don't like that method, because it distorts what you really have. The market value of my investment is real to me only on the day I sell shares. Otherwise, it's a paper number. To calculate return on investment, I prefer to multiply the numbers of shares I currently have by the share price when I bought them. When I subtract my initial investment, I have the amount of actual gain over the period I've held the shares. That gain, divided by my original investment, gives me a percentage. When I divide that percentage by the number of years I've held the investment, I can figure the annual rate of return. If it's close to 10 percent, I'm happy.

What about the actual market price? Doesn't that impress me? No, not unless I'm selling that day. Markets go up and down. I want to see the number of shares I own grow in number from reinvested dividends and capital gains.

Calculating return on investment the more traditional way gives you the higher rates of return you sometimes read about. If you do it the way I suggest, your calculations are complicated by periodic purchases of blocks of shares, but the method can work under virtually any circumstance. You can even use it for load funds. It provides a real eye-opener on the amount you're being charged.

PICKING AN INVESTMENT

Almost all mutual funds have 800 numbers. Call directory information (1-800-555-1212) for the family that interests you. I recommend Vanguard as a good no-load family of funds. It's especially suited to the beginning investor because the number of funds in the family is sufficient to provide diversity but not so overwhelming you feel you have no chance to get a handle on what's happening.

When you call the family, tell the agent you'd like a prospectus and annual report for funds X or Y or Z. (Prior to making the call, go through the newspaper listing and pick out some funds that strike your fancy.) Or, better yet, tell the agent your age and tell him to send prospectuses on funds people your age usually invest in. The agent knows the business and should be willing to help you.

Vanguard publishes a booklet that arranges its funds by level of risk. I find this very helpful to clients as they sort out the difference between growth-and-income funds versus growth funds, for instance. The booklet is called *Facts on Funds* and is free for the asking. Also request an application to open an IRA, SEP-plan, or Keogh-plan account. In the case of Keoghs, indicate profit-sharing or money purchase.

You won't be pressured to buy. Reputable funds don't make follow-up calls, relying instead on their performance to do their talking for them. Never buy anything under pressure. For every bargain available "only if you sign up today!" there are three others waiting in the wings. In a week or so you'll receive in the mail the prospectus and annual report on several funds. Where do you begin? Start with the prospectus and look for three items: what it costs to get into the fund, what it costs to get out of the fund, and how the fund charges its operating expenses.

It's hoped that what you find is a flat administrative fee, which signals you've found a true no-load fund. If you see information on 12(b)1 provisions for charging expenses, drop the fund like a hot potato unless you're buying it for other than financial reasons. Maybe you're committed to the social cause the fund addresses. That's okay, but you'll pay for the privilege.

A prospectus contains lots of other information. Don't be intimidated by it, and don't be too impressed (or depressed) by the overview of past returns. Past performance is a good indicator of future performance, but doesn't guarantee anything. In a similar vein, do not invest in the latest "hot" fund; it probably has nowhere to go but down.

In the annual report you'll look for a listing of the kinds of companies the fund invests in. See if the mix is agreeable to you. If you are dead-set against owning anything connected to the defense or tobacco industries, then you're better off pursuing one of the socially conscious funds, most of which charge a full-load commission.

The number of funds you select depends on the size of your initial investment. If you're opening an account with $2,000, choose one fund. It's not worth cluttering your file cabinets with a second file for such a small investment. If you have Keogh money to invest, say $10,000, put it in no more than two or three funds you think you can live with happily for the next ten years.

You'll send a check with your completed application. In the application you'll designate how you want your money invested, and you'll designate the year you want it applied to. Generally you'll designate the prior year, since you're working on that year's tax return and want the tax break to apply to that year. For each fund you designate, establish a separate file folder to keep track of the information you'll receive on that fund during the year. While information on a retirement account isn't reportable on your tax return, you will want the information for periodic review and evaluation. Don't toss all the materials in one folder. Everything will be so jumbled together that you'll never use the information in it.

Make sure you enter your contribution on the appropriate line in the adjustments-to-income section on the front of Form 1040 before you do the final calculations. Allow at least a week between the time you send your check to a mutual fund and the time you file your tax return.

Perspective

Contributing to a retirement plan is the primary means of guaranteeing your financial security. It's been estimated that a retiree's budget will equal about eighty percent of his or her preretirement budget. Items such as housing costs drop as a home mortgage is paid off, but medical expenses rise. Of that retirement budget, approximately one-third will be provided by Social Security, one-third by the pension plan where you worked, and the other third needs to come from retirement plans and savings.

It doesn't take a rocket scientist to see that these estimates are directed toward the person who worked for a corporation all his life and then retired with full benefits. It doesn't take a Nobel Prize-winner in economics to see that this model is becoming more and more unusual as companies scale back retirement benefits or lay off older employees. Needless to add, normal retirement planning bypasses the self-employed worker.

One part of the model holds: the Social Security part. It's advisable to check in with the Social Security Administration every three years to make sure your Social Security or self-employment tax payments are being credited properly. Use Form SSA-7004 for this purpose. While you're at it, complete the few additional questions it takes to get an estimate from the Social Security Administration of what your benefits are likely to be at age 62 or 65. You'll be sent a great printout that can help with retirement planning.

For most individuals, figure that Social Security will provide about one-third of what you'll need to live on. For the self-employed person who doesn't work for a corporation and has never become eligible for a corporate retirement program, that means two-thirds of what you'll need to live on needs to come from retirement plans and savings accounts. Sobering thought, right?

Don't despair. Don't *delay*, but don't despair either. If you start socking money away when you turn forty, chances are you'll have what you need to have by the time you retire. This assumes you make retirement plan contributions a priority in your finances. The sooner you start, the easier it becomes. If you're in your twenties or thirties, you may want to put money away simply to cut your tax bill. That's okay. Say you're in the 28 percent marginal bracket on your federal taxes and cough up another 7 percent on the last dollar you earned to the state tax department. For every dollar you contribute to a retirement plan, you'll save 35 cents on taxes. That's like having an employer say: "For every dollar you contribute, I'll add 50 cents to the pot."

What a deal! Your "employer" in this case is your good old Uncle Sam. Spend it on taxes or spend it on yourself. Not too many folks have trouble deciding.

For More Information

See IRS publication 560, "Retirement Plans for the Self-Employed," or publication 590, "Individual Retirement Arrangements (IRAs)."

□ 20 □

Paying Your Taxes

Overview

Taxpayers are required by law to pay tax on their income as they receive it. That's easily accomplished with W-2 income, which has taxes withheld before it reaches the hands of the wage earner. Earned income from self-employment activities, or unearned income from interest, dividends, and capital gains, requires the taxpayer to do his own withholding and to forward the amounts withheld to the government as quarterly estimated tax payments.

Estimated Taxes

If you are self-employed, you are earning income from which no tax has been withheld. Because there is no withholding at the source and no employer is making periodic payments of your money on your behalf, you must make those payments yourself. You make periodic estimated tax payments using Form 1040-ES. Chances are good that if you need to make quarterly federal payments, you also need to make state payments. Check with your state tax office for the appropriate forms to file to make estimated state tax payments.

Self-employed people pay estimated taxes quarterly, on the fifteenth days of April, June, September, and January. State deadlines usually conform to federal deadlines. If the fifteenth falls on a Sunday or holiday, the deadline is moved to the following business day. Failure to make payments on time results in interest penalties. A postmark is considered proof of filing on time.

There are two ways to make tax payments: through withholding at your W-2 job, and through quarterly estimated payments. Any combination of the two can cover your liability. If you are wholly self-employed and have no regular employment on which withholding is taken, then, of course, your entire tax payment must come from quarterly filings of estimated payments.

The estimated tax payment is just that—an estimate of how much tax you need to pay for a given year. But what sounds easy is difficult to calculate. At a minimum you need to know the rules on deductibility and to keep scrupulously accurate books. If in March you calculate your total tax liability for the prior year at $10,000 and you've paid only $8,000 in quarterly tax payments, you may be facing an underpayment penalty on that $2,000 shortfall, which could run as much as $200 or more.

In the example just described, if you had paid $9,000 in quarterly tax payments, you would still owe the IRS another $1,000 but at least you would be able to file Form 2210 with your tax return to exempt you from the penalty for underpaying your estimated tax bill through 1991. Form 2210 provides exemption from the penalty for underpaying your taxes under either of two conditions: 1. payment of 90 percent of the current year's tax liability (this is the exemption you would use in the situation described above); or 2. payment of an amount equal to the previous year's tax liability. Beginning in 1992, upper-income taxpayers generally need to pay 100% of their current year's tax liability to avoid the underpayment penalty.

If you had paid only $8,000 of the $10,000 you owed, you would try to use the second exemption to avoid the underpayment penalty. Look at your total federal tax liability for the prior year. If that figure is $8,000 or less, there will be no penalty for underpaying your estimated taxes, although you will still need to cough up the additional $2,000.

Let's assume you escaped unscathed this time. How do you plan your quarterly payments for the current year, the first of which is due on April 15, the same day you need to pay off the remaining liability on last year's taxes? There are two ways to calculate your payments. The first involves more work and a strong grasp of tax law and is risky; the other is simple and sure, but may result in an overpayment to the IRS during the year.

With the first method you calculate your tax liability at four points during the year: March 31, May 31, August 31, and December 31. Calculate your tax liability for each period, prorating your deductions and personal exemptions. The figure you come up with for each date will be the amount you need to pay for that quarter. At the end of the year, if you owe the IRS more than $500, use the work sheet accompanying Form 2210 (Annualized Income Worksheet) to see if you can escape the penalty or, at least, see where your calculations failed you.

A more certain method for calculating your estimated tax payments is to base your payments on the prior tax year's liability. If you know in March that last year's tax liability is $10,000, divide that figure by four and use that $2,500 figure as your quarterly payment. Next February or March, when you sit down to this year's tax return, file Form 2210 to claim exemption from the penalty by virtue of having paid an amount equal to the previous year's tax liability.

What happens this year if your business drops off and you don't make nearly as much as you did last year? Do you still need to send the $2,500 each quarter? No. If by December you know your net profit is well below the previous year's, or you've added a part-time job and had taxes withheld, you may decrease that last payment. Alternatively, you can skip the January 15 payment altogether, provided you file your tax return and pay any outstanding liability in full by January 31.

Practically, it's unusual for income to drop. Income generally increases from year to year. What this means for your quarterly estimated taxes is that you are paying the minimum required by law. By April 15 of the following year, you need to pay up the remaining balance due and make the first payment on the following year's tax liability. And so it goes, year after year.

What happens in a given year if you overpay your quarterly taxes and the IRS ends up owing you $200 or $300? Generally you roll this amount over toward the first-quarter estimated payment (which then is $200 or $300 lower than the other three) to avoid checks crossing in the mail or a slip-up in recordkeeping.

It's difficult to get on the quarterly payment bandwagon because the first year of self-employment usually sets you back financially. You need to pay up on the previous year's taxes and then also make a dent in the upcoming year's tax liability. It's tough, but those who pay quarterly not only avoid throwing money away on penalties (it's cheaper to borrow against a credit card), but also avoid having to come up with large sums of cash on demand as they discipline themselves to anticipate these payments. Paying quarterly estimated taxes is about as much fun as going to the dentist, and about as necessary.

Short of Cash?

A medical emergency, an unplanned expense, a check you've been promised but that hasn't quite found its way to your mailbox, any host of circumstances can find you short of money to pay your tax liability.

Assume in this instance that you only have $4,000 in your account for taxes. The IRS wants $2,000 for last year and $2,500 for the first quarter of this year, the state wants $600, and your state estimated payment is $400. How do you make that $4,000 stretch into $5,500? It depends somewhat on when you think you'll have the additional $1,500. Remember, on June 15 you'll need to send another $2,500 to the IRS and $400 to the state for the second-quarter estimated tax payment.

Under no circumstances should you delay filing your tax return. If you'll have the $1,500 in a few weeks or so, send the IRS $500 with last year's tax return and make all the other payments in full. Do not, repeat, *do not* write the IRS a letter and enclose it with your tax return. Just the check, please, with the tax return.

In about six weeks you'll receive a notice of payment required from the IRS, adding interest to the $1,500 you still owe the government. Accompanying the notice is an envelope. Write the IRS a check, noting in the memo section the tax year, Form 1040, and your Social Security number. Return it to the IRS with the payment voucher at the bottom of the notice in the envelope accompanying the notice.

What if you receive a notice for payment and you still don't have the money to pay it in full? Continue to make quarterly estimated tax payments on the current year and send the IRS as much money as you can with the notice, identifying in the memo section of the check the tax year, Form 1040, and your Social Security number. Tear off the payment voucher at the bottom of the notice and send it to the IRS in the envelope enclosed with the notice. Continue this until the bill is paid in full.

What if you're *really* having trouble finding the money to pay the IRS? Eventually you'll receive a certified letter announcing an intention to levy. This is the first in a series of four notices that culminate in the IRS seizing your bank account or putting a lien on your property. When you receive the certified letter, call the IRS at the number listed on the notice and explain your circumstances. Tell the agent you want to begin payment plans of so many dollars per month. If the plan is at all reasonable, the IRS will accept it and you'll start making monthly payments. You'll notice that, by this time, you're seeing late-payment penalties added to the interest the IRS is charging you on the unpaid balance. These late-payment penalties are charged on your entire federal tax liability, not just the amount you couldn't pay by April 15. They can be significant. This is where it's cheaper to borrow against a credit card than from your Uncle Sam.

If that certified letter sends you into denial or avoidance, you'll find a string of notices, increasingly threatening in tone, winding its way to your door. By the fourth notice, the "levy" word is in red. The next notice is of intent to impose a lien. If you haven't called to set up a payment plan with the IRS by the time the words are red or a lien is threatened, you must do so immediately.

In cases where you owe the IRS a lot of money, you may need to complete a rather detailed financial statement, disclosing the location of all your assets. That way, if you default on the payment plan, the IRS can move expeditiously to seize what it can. Don't panic at the thought of telling the IRS where everything you own is. It's the price you pay for being a borrower. The reality is that you will pay off the government. About the only option is leaving the country. Forever.

Payment plans ideally result in the payoff of a taxpayer's liability in twelve months or less. The IRS likes to see that kind of payoff schedule because it doesn't want to see you in another tax year still plagued by an old liability. In some cases, eighteen months is allowed. I've seen extreme situations where the IRS has accepted a two-year payment plan.

Some Myths

Myth #1. *Your first year in self-employment you have a grace period and the IRS won't fine you for not making quarterly tax payments.*

Wrong. Each year any taxpayer is required to pay an amount equivalent to the prior year's tax liability or ninety percent of the current year's tax liabilities through regular, periodic payments (either withholding or quarterly estimated tax payments). There is no grace period.

Myth #2. *It's better to owe the IRS a whole lot of money on April 15 because that way you have use of your money during the year instead of the IRS having it.*

Costly miscalculation. I've had clients who believed this watch as their penalties for not making quarterly estimated tax payments steadily climb. Usually by the time the penalty hits the $400 mark, they begin discussions of how to make quarterly estimated tax payments.

Myth #3. *The feds will throw me in prison if I don't have the money to pay my taxes. I just won't file and hope they don't find me.*

The only people the IRS throws in prison are tax evaders. Fail to file a return enough years in a row, though, and you might find yourself in that category. Most taxpayers who end up owing the government money are not tax evaders.

Always file your taxes on time, whether you have the money to pay what you owe the IRS or not. In addition to interest penalties on unpaid balances and underpayment penalties on total tax liability, there's also the late-payment penalty. Penalties will never be more than 47.5 percent of your total tax liability. Interest accrues on your account until it's paid in full.

It's almost impossible to escape the computer network virtually every institution in the country plugs into, and your Social Security number tells the IRS where to find you. This may happen sooner or later, but it *will* happen. Changing your Social Security number is not an answer. That's a federal crime.

To put some perspective on this payment business, remember the cardinal principle of the tax system: The government wants your money, not your life (or that of your firstborn).

A Note on Employer Taxes

This discussion has focused on paying individual income taxes. It has nothing to do with garnishments imposed on you for failure to pay child support or a student loan. It especially has nothing to do with failure to pay employer taxes.

Failure to pay individual income taxes may result, for some professionals, in suspension of their licenses. Failure to pay employer taxes results quickly in seizure of your business and its assets. You're shut down, put out of work, and hounded mercilessly.

Why the harsh treatment? Employer taxes consist primarily of withholding from employees: the employee's share of Social Security plus the employee's federal and state withholding. When you fail to pay employer taxes, you're stealing from your employees. That's a crime, not a cash-flow problem. Whatever else happens in your life, make sure those employer tax reports are filed on time and the liabilities are paid in full.

A note to corporations: Corporate officers are personally responsible for employer taxes. Even if a corporation declares bankruptcy or ceases operations and files a corporate dissolution, liabilities stemming from unpaid employer taxes become the personal liability of corporate officers. This is a noteworthy exception to the liability protection feature of a corporation.

For More Information

See IRS Publication 505, "Tax Withholding and Estimated Tax," for further information.

▫ 21 ▫

"Qualified Performing Artist"

Introduction

The Tax Reform Act of 1986 included a provision giving a significant tax break to certain people, among them the "qualified performing artist." It marks an attempt to encourage low-income artists to pursue their art by allowing them to deduct employment-related expenses directly on the front of Form 1040.

For most taxpayers, employment-related expenses are deductible only on Schedule A, Personal Itemized Deductions. Most low-income taxpayers don't use Schedule A because the standard deduction gives them a higher deduction than itemizing would. This means that for low-income taxpayers, ordinarily, employment-related expenses are out-of-pocket expenses for which the tax code provides no solace.

While it's true that the Tax Reform Act of 1986 eliminated tax breaks for all classes of the citizenry, what's real is that breaks formerly enjoyed by the monied classes were eliminated and some efforts were made to help the working poor. This "qualified performing artist" provision is one example.

Criteria

A "qualified performing artist" is defined as a performing artist (dancer, musician, actor) who: 1. receives at least two W-2 forms from performing arts activities, amounting to at least $200 each; *and* 2. has expenses that exceed ten percent of performing arts income; *and* 3. has adjusted gross income (AGI) less than $16,000.

If you're married, you must file a joint tax return with your spouse. The $16,000 AGI limit applies to a single person or to a married couple.

How It Works

Complete Form 2106, entering your employment-related business expenses in the appropriate places. You may also want to refer to Chapter 10 for information on how to report expenses on those out-of-town gigs.

When you arrive at a total deduction, instead of transferring it to Schedule A, enter it in the adjustments-to-income section on the front of Form 1040 and note next to it "Form 2106." Include Form 2106 in your tax return, labeling it "Qualified Performing Artist" across the top of the form in bold print.

Who Uses This Option?

Performing artists, of course. Beyond that, the clients for whom I most often use this reporting option are the ones who call me from

Oregon or from Texas or from Indiana to let me know they'll need an extension because they won't be back in the Twin Cities until midsummer. Or they're the ones who come in for a tax appointment on a Friday and need to pick up their completed returns the following day because they're taking off for Boston.

Believe me, I'm not singing the blues because I work for artists. It's downright exhilarating to get that call through a Hong Kong operator or to answer the phone at 3:00 A.M. and find my client at the other end of the world, not quite sure what time it is back there in the Midwest. It's nice knowing I can call the theater crowd late at night (but never early in the morning), a time when most accountants have to call it a day because no one wants to talk to an accountant then. It's also fun to run across their names in the papers. I keep their clippings in their regular tax files, partly for audit purposes, partly to try to keep up with their activities and whereabouts.

Performing artists who can make use of this option are not the ones who have made it. Instead, they're the ones on the road, doing the small-time touring gigs for experience and exposure. The $16,000 threshold may seem unfair—at least it should be indexed to inflation—but it provides a slim margin of relief for those who need it most.

If you're going to be touring, or if you're in a residency or summer stock or other short-term program that takes you away from your tax home, see Chapter 10 to gain an initial appreciation of what you can deduct and learn how to keep track of expenses while you're away from your tax home.

What happens if you end up making more than $16,000? Well, the bad news is that you lose the qualified-performing-artist tax boost. The good news is that you have more money. But as your income and expenses increase, also be sure to figure out whether the standard deduction still works better for you than itemizing your personal deductions, even if you don't own your own home.

I have some clients who earn a lot of money as performing artists who don't own their own homes. Ordinarily you'd suspect they're better off taking the standard deduction than itemizing their personal deductions. What's true is that they spend so much on the road, they need to complete Form 2106 and then Schedule A to take advantage of the maximum deduction allowed them.

I'm reminded of what's considered in some circles to be the greatest audit story of all time. It concerns the issue of what constitutes a legitimate business expense, specifically the costume of a performing artist. It doesn't exactly fit into this section of the book, but it's such a great story I hope you indulge me.

The issue of deducting the cost of costumes used in performances arose in the audit of one Walter Liberace, a native of Milwaukee, my hometown. Walter had progressed from honky-tonks on the south side of Milwaukee to the big hotels downtown and, from there, to major stages and opera houses throughout the world. For a while in the 1950s he even had his own television show.

Well, Liberace, as he called himself on stage, appeared for the audit as would any normal citizen—suit and tie, accompanied by his accountant. Word has it that the auditor was unsympathetic to the claim that the vast amounts of money Liberace spent on his costumes were legitimate business expenses. The rule states that if you can convert a costume to personal use, you lose it as a deductible expense. Any fool knows you can remove all those sequins and ermine accents and make that shirt look just like the one Harry down the street wears. Or at least that's what the auditor argued.

Liberace and his accountant asked for a second meeting with the auditor. About the time Liberace was to appear, the auditor became aware of a massive disturbance in the office. People were running by his desk toward the appointment desk. When he went to investigate, he found his fellow auditors massed in a circle, waving notepads and ledger sheets and anything else they could find, as though they were seeking autographs. Who was it in the midst of the mob? When the crowd parted, it was none other than the auditee. It was Liberace.

It was Liberace the performer, not Walter Liberace the taxpayer. Walter Liberace hadn't been mobbed when he came into the office wearing a business suit. Perhaps the receptionist recognized the name, but there was no cause for bedlam. But when Liberace came in wearing a costume, he was recognizable and he became a celebrity even to IRS personnel.

Liberace and his accountant made their point in a flamboyant display, commensurate with the total deductions under question. I don't advise the same for my clients (see Chaper 18), but I like the story for this reason: An artist frequently underestimates herself, especially a maturing artist. Don't sell yourself short. Understand what legitimate deductions you can take and then don't be afraid to take them, or be ignorant about how to take them.

For More Information

The qualified-performing-artist provision is described in Publication 529, "Miscellaneous Deductions," in a subheading under deductions not subject to the 2 percent AGI threshold. If you are a qualified performing artist, be sure to read Chapter 10 to maximize your travel deductions.

PART

III

APPENDICES

Glossary of Terms

Accrual System A system of accounting that requires your income to be "recognized" (entered in your books) when you send a bill or invoice, and allowing expenses to be recognized when you receive a bill for these. Bad debts are possible only with the accrual system.

Adjusted Gross Income (AGI) The sum of your income for the year after subtracting allowable adjustments (retirement plan contributions, alimony payments, 25 percent of health insurance costs, employee business expenses for qualified performing artists, a penalty assessed by a bank on early withdrawal of savings); last line on the front of Form 1040.

Amortization

A method of writing off costs over a period of years (generally no fewer than five). Differs from depreciation, which decreases the value of an asset for each year it's in service. Examples of expenses commonly amortized are start-up expenses (Internal Revenue Code section 195), organization expenses (IRC section 248 for corporations and section 709 for partnerships), and costs incurred for research and experimentation (IRC section 174).

Audit

Also known as "examination of return." A review by the Internal Revenue Service of your tax return for a particular year. Generally you are notified of an intention to audit about one year after you file the return. The audit may be done without further information from you, or the IRS may require that you provide documentation by mail (mail audit) or in person (office audit, if held in a local IRS office; or field audit, if held in your home or place of business).

Since 1980, the audit rate has declined from more than 2 percent of all returns filed to less than 1 percent of all returns filed. The single factor most likely to trigger an audit: unreported income. Other likely factors: self-employment, employee business expenses, moving expenses, limited partnerships, and travel and entertainment expenses.

Bad Debt

For use only with the accrual system of accounting. A bad debt occurs when a payment owed you and already recognized as income proves uncollectible.

Example: Bill Sweeney billed Karin Nelson sixty dollars for pottery sent to her the previous week. The invoice date is the date on which sixty dollars is entered as income into Bill's books. Two months and four telephone calls later, Bill learns that Karin's gone out of business and will not be paying him. Bill now has a bad debt.

On his income books, Sweeney makes a note (but no entry) on the date he learns his invoice is uncollectible. He removes Nelson from his accounts receivable list, and enters the amount of the bad debt ($60) as an expense in the "Miscellaneous" category, referencing Nelson and the original invoice. On his tax return, he'll list this and other bad debts as an expense on Schedule C.

Notice that a bad debt only cancels out income previously reported. There is no "loss," even though Bill has suffered the actual loss of some materials and his time and craftsmanship. For tax purposes, the materials have already been written off as expenses, while Bill's time is not money and never shows up in the books. Moral of the story: Collect on those bills! Better yet, get your customers to pay on receipt of merchandise.

Barter

Trading your goods or services for another person's goods or services. To the IRS, the fair market value of the goods you receive through barter is unreported income. Since you're already writing off as deductions materials and supplies used in the goods you barter, barter becomes a fraudulent attempt to underreport income.

Recommendation: Do not barter. It's not allowed by the IRS and it's unprofessional. If you want something, pay for it; if the goods or the service you offer are valuable, sell them.

Basis

A tax term meaning your current investment in an asset. Basis changes throughout the life of an asset. When you purchase a new piece of equipment, for example, basis equals purchase price. As that equipment is depreciated, the amount of depreciation reduces the basis. When an asset is fully depreciated, your basis in it is zero.

Basis is used to calculate the gain or loss from disposition (sale) of an asset.

Capital Asset

Purchase of an item costing more than $200. Any capital asset must be tracked individually on your tax return, in contrast to noncapital assets, such as office supplies, art supplies, or small equipment, all of which are written off under one of the expense categories on Schedule C. A capital asset must be individually entered on Form 4562, where it is either "expensed" (totally written off in the year of purchase) or depreciated.

Disposing of a capital asset results in a capital gain or a capital loss, and is calculated on Form 4797.

Capital Gain/Loss

The difference between the basis and the sale price of a capital asset used in business. If your basis in an asset is lower than the amount you receive for it when you sell it, you have a capital gain. If your basis is higher than the sale price, you have a capital loss. Sale of any capital asset used in business results in either a capital gain or a capital loss.

An exception: When you sell an automobile for which you've been deducting expenses using the standard mileage rate deduction and come up with a paper gain on the sale, that gain is automatically reduced to zero. In other words, you cannot "overdepreciate" a vehicle, or reduce its basis to less than zero, by taking the standard mileage rate deduction.

Cash System

A system of accounting under which income is recognized (entered in the books) when it is received and expenses are recognized when paid. You cannot use the cash method of accounting if you have an inventory that materially affects how you report income and expenses. A guideline: If you regularly have on hand raw materials and finished or unfinished goods the value of which (cost or current market value, whichever is lower) exceeds 10 percent of your usual annual gross revenues, you must keep track of that inventory and use the accrual system of accounting.

Recommendation: Keep your inventory low. Goods sitting around your studio cannot earn money for you. Stick with the cash system of accounting, as long as it meets IRS requirements, because it's easier and because you aren't paying tax on money you haven't yet received.

Commuting

First trip out of your home each day and last trip back, except for temporary job assignments. A self-employed person working at multiple job sites has no commuting mileage, per Internal Revenue Ruling 90-14, issued in March 1990 and retroactive to the start of 1989.

Credits

Items allowed by law to offset a tax liability, dollar for dollar. Some commonly used credits: child-care credit, foreign tax credit, earned income credit.

Depreciation

A method of spreading the cost of an asset over its useful life. Each year, the asset loses a portion of its value (it's "depreciated") until the cost of the asset is used up. At that time, the total depreciation taken on the asset will equal its original cost, and its basis to you will be zero.

The useful life of an asset is determined by the IRS. IRS Publication 534, "Depreciation," lists all classes of assets and the useful life assigned to each. (See Chapter 7 for an in-depth discussion of the topic.)

Earned Income

Payments received for work performed or services rendered. Does not include prizes, fellowships, or awards. Alimony, however, is considered earned income for the purpose of calculating eligibility for an Individual Retirement Account (IRA) contribution.

Employee

A person who works for you at regularly scheduled hours, on your premises, for more than seventeen weeks of the year. As an employee, that person is entitled to have you pay half her Social Security tax (FICA), and all of her Workers' Compensation and unemployment insurance and is, moreover, eligible for any retirement programs you have for the business you operate.

Employer Identification Number (EIN)

Also known as Federal Employer Identification Number (FEIN). It is required if you have employees or a Keogh plan.

You must have an EIN in order to file quarterly wage reports on income tax withholding and FICA taxes. Also required if you are a sole proprietor with a Keogh account. Apply for one using IRS Form SS-4. Do not apply for one if you do not have employees or a Keogh retirement plan.

Exempt Organization

A corporation that does not pay taxes on most corporate profits because it fits certain criteria. Must file an annual tax return (Form 990) if gross receipts equal or exceed $25,000 in the fiscal or calendar year.

An organization obtains tax-exempt status by incorporating under state law as a nonprofit entity and then filing with the IRS Form 1023 to request tax-exempt status. If the IRS determines that the organization meets the legal criteria for exemption, the organization is given tax-exempt status. If Form 1023 was filed within the first fifteen months after incorporation, the tax-exempt status is retroactive to the date of incorporation. If Form 1023 is filed after the fifteen-month period has elapsed, the organization is subject to corporate tax rules and corporate tax rates until that tax-exempt status is granted.

Because an exempt organization is a corporation, it must have employees. Do not incorporate yourself as a nonprofit organization and expect to draw money from that organization unless you establish a salary for yourself and withhold things required of an employer.

Exempt organizations can hire independent contractors and issue 1099-MISC forms at the end of the calendar year for money they have paid. By regulation, no shareholder or officer of the exempt organization can be treated as an independent contractor.

Expenses

The costs of running a business, some of which are tax-deductible.

Expensing

A decision to deduct the full cost of a capital purchase in one tax year, rather than to depreciate it. Also called a "Section 179 election to expense." Up to $10,000 in capital assets purchased during the year can be expensed, but not more than your profit for the year. In other words, expensing cannot give you a tax loss for the year.

Fellowships

A fellowship or grant is a cash award to an individual from a nonprofit organization or exempt foundation or government agency in recognition of that individual's professional contributions or promise.

A fellowship is fully taxable and should be reported on the "other income" line on the front of Form 1040.

A fellowship is considered a prize or award, not earned income. Hence it is not subject to Social Security tax (FICA) and should not be reported as income on Schedule C. It cannot be included as earned income in calculating eligibility for an IRA, Simplified Employee Pension Plan (SEP), or Keogh retirement plan contribution.

Filing

To file a tax return is to complete the forms and schedules needed to report your income and claim your deductions, and to mail those forms and schedules to the IRS district office assigned to your area of residence by April 15 of the year following the close of the tax year.

Filing Deadlines

April 15 for an individual tax return. Quarterly estimated tax payments are due the fifteenth day of April, June, September, and January, unless the fifteenth falls on a Sunday or a holiday, in which case the due date is the next business day. Failure to file on time can result in penalties, in addition to the interest due on underpaid tax liabilities.

March 15 for a corporate return. If the corporation has a fiscal year, the filing deadline is two and one-half months after the close of the fiscal year.

April 15 for a partnership return, but March 15 for partnerships with more than 250 partners.

The fifteenth day of the fifth month following the close of a fiscal year for an exempt (nonprofit) organization.

Note that the 1986 Tax Reform Act eliminated the use of fiscal years for most partnerships and S-corporations.

Filing Extensions

Use Form 4868 to obtain an automatic four-month extension of the filing deadline. The extension is for filing only, not paying. Taxpayers are required to calculate their liability and send it with Form 4868.

An extension from August 15 to October 15 is available, with written explanation for the extension, by using Form 2688. Further two-month extensions can be requested but are rarely granted.

Use Form 8736 to apply for a three-month filing extension for a partnership, and Form 7004 to apply for a six-month filing extension for a corporation.

Fiscal Year

A twelve-month period that is different from a calendar year. Most taxpayers are calendar-year taxpayers. In the past, some partnerships and S-corporations were allowed to adopt a fiscal year. Under the Tax Reform Act of 1986, almost all partnerships and S-corporations adopted calendar-year reporting at some time during 1987.

401(K) and 403(B) Plans

Retirement plans through private [401(K)] or public or nonprofit [403(B)] employers that deposit pretax earnings in retirement savings that are tax deferred until you retire. Since these deposits are pretax dollars, your reportable wages (box 10 of your W-2) are lower than the total wages shown on your wage stub and in the W-2 box showing Social Security wages. This is one form of tax savings.

Depending on your overall income, you may also be eligible for an IRA plan or a Keogh or SEP retirement contribution (the latter two are based on your net profit from self-employment).

Grants

See "Fellowships."

Hobby

An activity pursued primarily for pleasure or relaxation, not for profit. Expenses incurred in running a hobby can be used to offset income generated by that hobby to the extent of that income. A hobby can never generate a tax loss to offset other income.

Income

Most money—wages, prizes, awards, gambling winnings, stipends, alimony—you receive is considered income. Important exceptions are: scholarships for undergraduates and tuition scholarships for graduate students; inheritances; legal judgments resulting from pain and suffering; child support.

Income Averaging

Repealed for 1987 and subsequent years.

Independent Contractor

A self-employed person who does not have income taxes or Social Security taxes withheld from gross pay prior to receiving it. An independent contractor pays his or her own Social Security and income taxes on all income received and has none of the benefits employees normally enjoy, such as unemployment insurance, Workers' Compensation protection, or health-care benefits. Independent contractors report their income and expenses on Schedule C. They must complete the long form (Form 1040) to file their federal income taxes.

Individual Retirement Account (IRA)

All taxpayers with earned income are eligible to have an IRA and to make contributions to it. Any contributions to an IRA earn tax-deferred income. The deductibility of an IRA contribution after 1986 depends on your adjusted gross income (AGI) and on whether or not you are covered by a pension plan where you work. (See Chapter 19 for a complete discussion of eligibility and deductibility of IRA contributions.)

Inventory

Finished goods or goods in progress when their cost in materials represents a major factor in the way a net profit is calculated.

Everyone in business has an inventory of some size. A writer has notepads and pencils; an artist has sketchpads, paints, and framing pieces. But these "inventories" are too insignificant to declare. Whether an inventory is declared for tax purposes depends on the size of the inventory and whether the cost of the inventory has a material impact on the way a profit or loss is figured.

As a general rule, if the cost of your inventory usually exceeds 10 percent of your annual revenues, that inventory has an impact on how you report your profit, and must be tracked. Having a collection of reproductions or a stock of books will require you to keep track of and declare an inventory.

Investment Tax Credit (ITC)

Repealed for most real property by the Tax Reform Act of 1986. Use Form 3800 to calculate allowable current credits and remaining portion of old credits. An ITC can offset only income tax, not Social Security tax.

Keoghs (H.R. 10)

Shorthand notation for Keogh plan. A retirement plan variety (like IRA or SEP), it is named for a congressman and the number of the bill he sponsored establishing this retirement account for self-employed people. A Keogh plan can be used in conjunction with or separate from an IRA. (See Chapter 19 for more information about this option.)

Limited Partnership

A partnership that has at least one general partner and one or more limited partners, but no more than thirty-five partners total. Only the general partner or partners are legally responsible for the debts and liabilities of the partnership, and only they can participate in managing the partnership. A limited partner shares in profits or losses but is limited in liability to the amount originally contributed to the partnership. A limited partner is prohibited from participating in management decisions.

Limited partnerships became popular investment vehicles in the go-go eighties as drastic tax-sheltering devices. An absence of underlying value began to be evident in the late 1980s, and by 1990 the market for them had virtually evaporated. They remain highly speculative investments.

Marriage Penalty

Refers to a condition under previous tax law that levied higher taxes on married couples than on unmarried couples (two single people) when both work. The penalty was a result of the progressive tax structure, which taxed higher earnings at a proportionately higher rate. Under the Tax Reform Act of 1986 a flatter tax structure lessened but did not eliminate this penalty.

Midyear Convention

A rule used in depreciating assets. It requires reducing first-year depreciation by half.

If more than 40 percent of the cost of all assets purchased during the year falls in the final quarter of the year, you must use a quarter-year convention for each depreciable-asset group.

Net Operating Loss (NOL)

Calculated using Form 1045, an NOL usually arises from a severe downturn in business that causes losses to exceed all other sources of income. Calculate the potential NOL if adjusted gross income in any particular year is a negative number.

An NOL can be carried back three years to offset income taxes in any of those years, or you may elect to carry it forward for up to fifteen years, offsetting income tax in each year following the NOL year, until the NOL is used up. Your decision on where to apply the NOL must be made by the end of the calendar year following the NOL year.

NOLs that occur year after year may

mean imminent bankruptcy of the business and/or individual involved.

Most state tax laws allow you to calculate an NOL, although state rules about items eligible for inclusion may differ from federal rules. Check with your state revenue department for forms and instructions.

Nonprofit

Shorthand for a nonprofit corporation. See "Exempt Organization." Nonprofits are required to file an annual tax return for any year revenues exceed $25,000 or any year in which they receive income unrelated to tax-exempt purpose exceeding $1,000. Must have at least one employee.

Penalties

Charges levied when tax liabilities are not paid on time or when tax returns are not filed on time. The penalty for not paying your tax liability on time is 0.5 percent per month, up to 22.5 percent of the amount owed. The penalty for late filing is 4.5 percent per month, up to 25 percent of the amount owed. There is an exception. More than sixty days after the due date for the return, you will be assessed a penalty equal to $100 or the amount owed, whichever is less. The combined penalty for filing late and not paying on time is 47.5 percent of the amount owed.

In addition to these penalties, interest will accrue on the unpaid amount at the IRS interest rate in effect during the period of the unpaid liability.

Penalties are not deductible, nor is interest after 1990.

Profit and Loss Statement (P&L)

Required by banks and mortgage companies to assess a sole proprietor's credit worthiness. A P&L contains the same type of information as that found on Schedule C.

Recapture

Shorthand for recapture of investment tax credit (ITC). Most commonly occurs when business property used to gain an ITC is sold or returned to personal use. Depending on when the disposition occurs in the life of the property, some or all of the previously claimed or used ITC must be returned to the government. Use Form 4255 to calculate.

Can also apply to recapture of depreciation when accelerated depreciation has been used and business use of an asset falls to less than 50 percent.

Receipts

Issued by vendors, receipts are records verifying expenditures you make.

Refund

Not the same as a bad debt. A refund most often occurs after an overcharge or settlement of a disputed payment.

Example: John Smith sells the XYZ Corporation the layout for its annual report and bills the corporation $3,000. In thirty days, a check is sent to John for the full $3,000. Six weeks later the head of marketing for XYZ calls John. She tells him how much heat she received because he mixed up the bar graphs for the international and national sales groups, and she demands a refund of half the original fee. In the interest of goodwill, John agrees to a $1,000 refund. In his books, John shows the $3,000 check as income, with a $1,000 refund entry in his miscellaneous expenses, identified as "refund."

Self-Employment Income

Any money you earn from which Social Security tax is not withheld by the payer.

Self-employment income can be reported only on Schedule C. If you use a Schedule

C, you must also use the long form (Form 1040), even if the bulk of your earnings are reported to you on W-2s.

Simplified Employee Pension Plan (SEP)

SEPs offer most of the advantages of Keogh plans without the usually higher contribution requirements built into Keogh plans. The maximum SEP contribution is around 13 percent of net profit from self-employment (13.043 percent times net profit reduced by the self-employment tax adjustment made in the Form 1040 adjustments-to-income section). Keoghs can be structured to allow 20 percent of net profit less that self-employment tax adjustment. (See Chapter 19 for a more complete discussion of SEP plans.)

Taxpayer Identification Number (TIN)

Your Social Security number. The TIN for a partnership or a corporation is its federal employer identification number, obtained by filing Form SS-4.

Underpayment of Tax

Failure to pay or overpay your federal tax liability in a given year. A penalty for underpayment of taxes may result if you owe more than $500 to the federal government at the end of the tax year. This penalty or the exemption to the penalty are figured on Form 2210.

The penalty for underpaying federal taxes can reach 20 percent of the amount underpaid. The moral is that you must file quarterly estimated tax payments (Form 1040-ES) if amounts withheld from you by external sources (employers, for instance) do not exceed 90 percent of your total tax liability for the year. Underpayment can result from untaxed income, self-employment income, or underwithholding at your place of employment. Make sure your W-4 does not overstate the withholding allowances to which you are entitled. (See Chapter 20 for a more complete explanation of this subject.)

Uniform Gifts to Minors Act (UGMA) Refers to a good estate-planning tool, under which money can be given to a child in the child's name and held in trust until the child reaches the age of majority. This is still a good way to establish a college fund for a child, despite 1988 changes in tax laws that made the income of children under the age of fourteen taxable at their parent's marginal tax rate.

Open an UGMA account at a bank or brokerage house in the name of a minor child, usually with a parent as trustee. The money put into the account is a gift and becomes the property of the child (trust beneficiary) when he or she reaches the age of majority (eighteen years, in most states). At that point, the money is the property of the child, no strings attached.

The trustee of an UGMA cannot pledge the UGMA as security for any loans the trustee may seek, nor may the trustee withdraw funds from the account for the basic living needs (food, clothing, education) of the trust beneficiary.

The earnings are taxed at the child's rate (usually zero) until annual earnings exceed $1,000, at which point the parents' highest tax rate is used.

A Quick Guide
to Income and Deductions

Income

If you receive income from:	Enter it on:	Comments:
WAGES, defined as income on which some withholding has been taken—federal income tax or Social Security tax—and for which you receive a W-2 form at the end of the tax year.	the "wages" line of Form 1040.	Only W-2 income appears on this line.

If you receive income from:	Enter it on:	Comments:
INTEREST on savings or checking accounts, certificates of deposit, U.S. Savings bonds, or land contracts/contracts for deed.	the "taxable interest" line of Form 1040 if the total received is less than $400, or on Schedule B if the total received is more than $400.	
DIVIDENDS from stocks or mutual funds (even if the dividends are reinvested).	the "dividend" line of Form 1040 if the total received is less than $400, or on Schedule B if the total received is more than $400.	
SALE OF PROPERTY: PERSONAL RESIDENCE	Form 2119, or on Form 4797 if you claimed home-office use.	Remember that selling your residence at a loss does not result in a tax deduction.
SALE OF PROPERTY: STOCKS, BONDS, MUTUAL FUNDS	Schedule D.	Remember to adjust your basis in bonds downward by any nontaxable returns of principal and to adjust your basis in mutual funds upward by any reinvested dividends.
SALE OF PROPERTY: BUSINESS PROPERTY	Form 4797.	Remember that sale or disposal of a personal automobile you used in your business

If you receive income from:	Enter it on:	Comments:
		is a taxable transaction, resulting in either a taxable gain or deductible loss.
SALE OF PROPERTY: INSTALLMENT BASIS	Form 6252.	Interest on an installment contract is reported on Schedule B. Calculate the taxable part of principal received on Form 6252; from there it becomes capital gain on Schedule D.
BUSINESS you operate as a sole proprietor.	Schedule C.	Remember that the net profit generated is subject to self-employment tax.
BUSINESS you operate as a partnership.	Schedule E.	A partnership files its own tax return, Form 1065. Each partner's share of the partnership's profit or loss, plus each partner's draw, is reported on Form K-1 of the partnership's return. Both profit and draw are subject to self-employment tax. A loss can offset draw.

If you receive income from:	Enter it on:	Comments:
BUSINESS you operate as an S-corporation.	Wages line of Form 1040 and Schedule B.	As an employee of the corporation, you receive a W-2 form at the end of the year for your salary, which is reported on the "wages" line of Form 1040. As a shareholder, you receive a Form K-1 from the corporation's tax return, Form 1120-S. That K-1 lists your share of the corporation's profit or loss. It also lists the amount distributed to you, from profits, over the period covered by the tax return. Although this distribution is not taxable income (since you've already paid tax on the corporation's profit), the IRS monitors the figure as one guide to whether you're paying yourself a market-level salary.
BUSINESS you operate as a Standard (C-) Corporation.	Wages line of Form 1040, and possibly Schedule B.	A standard corporation files its own tax return (Form 1120)

If you receive income from:	Enter it on:	Comments:
		and pays its own taxes. You receive a W-2 form from the corporation at the end of each calendar year on the wages it paid you. You report those wages on the "wages" line of Form 1040. Any dividends paid to you by the corporation are reported on your Schedule B.
PENSIONS and ANNUITIES	The pensions and annuities line of Form 1040.	Report the gross amount on the "a" part of the line from the 1099-R form you receive at the end of the year. The taxable portion of a pension is less than the gross amount if you made after-tax contributions to your pension fund. The taxable portion of an annuity represents the annual share of the annuity's pretax growth. Your payments to an annuity are part of the gross amount you receive, but are not included

If you receive income from:	**Enter it on:**	**Comments:**
		in the taxable portion. Both the "gross distribution" and "taxable distribution" figures are listed on the Form 1099-R issued to you at the end of a year.
IRA, SEP, or KEOGH plan distributions; 401(K) or 403(B) distribution.	The IRA distributions line of Form 1040, and possibly Form 5329.	A distribution includes money you withdrew and rolled over to another qualified account as well as money you withdrew and kept. Report the gross amount distributed on the "a" portion of the line; the "taxable amount" is the amount you kept. Unless you're 59½ years of age or older, that taxable amount is subject to a 10 percent penalty, figured on Form 5329. Some retirement plan withdrawals are exempt from the 10 percent penalty tax: involuntary distributions of your company's employee stock option plan (ESOP); dis-

If you receive income from:	**Enter it on:**	**Comments:**
		tributions resulting from a divorce decree; withdrawals used to pay medical bills (the amount withdrawn must be less than medical bills paid and itemized on Schedule A). Only a handful of narrowly defined exemptions apply. See the instructions for Form 5329 on the proper notation to make to avoid the 10 percent penalty. Note that premature withdrawals from a retirement plan may also be subject to penalty at the state level.
ESTATE or TRUST FUND	Schedule E, possibly Schedule B or D.	Use the K-1 form the estate or trust fund issues to you to make entries in the appropriate part of Schedule E. Some estate or trust fund income should be reported directly on Schedule B or Schedule D. Follow the K-1 directions.

If you receive income from:	Enter it on:	Comments:
ALIMONY	Specific line on Form 1040.	Alimony is considered earned income for the purpose of qualifying to make an IRA contribution, but is not earned income for the purpose of qualifying for the earned income credit.
FARMS	Schedule F if you operate the farm directly; Form 4638 if you rent out farmland.	
UNEMPLOYMENT COMPENSATION	Unemployment compensation line of Form 1040.	Unemployment payments have been fully taxable since 1987.
SOCIAL SECURITY PAYMENTS	Social Security line of Form 1040.	The gross amount you receive is reported to you at the end of the year in box 5 of Form SSA-1099. Report it on the "a" section of the Form 1040 line and use the worksheet in the Form 1040 instructions to calculate the "b" section, the taxable amount. No more

If you receive income from:	Enter it on:	Comments:
		than half the gross amount received is subject to tax.
PRIZES, AWARDS	The "other income" line of Form 1040.	
JURY DUTY	The "other income" line of Form 1040.	If you were required to turn over payment for jury duty to your employer, enter the gross amount received followed by "less payment of same to employer = 0."
GAMBLING WINNINGS	The "other income" line of Form 1040.	Deduct the cost of tickets you can prove you bought as a miscellaneous deduction on Schedule A, up to the amount you won.
GRANTS or FELLOWSHIPS	The "other income" line of Form 1040.	Identify by source. Grants and fellowships have been fully taxable since 1987.

Income can also come from:	Enter it on:	Comments:
GOODS or SERVICES you receive in lieu of cash payments.	Same form or schedule you would have used to report the cash payment of the same thing.	Example: You "trade" some of your work for a computer. The fair market value of your work becomes Schedule C revenues and the basis of the computer.
RENTS	Schedule E.	Exceptions: If you rent property as a business, use Schedule C. If you are a sole proprietor and occasionally rent out your equipment, report rents received as part of your Schedule C revenues.
ROYALTIES	Schedule E or Schedule C.	Royalties on oil or gas wells you do not operate belong on Schedule E. Royalties derived from oil or gas wells you have a hand in operating belong on Schedule C. Royalties on works you write or create are always reported on Schedule C.

Income can also come from:	Enter it on:	Comments:
DEFAULTS on contracts	Form 4797.	The "selling" price is the balance remaining to be paid on the contract.
BANKRUPTCIES involving forgiveness of debt on business equipment.	Schedule D.	With debt forgiven on, say, an office communications system, your basis in the property drops from the price you agreed to pay to the amount you actually paid before the debt was absolved. The difference between the two is capital gain to you.

You may also receive money that is not considered taxable income from such sources as:	Enter it on:	Comments:
CHILD SUPPORT		Not income to the receiving parent nor a deduction to the paying parent.
GIFTS		Never taxable to the recipient, gifts of more than $10,000 in a single calendar year force a gift-tax return to be filed by the donor.
SCHOLARSHIPS		Not income if paid directly from a donor to an educational institution for tuition and fees. Payments for books, supplies, or room and board are taxable income.

Deductions

Academicians

If you produce art primarily as a professional requirement of your teaching duties, report your art expenses as part of the miscellaneous business deductions on Schedule A. Itemize your expenses as employee business expenses on Form 2106 and transfer totals to the miscellaneous deductions section of Schedule A. Only that part of your miscellaneous expense total that exceeds 2 percent of your adjusted gross income is deductible.

If, on the other hand, you have established marketing channels and an ongoing history of sales of your work, you can instead file as self-employed in addition to your regular employment as a teacher. Use Schedule C to report income and expenses from your art business.

Actors

If you are an actor or other public performer who receives more than two W-2 forms for acting gigs, you can report expenses connected with your performing (e.g., voice lessons, costumes, makeup, theatre tickets) on Form 2106 and, from there, directly on the front of Form 1040, thereby escaping the 2 percent threshold on deductibility mentioned earlier.

Use Form 2106 to report these professional expenses. If your income is less than $16,000, you can deduct these expenses without regard to the 2 percent threshold that affects deductibility of miscellaneous expenses. If your income exceeds $16,000, or if you have only one W-2 employer, these professional expenses are deductible on Schedule A only, where they are subject to the 2 percent of AGI threshold.

Automobiles

A deduction is allowed for business use of your car. Certain rules apply: The vehicle must be yours, and you must keep a written record that identifies business use in the context of overall use of the vehicle. Generally this means you must keep a daily log of odometer readings for business use of your car.

For most workers, the first business trip out each day from the home and the last business trip back each day to the home are considered commuting mileage and cannot be counted in the total number of business miles driven. If, however, you are self-employed and work at multiple job sites or if you are an employee who travels to various locations as part of your job, this rule does not apply.

There are two methods of deducting automobile expenses. The first is the standard mileage deduction; the other is the actual expense method.

The standard mileage deduction changes each year according to federally determined criteria on the cost of operating a vehicle. If you use the standard mileage deduction, you may claim in addition only business parking costs and the business portion of the interest paid on your car loan. All other auto expenses (insurance, repairs, maintenance) are assumed to be covered by the standard mileage rate.

The second method of deducting automobile expenses is the actual expense method. This method requires you to keep a daily mileage log plus receipts for all automobile expenditures: gasoline, oil, repairs, maintenance, license plates, and insurance. First you calculate your percentage of business use from your mileage log. Then you multiply that percentage of business use by the total auto expense to get the amount you can deduct as business-related automobile expense. To this expense total can be added depreciation on the vehicle, business parking fees, and interest on an auto loan.

Since 1987, all autos have been depreciated over a five-year period using the double-declining balance method of depreciation. Luxury cars are subject to special limits on the amount of depreciation allowable each year. (See Chapter 8.)

Expenses for a leased vehicle are deducted using the actual expense method, with the lease payments replacing the depreciation part of that method.

Bank Charges

Charges on personal accounts are not deductible. Business-account charges are deductible on Schedule C if you are self-employed. Charges for mixed accounts (business and personal) are deductible only if the bank charges a per-check service fee. In that case, your Schedule C deduction equals the number of business checks written times the per-check fee.

Bankruptcy

Nondeductible. May in some cases lead to taxable income, due to writing off debts. If you are considering filing for bankruptcy, consult a tax advisor first.

Books

Deductible in year of purchase for self-employed persons (Schedule C) or regularly employed professionals (miscellaneous section on Schedule A). If you are a photographer and you buy books used in both your regular employment and self-employment, it's more advantageous to deduct the cost of those books on Schedule C. If, however, a particular book deals only with your regular employment, the deduction belongs on Schedule A.

Casualty Losses

Personal losses are reported only as a personal itemized deduction on Schedule A only to the extent the loss exceeds the insurance reimbursement and 10 percent of adjusted gross income. Use Form 4684.

Business items lost or destroyed through casualty or theft are reported on Form 4684 to determine the loss; the loss is then transferred to Form 4797 for inclusion on Form 1040. Frequently a casualty loss may turn into a taxable gain due to depreciation taken on an item in prior years.

Child Support Payments

Neither deductible to the payer, nor taxable to the receiving parent.

Conferences/Continuing Education

Deductible if they pertain directly to your business and professional activity. Conference fees are deductible on Schedule C for self-employed people and on Schedule A for regularly employed people.

Travel and lodging costs incurred to attend a professional conference are listed on the "travel" expense line of Schedule C. Meal costs are only partly deductible, even if the costs are incurred as part of an out-of-town conference.

Conference costs that seem high in the overall context of running your business (e.g., $2,000 in conference fees for a self-employed professional grossing $6,500 in a given year) will invite IRS scrutiny and subject you to questions about whether you are pursuing the activity for profit.

Contributions

Claim a deduction on Schedule A for cash or personal materials given to nonprofit organizations. Contributions of your time and/or artwork are not deductible anywhere, any time. A deductible contribution represents contributions from previously taxed income. If you contribute one of your paintings valued at $500, you never claimed that $500 as income and hence do not have a $500 contribution. You do have a contribution of materials (generally already included on Schedule C) and perhaps some mileage to deliver the donated material to the donee.

Volunteers working in nonprofit organizations can also, on Schedule A, deduct expenses they incur in the act of volunteering. Examples of such costs include airfare to a national conference for board members, or mileage to and from the organization (at the rate of twelve cents per mile).

Costumes

Deductible for actors, musicians, and other public performers. Costumes are defined as clothing that causes you to stand out in a crowd or that is not ordinarily seen otherwise. Furthermore, a costume cannot be converted to standard dress. Hence, tuxedos are not deductible in New York City but are deductible in Des Moines. Corporate suits are not deductible anywhere.

Credit Card Interest

A form of consumer interest no longer deductible in most cases. For credit cards used exclusively in business, the interest is fully deductible on Schedule C.

Day Care
Payments made by taxpayers qualifying for tax credit. Use Form 2441 to compute. Not deductible as a business expense unless you are the employer who provides the service for your employees' children.

To claim the credit, you must enter the Federal Employer Identification Number (FEIN) or Social Security number of each day-care provider on Form 2441. Use Form W-10 to obtain the information you'll need to complete Form 2441.

Dependents
Blood relative, relative by marriage, or any other person who has lived in your home for a full year whom you support and whose presence does not violate existing law.

Disability Insurance
Not deductible.

Dues and Publications
Dues to professional organizations and associations, and periodicals and publications used in your trade or business, are deductible on Schedule C for self-employed people. If you are a regular employee, fees for dues and publications are deductible in the miscellaneous section of Schedule A only to the extent the total miscellaneous deductions exceed 2 percent of your adjusted gross income.

Education
See "Conferences/Continuing Education."

Employees
Wages you pay your employees are deductible on Schedule C, as are amounts paid by you for FUTA (federal unemployment insurance), FICA (Social Security), Workers' Compensation, health and life insurance, and any pension or disability plans you fund. Each employee must be sent a Form W-2 by January 31 of the following year; the Social Security Administration must receive

Form W-3 (as a cover or transmittal document), along with the original (colored) W-2 form, by February 28 of the following year. Other reports required to be filed if you have employees include Form 941 (quarterly report of withholding) and Form 940 (an annual report for FUTA). In addition, state forms for withholding, unemployment insurance, and Workers' Compensation must be completed and filed with the appropriate state agencies.

Entertainment

Deductible only if directly related to the production of income and then only 80 percent deductible. Do not include nightclubs, theatre tickets, sports events, cocktail parties, or yacht cruises. The IRS has declared that these activities are primarily recreational, regardless of who accompanies you.

You may include the cost of your own meal if there is demonstrable proof of additional cost to you due to the business nature of the outing. You may also include the cost of business gifts (not to exceed $25 per person per year).

Fees

Payments to independent contractors are deductible on Schedule C if payments are made for services incidental to the self-employed person's trade or business.

Fellowship Exemption

Eliminated for 1987 and after.

Foreclosures

See "Repossessions/Foreclosures."

Gifts

Neither taxable to the recipient nor deductible to the donor. Any donor can give any donee up to $10,000 per year; amounts exceeding $10,000 require donor to file a gift-tax return.

Health Insurance

All taxpayers can itemize 100 percent of health-care payments on Schedule A. The portion of health-care costs that exceeds 7.5 percent of adjusted gross income is deductible. Self-employed persons who pay their own health insurance premiums are better off deducting 25 percent of the premiums on the front of Form 1040, with the other 75 percent of the insurance premium cost and other medical costs deducted on Schedule A.

Home Mortgage Interest

Reported to the payer on Form 1098 by the bank or mortgage company holding the mortgage on the property. Fully deductible on Schedule A or partly deductible on Form 8829 (to the extent you claim an office in the home), with the balance deductible on Schedule A.

Home Office

Deductible only to the extent you have a profit. Space must be definable and used exclusively for business. The IRS recognizes two methods of determining the percentage of your home used for business: square footage or number of rooms. Use the square-footage method if rooms in your home are not the same size. Bathrooms do not count in square-foot total or room-number total.

Renters: Deduct a percentage of rent and utilities costs equal to the portion of your residence used for business, up to the amount of your net profit prior to the home-studio deduction.

Homeowners: Deduct a percentage of mortgage interest, real estate (property) tax, insurance, and utilities costs, plus depreciation, equal to the portion used for business. Don't skip deducting for depreciation to simplify your future tax situation. If you claim home office and deduct a portion of your expenses for everything except depreciation, the IRS will impute that deduction to you at the time you sell your home. Remember that depreciation is an allowed or an allowable expense; take it or lose it.

From 1991 on, you must file Form 8829 as part of your return in order to claim a home-office deduction.

Independent Contractors

Persons to whom you pay fees for specific services. Only the fees themselves are deductible by the payer. The payer must issue Form 1099-MISC by January 31 of the following year if payments exceed $600 in the calendar year to any independent contractor.

Inheritances

Not income to the recipient. If property is transferred to a beneficiary, the value of the property listed in the estate return becomes the beneficiary's basis in the property. This is important when the asset is sold, since that is when a long-term capital gain (or loss) is incurred.

Legal Fees

Deductible to the extent they are related to income-producing activities. Deductible legal fees related to self-employment appear on Schedule C; fees related to regular employment appear on Schedule A as miscellaneous deductions (the sum of which is deductible to the degree it exceeds 2 percent of adjusted gross income).

Loans

Not deductible as an expense; not reportable as income.

Local Transportation

Deductible for the self-employed person who uses bus, railway, boat, or auto to travel to work. Not deductible for employee commuting.

Loss

There is no tax-deductible loss if a vendor defaults on a payment to you, unless you have already counted that payment as income. In that case, you are using the accrual system of accounting and have a bad debt. For other information on losses, see the Glossary under "Capital Gain/Loss."

Medical Expenses

Deductible on Schedule C only if a specific injury occurred in the line of work. Example: An actor who has his teeth punched out while filming a western could deduct the cost of dental repairs and restoration on Schedule C.

Effects of long-term wear and tear, however, are not deductible on Schedule C. Example: Dancers cannot deduct chiropractic fees on Schedule C, or the cost of contact lenses or cosmetic dental work, even though without those services the dancer would be less likely to be employed.

Medical costs (insurance, fees to practitioners, hospital expenses, travel to medical care) are deductible on Schedule A to the extent they exceed 7.5 percent of adjusted gross income. Medical expenses for dependents are deductible. Medical expenses for friends or blood relatives who are not dependents are not deductible.

Moving Expenses

Deductible only if you find new employment more than thirty-five miles away from where you currently work, and then deductible only as a miscellaneous deduction on Schedule A. A move for your convenience or preference is not deductible. The move must result in regular employment in 39 of the 52 weeks following the move; for a self-employed person, in 78 of the 104 weeks following the move.

Points

Deductible in the year of payment for home purchase if paid by a separate check at closing. Not deductible (even if paid by separate check) for home refinancing. Refinancing points must be amortized over the life of the loan on the "deductible points" line of Schedule A. Not deductible at all if rolled over into the mortgage principal.

Political Candidates

Contributions to political candidates and political campaigns are not deductible.

Real Estate Taxes

Also known as property taxes. Deductible on Schedule A. If you claim a home office on Schedule C, the home-office percentage of property taxes on your home is deductible on the "taxes" line of Schedule C. Whatever is claimed on Schedule C cannot also be claimed on Schedule A. You can't deduct more than 100 percent of your property taxes.

Repossessions/ Foreclosures

Gain results most frequently from repossession of property or foreclosure on real estate. For a self-employed person using the accrual system of accounting, a repossession will trigger income because a deduction was already taken for the property, even if it was not paid for in full. A gain may also result for a self-employed person who depreciated or expensed the item repossessed.

You must figure your basis at the time of repossession to determine whether you have a gain or loss and how much it is. Foreclosure on real estate also requires calculation of your basis at the time of the foreclosure to determine the size of the gain.

A loss is possible in the case of a repossession or foreclosure, but it is rare.

Safe-Deposit Box Fees

Deductible on Schedule A only if you keep tax records or income-producing documents in it; deductible on Schedule C only if you use the box to keep your copyrighted work safe from theft or damage.

Sales Tax

A state and/or local tax imposed on sales of goods within a specified political jurisdiction. No longer deductible as a separate item on Schedule A. Sales tax you pay on supplies used in your business is deductible as part of the total cost of an item on Schedule C.

Scholarships

Not taxable as income so long as the scholarship pays only for books and tuition and is paid directly to the institution. If a scholarship includes a stipend for housing, that portion is taxable income to the recipient; if it's paid to you with no strings attached, it's fully taxable. Tuition paid for by scholarships is not deductible as a business or personal expense.

Seminars

See "Conferences/Continuing Education."

Start-up Costs

Not deductible in the year of expenditure, they must be amortized over a minimum of five years (Internal Revenue Code 195). Amortization expense is calculated on Form 4562 and deducted on the "other expense" line of Schedule C.

Tax Preparation Costs

Deductible only as a miscellaneous deduction on Schedule A, the total of which is deductible to the extent it exceeds 2 percent of adjusted gross income.

Theft

See "Casualty Losses."

Travel

Deductible for a sole proprietor on Schedule C only to the extent it pertains to self-employment activities. May be deductible for regular employees, whether or not reimbursed by employer, on Form 2106 (and transfer the allowable deduction to the miscellaneous section of Schedule A).

Personal travel (recreational or avocational) is not deductible. Trips that mix personal and business affairs must allocate trip days by activity. Trips undertaken primarily for personal reasons—even though some business may be done on them—are not deductible. You can take the business expenses for the business days, but that's the limit. (See Chapter 10 for further guidelines.)

Index

Academicians 252
Accounting methods
    Accrual defined 223
    Cash defined 227
ACRS (Accelerated Cost Recovery
    System). See Depreciation.
Actor 252–253
    See also Qualified Performing
        Artist 215–219
Adjusted gross income defined
    223
ADR (Asset Depreciation Range).
    See Depreciation.
Alimony 247

Amortization 263
    defined 224
Assets, business, sale of
    life of 71
    mixed use 77
    tax treatment 79–81
Audits 181–189
    chances of 182–183
    mail 183–186
    office 185, 186–188
    types 183–185
    what happens 186–188
Automobiles, business use of 86–
    95

allowable deductions 89–91, 253–254
commercial vehicles 94
how to document 16–17, 86–89
limits on luxury vehicles 71, 136, 170
luxury vehicles defined 76
rental 94–95
sale or trade-in 164–169
Awards. See Fellowships.

Bad debts 83, 133–134
defined 224–225
Bank charges 254
Bankruptcy 250, 254
Barter
defined 225–226
Basis
defined 226
Books 254–255
Books/bookkeeping 3–47
business versus personal 8–9
choosing categories 13–25
evaluation techniques 32–47
examples 23, 24, 26–27
organizing 3–11
overcoming your fears 3–7
storage 29, 31
time required 12–13
Special topics:
automobiles 16–17
home office 17–18
travel 18–19
Budget sheet 174

Capital assets
defined 226

sale of assets 94
examples
automobile 164–169
equipment 158
residence 158–164
tax consequences 156–158
where to report 241–242
See also IRS publication 544.
Capital gains
defined 226–227
Capital loss
defined 226–227
Capitalization 61–66
defined 62
how it works 62–63, 64, 65–66
Cash system
defined 227
Casualty loss 255
Childcare credit 257
Child support 251, 255
Commuting
defined 227
Conferences/continuing education 255–256
Contract laborer. See Independent contractor.
Contributions 256
Corporations 111–112
advantages and disadvantages 116–118
comparison chart 119
defined 229
nonprofit (also known as "exempt" organizations) 118, 120
Also see IRS publications 583, 542, 589, 334, and 937.
Costumes 256
Credit card interest 256
Credits

defined 227–228

Dancer
See Qualified Performing Artist
215–219
Daycare 257
Defaults (on contracts) 250
Dependents 257
Depreciation 69–85
definition 71, 228
limits on luxury vehicles 76–77
methods 71–75
midquarter convention 73, 74
midyear convention 70, 72, 73,
74, 235
overview 69–70
recapture
defined 75, 237
how it works 75–76
sale of assets 170–171
tables 81–85
tables 78, 79, 80, 81, 82, 83
thresholds 79–81.
See also Capital assets.
See also IRS publication 534.
versus expensing 17, 71–73
Disability insurance 257
Dividends received 48, 54, 56, 78,
96
where to report 241
Double declining balance (DDB)
71. See also Depreciation.
Dues 257

Earned income, defined 228
Employee
defined 122, 228
versus independent contractor
121–124
Employer identification number.
See Federal Employer Identification Number.
Employer taxes 213–214
Entertainment 258
Equipment, large. See Capital assets.
Estimated tax payments 207–209
penalties for underpayment
209–210
rationale 207
Evaluation methods 23–35
Exclusive use
automobiles. See Automobiles—
commercial.
home office 96–98
See also Assets—mixed use.
Expenses
defined 230
Expensing 74
defined 230
See also Depreciation.

Federal Employer Identification
Number (FEIN) 52
defined 228–229
Fellowships 230, 248
exemption 258
FICA. See Social Security tax.
Filing 230
due dates 230–231
extensions 231
Filmmakers/video artists 63–66
See also Capitalization.
Fiscal year 231–232
Foreclosures 258
Form 940 (federal unemployment)

57, 58
Form 941 (quarterly federal with-
    holding and FICA tax) 56–57,
    58
Form 1040-ES (estimated tax pay-
    ments) 59, 208
Form 1065 (partnership return)
    119
Form 1096 (transmittal document
    for 1099s) 50
Form 1099-MISC (payments to in-
    dependent contractors) 51
Form 1120/1120S (corporate re-
    turn) 119
Form 2210 (underpayment of esti-
    mated taxes) 208–209
Form 4562 (depreciation) 70, 75
Form 8109 (federal deposit
    coupon for employers) 56, 59
Form 8606 (nondeductible IRA
    contributions) 193
Form 8829 (home office deduction
    for homeowners) 77
Form SS-4 (application for a
    FEIN) 52
Form W-2 (wages paid) 58
Form W-3 (transmittal sheet for
    W-2) 53
Form W-4 (withholding allowances)
    53
401 (K) or 403 (B) plan 191
    defined 232

Gambling winnings 248
Gifts 251, 258
Grants. See Fellowships.

Half-year convention. See Mid-
    year convention.
Health insurance 259
Hobby 125–132
    criteria 129–131
    defined 126–128, 232
    tax effects 131
    three-of-five-year rule 128–129
Home office 96–102, 259–260
    exclusive use defined 96–97
    how to depreciate 77–79
    rules for homeowners 99–101
    sale of residence 158–164
    rules for renters 101–102
    See also IRS publication 587.

Income 56–57, 147–150
    defined 232
Income averaging 232–233
Incorporating 116–118
Independent contractor 260
    defined 233
    versus employee 121–124
Inheritance 260
Interest received
    where to report 241
Inventory 142–155
    defined 142, 233–234
    example 150–154
    how to report 149–155
    requirements 145–146
    See also IRS publication 334 and
        Internal Revenue Code section
        471.
IRA (Individual Retirement Ac-
    count) 192–194

deductibility 192–193
defined 233
distributions 245–246
early withdrawal penalty 193
eligibility 192
nondeductible contributions 193–194
tax implications described 142–145, 146–148
See also Retirement Plans.
Itemized deductions (personal) 56, 60, 75–78, 96, 106

Journals. Same as Dues.
Jury duty 248

Keogh plans 195–196
defined 234
distributions 245–246
See also Retirement plans.

Leasing
a luxury vehicle 92–93
an automobile 91–92
strategies 93
Legal and professional costs 260
Limited partnerships 234–235
"Listed property"
automobiles as listed property 91
defined 75
Loans 260
Local transportation 260–261
Loss 261
Luxury automobiles 71, 136, 170

defined 76

MACRS (Modified Accelerated Cost Recovery System).
defined 71–72
how it works 72–74
See also Depreciation.
Marriage penalty 235
Medical expenses 261
Medical insurance. See Health Insurance.
Mileage log 16–17, 86–89
Midyear convention
defined 235
Mortgage interest 259
Moving expenses 261–262
Musician
See Qualified Performing Artist. 215–219

Net operating loss 235–236
Net profit
how to calculate 28–29, 30
Nonprofit organization 236
See also Corporation–nonprofit

Partner/Partnership 111
advantages and disadvantages 113–116
comparison chart 119
rental property 116
See also IRS publications 541, 583, 334, and 937.
Payroll 53–56

format 54
Penalties for underpaying taxes.
    See Estimated tax payments—
    penalties.
Penalties for underpayment of tax
    236
    defined 236
Pensions. See Retirement plans.
Per diem rates for meals 107–110
Points 262
Political contributions 262
Pricing 173–180
Prizes 248. Also see Fellowships.
Profit, 3-of-5 year rule 128–129
Profit and loss statement 236–237
Proprietor. See Sole proprietor.

Qualified Performing Artists 215–
    219
    See also IRS publication 529,
    "Miscellaneous Deductions."
Quarter-year convention
    defined 216
Quarterly payments. See Estimated
    tax payments.

Real estate taxes 262
Recapture. Same as Depreciation
    recapture.
Receipts
    defined 237
Recordkeeping. See Books/Book-
    keeping.
Refunds 237
Rent 249

Rental property 94, 95
    partnership 116
Reporting requirements 48–60
    state sales tax 137–139
    See also Form 1099-MISC and
    Estimated Tax Payments.
Repossessions/foreclosures 262–
    263
Research 155, 165. Also see Capi-
    talization.
Residence, sale of 89
Retirement plans 190–206
    calculating return on investment
    201–205
    implications if you have employ-
    ees 196–197
    IRAs 192–194
    Keoghs 195–196
    overview 191–192
    rationale 190–191
    SEPs 194–195
    See also IRS publication 560 and
    590.
Revenues. See Income.
Royalties 249

S-Corporations 57, 94, 163–164,
    165
Safe deposit box 263
Safe harbor election 61–62
    ramifications 66
Sale of business property
    auto 164–169
    equipment 158
    home office 158–164
    recapture 169–171

Sales tax 60, 263
    business 86, 175
    defined 133
    interstate requirements 139–140
    state 98–99
    use tax 139
    which states have it 133–134
Scholarships 251, 263
Sec 263(A). Internal Revenue
    Code. See Capitalization.
Self-employment income
    defined 237–238
SEP (Simplified Employee Pension)
    Plan 194–195, 238
    distributions 245–247
    early withdrawal penalty 195
    See also Retirement plans.
Social Security payments 247
Sole proprietor/Sole proprietor-
    ship 111
    advantages and disadvantages
        112–113
    comparison chart 119
    See also IRS publications 583
        and 334.
Standard mileage rate
    what it includes 89–90
    leased vehicle exclusion 89
Start-up costs 263
State reporting requirements 52,
    57, 58
    sales tax 133–137

Studio in home. See Home office.

Tax preparation fees 263
Taxpayer identification number
    (TIN) 238
Theft. See Casualty loss.
Three-of-five-year-rule on prof-
    itability 128–129
Training. See Conferences/con-
    tinuing education.
Travel 103–110, 264
    deductibility 104
    documentation 105–106
    mixed use 104–105, 107–108
    per diem rates 107–110

UGMA (Uniform Gift to Minors
    Act) 239
Underpayment of tax 238–239
Unemployment compensation 247
Uniform capitalization. See Capi-
    talization.

Video artist/filmmaker 63–66. See
    also Capitalization.

Wages
    where to report 240, 243–244